retirement
on a budget

Help Us Keep This Guide Up to Date

Every effort has been made by the editors to make this guide as accurate and useful as possible. However, many things can change after a guide is published—establishments close, phone numbers change, facilities come under new management, etc.

We would love to hear from you concerning your experiences with this guide and how you feel it could be improved and kept up to date. While we may not be able to respond to all comments and suggestions, we'll take them to heart and we'll also make certain to share them with the editors. Please send your comments and suggestions to the following address:

The Globe Pequot Press
Reader Response/Editorial Department
P.O. Box 480
Guilford, CT 06437

Or you may e-mail us at:

editorial@GlobePequot.com

Thanks for your input, and happy travels!

retirement
on a budget

SIXTH EDITION

john howells

GUILFORD, CONNECTICUT

Text design by Nancy Freeborn

ISSN: 1934-3582
ISBN-13: 978-0-7627-4222-6
ISBN-10: 0-7627-4222-4

Manufactured in the United States of America
Sixth Edition/First Printing

Contents

chapter one

Golden Retirement Years

When people think of retirement, the term *golden years* naturally comes to mind. Golden, because retirement years are considered to be a reward— a substantial reward for a lifetime of productive work and loyalty to the workplace. Most workers eagerly look forward to these happy years as the time when they can enjoy the fruits of their labor and bask in the sunshine of leisure. A company pension, stock dividends, annuities, interest on savings, and Social Security provide the income to enjoy this new, carefree career as a retiree.

For the majority of those entering the retirement phase of their careers, this rosy scenario will probably play out. However, in today's world of economic uncertainty, there are no guarantees. Many people find themselves facing some tough choices that could make their "golden years" look somewhat tarnished. This is particularly true at the time of revising this sixth edition of *Retirement on a Budget*. Some people may have to look at *all* their retirement options.

At the time of revising this book, the U.S. economy was improving, with many new jobs being added to the workforce. However, the vast majority of the jobs were semiskilled jobs, paying between minimum wage and $10 an hour. Not enough income to encourage many to keep working, and making retirement more attractive. Those of you who saw your well-paid and high-skilled jobs outsourced to India may never again find similar employment. So maybe it's time to go into retirement, or perhaps semiretirement while working parttime.

Shaky Pension Plans

Lately, bankruptcy has forced some large corporations to default on their pension plans. But some of you who work for financially sound corporations also could be in for a surprise when retirement time comes. In mid-2006, Congress was busy considering a number of law changes designed to weaken existing pension plan protections. House and Senate bills were expected to pass that will lower corporate contributions to the already underfinanced pension system by $150 billion over a three-year period. This is bonanza for large corporations—not having to pay $150 billion into pension funds is the same as $150 billion extra profits. These extra earnings help make the economic picture look good, at least for corporate earnings.

Congress was adding dozens of escape clauses and loopholes for specific industries and those corporations that hire the most effective lobbyists in Washington. Lawmakers had already created a multibillion-dollar pension exemption to the nation's airlines as well as special breaks for dozens of favorite corporations, benefiting companies such as Smithfield Farms Hams, Bethlehem Steel, and many more. Add to the list General Motors, Lucent, Raytheon, United Airlines, Enron, JCPenney, and who knows what others? Hopefully, your company won't be next.

The bottom line is: For many people, the question of a pension is not settled until you start receiving your checks. Actually not even then. We

Not Your Parents' Pension Plans

Twenty-five years ago, when your parents retired, 40 percent of American workers were covered by company pensions. Today, only 20 percent of the workers in your generation expect retirement pensions. However, even that 20 percent may not be able to collect what they've been promised. It turns out that about 75 percent of all pension plans are underfunded.

have friends who retired from United Airlines after qualifying for the maximum benefits, adjusting their lifestyles to a comfortable income. Suddenly, retired pilots were looking at pension cuts of up to 50 to 75 percent. Lower-paid workers will lose as much as 20 percent of their pensions. You can imagine what happened to the promised lifestyles they thought they'd earned through loyalty to their company over the years.

Social Security

Despite the bad press the Social Security system often receives these days, many analysts maintain that the plan will be more than self-sufficient for several decades. Traditionally, retirees have depended on Social Security benefits as a welcome part of their retirement income. But today an increasing number of retirees are *totally* dependent on Social Security. Of the country's 48 million retirees drawing benefits, 60 percent count on Social Security as the majority of their retirement income. For more than 15 million, Social Security checks are virtually their *only* source of income!

Those who depend most on Social Security are single women. Women account for almost three-quarters of the older Americans who exist on poverty-level incomes. Because retirement income is tied to earnings and time spent on the job, women are deprived in two ways. First of all, they're traditionally paid less than men. Secondly, women who are covered by pension plans are more likely than men to lose their jobs before becoming vested in the plans. Low lifetime wages mean that women often cannot put aside enough money for a comfortable retirement. So Social Security is a lifeline for many.

Women's traditional role as family caregivers means many of them will have had gaps in their work histories to take care of children or will have spent a lot of their working lives as part-time help. This means reduced Social Security and pension benefits. The result? Women make only 70 percent of what men are paid. And the wage gap widens with age.

It isn't just those on Social Security who need to plan on getting by on a shoestring. Workers forced into early retirement because of corporate mergers or industrial doldrums, say at age fifty-five, won't qualify for Social Security until they reach the age of sixty-two. We all recognize that well-paying wage jobs are scarce for displaced workers fifty years old and above. This is partly because employers prefer to hire younger workers who aren't used to high wages and good benefits. It's also partly due to the fact that many thousands of highly skilled jobs have been outsourced to India and other low-wage countries. Some workers whose skills or crafts have been made obsolete by modern technology may find it tough to find jobs paying a living wage. These folks need to find strategies for living on savings and income from part-time jobs until they qualify for Social Security.

Baby Boomers and Social Security

Many of you who are considering retirement this year are members of the baby boomer generation, that titanic wave of children born in the decade after the end of World War II. This boom triggered a long-running expansion of home building and school construction and triggered a tremendous economic boom. An enormous number of tax dollars went to educate baby boomers, making this the best-educated generation in our history, the developers of Internet and other high-tech industry. You were the ones who used to say, "Don't trust anyone over thirty!" Remember? Well that was thirty years ago. Today, baby boomers are middle-aged and heading for retirement, with graying hair and sagging bellies. Welcome to old age, kids. Don't trust anyone over thirty, indeed!

A paradoxical twist is that baby boomers are now being subjected to old age discrimination as employers choose to replace them with younger workers who are so eager for work they will accept much lower salaries in this era of reduced employment opportunities. Age bias complaints by those between the ages of forty-five and fifty-five increased by 50 percent over the last five years. This is happening just as they are beginning to plan retirement ten years down the road. When retirement comes ten years earlier than expected, creative planning becomes necessary.

For years, retirement experts took it for granted that baby boomers, when they entered retirement, would step right into the affluent lifestyle enjoyed by their parents. Not necessarily so. For one thing, this younger generation was famous for "instant gratification," not for thrift. While their parents had memories of the Great Depression and World War II, and were always putting something aside for the future, many baby boomers spent their money on BMWs, fast lifestyles, and unaffordable homes. Ironically, some of these "unaffordable homes" have turned into fantastic reservoirs of cash, thanks to real estate appreciation. Unfortunately, only those lucky enough to have invested in the high appreciation regions of the country are so lucky. Furthermore, this is the group most affected by the disappearance of "dot-com" and high-tech jobs.

Those who fervently advocate drastic changes to the Social Security system point out that this massive wave of Baby Boomers will soon be moving into retirement, putting pressure on the system's finances. So-called experts keep making absurd claims that the problem is simply that people are living longer and will deplete the Social Security fund because they will be drawing more checks. Newspaper headlines proclaim: "Life expectancy rises to record level." A press release from the Centers for Disease Control recently announced: "Americans are living longer than ever before. If all goes well, you and yours may outlive previous generations, with record-breaking life expectancy!"

These predictions are based on statistics published in February 2005 showing that over the previous three years, the average U.S. male life expectancy had increased from a youthful 77.3 years to the ripe old age of 77.6 years! That's right, folks, a whopping *three-tenths* of a year! Yes, you might collect a couple more Social Security checks during that extra three-tenths of a year—and enjoy an extra couple of months living in a nursing home. But does anybody *really* believe that such a tiny fraction of a year is going to enable "you and yours to outlive previous generations with record-breaking life expectancy?" Don't hold your breath!

Well, then why will we be seeing this future overbalance of retired people versus their children who are working to support the system? I'll give you a clue: It has nothing whatsoever to do with people living longer (and they aren't really). The answer is (are you ready for this?) *the invention of birth control pills!*

Look, it goes like this: Baby Boomers were born in the late 1940s through the 1950s, okay? Probably the longest sustained population increase in history. Then in 1960, the first birth control pill (Enovid) became readily available. Because of the Pill, Baby Boomers were able to restrict their number of offspring dramatically. Thus, the end of the population explosion. The ideal was no more than two children, often no children. The result is that the U.S. birth rate dropped to the lowest level since the Census Bureau began collecting data. The trend is continuing—the rate of births among teenagers in 2005 fell to a new record low, continuing a decline that began in 1991.

So the answer to the question of why a future overbalance between young workers and old retirees should be a no-brainer: *fewer young people than old people!* (Duh!) Children who would have been born twenty years ago, are not here to work and pay into Social Security as you paid for your parents' retirement. Blame yourselves for using the Pill and not producing enough kids to pay the bills! There may come a time when you hear your grandkids saying, "Don't trust anyone over sixty-five!"

Actually, it isn't as bleak as it sounds. According to actuary experts, the system should be healthy for another twenty years without doing a thing. Should the government stop spending Social Security funds for other purposes, the system is good for forty more years and possibly forever. We'll discuss Social Security's future later on in this book.

Retirement on a Budget

For the past twenty years, my wife and I have been doing research on retirement lifestyles. Most of our books deal with *where* to retire, rather than how to retire. This book combines the two strategies: where *and* how. For some people, leaving their hometown and moving to a more affordable location is out of the question. Throughout the book we present retirement strategies that fit both situations: staying at home or moving away.

Our research method is to visit each potential location and investigate the town or city in person. We've traveled many thousands of miles by car, motor home, travel trailer, and airline—crisscrossing the country many times. As we visit cities, towns, and hamlets, we try to imagine ourselves actually living in each place. We routinely look at rentals and property for sale, and we check prices of various commodities. We examine newspapers, reading crime reports and classified sections for homes offered by owners. In each location, we estimate how much income we would need if we were to retire in that particular town. We try to visualize the lifestyle we could have in each community, whether on a high, medium, or low income. We take into consideration various kinds of hobbies, sports, and recreational opportunities.

The idea for *Retirement on a Budget* came about one day as we were having lunch in a small city on Washington's Pacific Coast. Housing prices and rentals were incredibly low and the cost of living surprisingly affordable. We began wondering how a retired couple might make out on an absolute minimum budget in this town. After all, millions of American retirees do live below the poverty level. What if our worst fears were realized and our only income came from a Social Security check? What kind of a lifestyle could we create for ourselves in this low-cost town?

We then visualized a need for a book not only on *where* to retire, but also on *how* to retire. How to retire on a shoestring. Given the fact that millions of folks must get by on Social Security benefits, then if they were to retire here, in this little coastal community, could they survive? And at what standard of living?

In 2006 the average married couple collected $1,648 a month in Social Security benefits, and a single male $1,129. A single woman's check averaged $870. Of course many people earn less than this amount, depending on the worker's earnings record. Finding a low-cost town for relocation could be a practical way to cope. For those who do not care to move away during retirement (and most folks don't), we'll take a later look at strategies to live within your income without moving away from home.

Average Social Security Benefit Checks	
Social Security couple (both eligible)	$1,648
Single or couple (one eligible)	$1,129
Single female	$870
Social Security Disability	$939
Average Supplemental Security Income (SSI) Checks	
Individual	$603
Couple	$904

The first thing we did was check a real estate office for their least expensive listings. We found an older, two-bedroom frame house in town selling for today's equivalent of about $45,000. We looked at another house, a brick ranch-style home, located on the edge of town and priced at $85,000. (These figures have been adjusted to reflect inflation and current real estate prices.)

Don't misunderstand, we're not suggesting that you can go just anywhere and pick up a house for $45,000 in today's market! These houses were priced exceptionally low because of several unusual economic conditions. The town's two major industries had shut down. Jobs had disappeared. Small businesses were struggling to survive and not making it. Houses were difficult to peddle because everybody wanted to sell, and nobody wanted to buy. Empty houses weren't renting because tenants were moving away to seek work elsewhere. For many retirees, employment opportunities don't matter nearly as much as affordable living costs.

We located the first house, a slightly run-down place not far from a supermarket and shopping center. As you can imagine, it needed paint, cleaning, and repairs. Yet the house looked like a fabulous bargain. Yes, we could easily imagine ourselves living here, and the price was afford-able even with the needed repairs. But suppose we couldn't afford to buy a house and needed to rent? The local newspaper listed several rentals, some furnished, for as little as $350 a month. We didn't look at mobile homes, but you can be sure that when conventional housing is that inex-pensive, mobile homes will be *really* inexpensive!

Next we figured out two "bare-bones" budgets for living modestly but comfortably in a town like this. The itemized budgets for a couple, given on the next page, call for monthly expenses ranging from $1,219 to $1,576. These approximate the average monthly income from Social Security checks for a couple who both qualify for Social Security and for a couple with only one qualifying for Social Security or Disability. Auto-mobile expenses account for a large portion of the more affluent budget. While car expenses might seem like a big chunk out of the finances, liv-ing in a small town without a car can be difficult because small towns are often without local bus service. Selecting a home within walking distance of shopping and bus transportation helps eliminate the need for an auto-mobile. The bare-bones budget allows for taxi fares when grocery shop-ping or other tasks where transportation is necessary. You can take several taxis every month for a fraction of what you'd spend on gasoline, car pay-ments, maintenance, and insurance.

These budgets don't allow for items such as life-insurance premiums, club dues, loan payments, or other expenses that vary with individual cir-cumstances. We are assuming that your auto is paid for, that you cashed in your life insurance policies after the children were grown, and you have no outstanding loans. Those are highly individual outlays that you have to add into your budget and adjust other expenses accordingly.

A unique condition that helped this particular budget was the town's ocean-tempered climate: cool year-round with no need for summer air-conditioning and mild winters without extreme heating demands that are

Bare-Bones Budget for a Couple
One qualified for Social Security ($1,129 a month)

Rent or mortgage payment	$500
Utilities (gas and electric)	100
Telephone	20
Groceries	200
Clothing, laundry, grooming	70
Cable TV (minimum service)	30
Bus, taxi, and other transportation	80
Medicare supplement B (one person)	88
Miscellaneous	131
Total	$1,219

Moderate Budget for a Couple
Both qualified for Social Security ($1,648 a month)

Rent or mortgage payment	$670
Utilities (gas and electric)	100
Telephone	20
Groceries	275
Clothing, laundry, grooming	80
Cable TV (all extra channels)	45
Automobile ins. (liability only)	32
Gasoline and maintenance	90
Medicare supplement B	88
Miscellaneous	176
Total	$1,576

routine in most parts of the country. (This is one of our strategies for cutting expenses: trimming utility bills.) Assuming we qualify for Medicare, we added $88 each to pay for Part B supplementary medical insurance.

Our conclusion: Yes, living in this small coastal city, we could cover all of our basic expenses with our Social Security benefits! No, it would not be easy, but a Social Security check the size of ours would barely cover rent in many of the towns we've visited!

As noted earlier, the term *cost of living* refers only to basic expenses, those items most people simply cannot avoid. Obviously, individual circumstances differ. When you retire, if you still have car payments, a mortgage, huge insurance premiums, back taxes, alimony, or gambling debts, you don't need a book on how to retire on a minimum income—you need a book on how to win the lottery. If you don't qualify for Medicare or Medicaid and you have no medical coverage, you don't need someone telling you that you are in trouble. Until our system catches up with the rest of the world in assuring medical care for all its citizens, millions of Americans will be without protection. Let's hope that you're among the lucky Americans who can afford the care you need. If not, your local hospital emergency room may be your access to medical care. The situation is particularly bad for early retirees, who can't get Medicare health insurance until age 65. For example, a healthy couple, both 60, can expect to pay $12,000 a year between them for a comprehensive health insurance policy from a private insurance company. (Those working even slightly above minimum-wage levels don't even *earn* $12,000 a year!)

Home Base

At first glance, our small coastal town looks like a great place to retire. With wooded hills, a lazy river, and lovely seascapes, summers here are always cool and often overcast because of the ocean. Temperatures rarely rise above 75°F, so air-conditioning is unknown. Because the town is on the ocean, winters never bring snow and rarely more than light frost. The winter downside is many damp and overcast days with shortened daylight hours. Some folks love cool weather like this, but our personal tastes lean toward hot summers and places where folks wear shorts and T-shirts instead of sweaters.

Even though we recognized that this town would not be the perfect retirement setting for us, we became interested in the possibility of using it as a home base. The home's large garage would make a great place to store our small motor home while we enjoyed inexpensive spring, summer, and fall weather here, living in a peaceful ocean setting. Then, when winter rain and overcast skies threaten, we could winter-proof the house and drive our motor home to Arizona, Florida, or even Mexico for inexpensive RV living. Small-town safety and neighbors would protect our valuables while we were on the road. Home base retirement is a concept that is gaining popularity. Of course, it's not for everyone.

The more we thought about having a home base to spend summers, the closer we came to actually buying the house! This often happens when we are researching a town. We become so enthusiastic that we begin scheming a way to live there part time. We came very close to buying a condo in Hawaii once, until we began considering how difficult it would be to commute to our work in California. We actually did buy a home on Oregon's Rogue River simply because we were so enchanted with the setting and the price. We later bought land and built a second home in Costa Rica while researching retirement there. Nowadays we spend most winters in Costa Rica to escape California's harsh winter climate. Where we live, it sometimes gets down to 45 degrees! (Okay, so we're weather wimps!)

Granted, places like this Washington town aren't representative of the normal, everyday real estate market. But dedicated bargain hunters can find similar conditions in many parts of the country. A factory goes bankrupt and workers follow jobs elsewhere. Logging and fishing industries fall into the doldrums. A military base closes its gates and the local economy collapses. Any number of business-related disasters can turn a wonderful residential community into a nightmare for people who must work for a living. This same disaster can be a windfall for those who don't have to work. Later in the book, we'll talk about ways to locate these bargains.

Mind you, finding depressed towns is just one solution for low-cost retirement. If we all crowded into these places, costs would soon begin to rise until they were no longer bargains. Furthermore, too many low-cost towns are depressed simply because they are boring places to live! Being able to buy a house for $45,000 does not guarantee you'll enjoy living there. If the most exciting thing to do is sit on your front porch rocker swatting flies, you might as well keep on working.

All of the above sounds wonderful, you might say, but suppose we don't want to move? What if we want to stay right here, in our hometown where we've lived most all our lives? We'll discuss this later on, and as we shall see, no matter where you live, it's possible to take *some* control of your budget.

Poverty and the Cost of Living

As we study retirement lifestyles and economic conditions in various sections of the country, my wife and I are always impressed by wide differences in the cost of living. Some couples reported they couldn't make it on less than $22,000 a year, while others get by on incomes of $12,000 a year. Of course, millions of folks in the United States would consider a $12,000 income a blessing.

Yes, the government does spend money on programs for the poor, if you can qualify as being poor. But do you earn more than $9,800 a year as a single person? Then congratulations! According to Congress, you are *not* poor, since you've earned $9,800. That would be a whopping $188 a week, before taxes and Social Security deductions, even less than minimum wage. Therefore you cannot qualify for perks such as food stamps or several other welfare-related programs.

If you're married and earn $13,200 a year—or $233 a week—you also earn too much to be considered poor. Your representative in Congress will tell you that you're too affluent to be entitled to many federal programs aimed at helping the country's poor. Can you imagine Congressmen struggling to get by on their $3,177-per-week paychecks, yet considering $233 a week adequate income?

Even worse, many politicos complain that today's retirement generation is *too* affluent! They feel that too much is being spent on the elderly at the expense of the country's youth. They want to cut Medicare benefits and slash Social Security payments while at the same time they increase their own salaries and medical benefits. By the government's own statistics, three and a half million retired senior citizens are living below the poverty line.

Women over sixty-five have double the poverty rate of men the same age; more than 15 percent fall into this category. Because women's wages historically have been less than men's, women's Social Security payments are also low—disgracefully low. Poverty among the elderly is highest among single black women over seventy-five (40 percent of them are poor), compared with 32 percent of Hispanic women and 18 percent of white women over seventy-five.

2006 Federal Poverty Guidelines: Incomes above Poverty Levels

	Yearly Income	Monthly Income	Weekly Income	Hourly Income
Single person	$9,800	$817	$188	$4.71
Married couple	$13,200	$1,010	$233	$5.83
—with one dependent	$16,600	$1,272	$294	$7.35
—with two dependents	$20,000	$1,533	$354	$8.85
—with three dependents	$23,400	$1,795	$415	$10.38

NOTE: Alaska and Hawaii have higher income guidelines. Programs using the federal poverty guidelines to determine eligibility include the Food Stamp Program and the Low Income Home Energy Assistance Program. In general, public assistance programs such as Aid to Families with Dependent Children, Supplemental Security Income, and the Earned Income Tax Credit Program do *not* use the poverty guidelines in determining eligibility.

This book isn't just for those who need to survive on minimal budgets. Many readers probably enjoy perfectly adequate incomes, but they'd rather not spend everything they have on basic living expenses. Cutting back on one area of the budget will release funds for travel, recreation, and luxuries. Keeping money aside for emergencies is prudent and reassuring. Besides, just knowing that it's *possible* to live on a lower income is a reassuring thought—you'll always have that "ace in the hole."

Other readers, while they may own property worth a small fortune, don't feel particularly rich. Owning a home doesn't do a thing toward boosting income. Home ownership usually absorbs money from the home owner's monthly income. After paying taxes, maintenance, and miscellaneous costs of home ownership, some folks are lucky to have enough left over to buy groceries—even though their home is worth hundreds of thousands of dollars. Later on, we'll discuss strategies for putting your home equity to work for you.

For those who aren't lucky enough to be comfortably affluent, things are not likely to change for the better. In fact, we must face the fact that the trend will continue—at least through the next decade. That is what this book is all about: facing facts and planning how to live with them.

Outsourcing Our Employment

- The United States has lost 1.3 million jobs to China in the last decade (CNN, January 12, 2005).

- U.S. employers eliminated 1 million jobs in 2004 (*The Week*, January 14, 2005).

Outsourcing of skilled and highly paid jobs overseas affects mature workers in two ways: First of all, when skilled jobs disappear, displaced workers are forced to either seek downgraded employment or choose retirement. Secondly, traditional opportunities for part-time work, vacation replacement, or consulting work with former employers or others in the industry no longer exist.

chapter two

Retirement Strategies

How do folks manage to retire on Social Security or its equivalent? Unless you're already accustomed to living on a limited income, it's going to take some adjusting. Not only adjusting financially, but mentally as well. The old notion of "keeping up with the Joneses" has to be set aside. Instead of feeling depressed because your neighbors buy a new Lexus every other year, you need to feel proud that you don't waste money on frills and that your old Toyota takes you just as many places, perhaps more, and that without car payments you can afford to keep $3.00-a-gallon gasoline in the tank.

Most folks who plan on retiring on a shoestring budget are familiar with ordinary tricks for saving money and economizing. Buying on sale, clipping coupons, finding bargains—you already know all the standard maneuvers. Chances are you could write your own book about keeping costs down.

But there's only so much you can save on many common expenses—items such as clothing, groceries, and so forth. That's because most of these prices don't vary significantly between one store and another, or one community and another. Most commodities are sold through national chain stores, so retail prices tend to be similar anywhere you go. Grocery costs can be lower in some communities, depending on competition from chain stores and availability of local produce. Food can vary as much as 10 percent from place to place, but food is one of the easier budgets to control—simply buy fewer steaks and serve more pasta dishes. You do what you have to do.

Gasoline prices *used* to vary widely, depending on state and local taxes, state regulations, and pricing strategies by local dealers. But gasoline prices don't vary as much today; prices are outrageous anywhere you go. The price of crude oil zoomed from $12 a barrel a few years ago (in 1998) to more than $70 a barrel at this writing, and future prices are impossible to predict.

There's not much you can do to reduce costs of groceries, clothing, or similar items other than cut back on the amount you use. Nevertheless, some monthly expenses can be cut considerably. The successful strategy for low-cost retirement is to take control of three most expensive budget items: housing, transportation, and utilities.

Cutting Housing Costs

First, let's look at the price of housing. Your largest savings potential lies in finding creative ways of keeping a roof over your head. This is typically

Top Ten Retirement Mistakes

1. Not having a retirement plan
2. Failing to change your lifestyle
3. Not planning life-and-death decisions
4. Assuming you'll need less money in retirement
5. Counting on company and government programs
6. Believing Medicare covers long-term care
7. Not taking inflation into account
8. Retiring abroad just because it is affordable
9. Relocating to your favorite vacation destination
10. Relocating without thoroughly investigating

the largest single outlay in any budget. According to the Census Bureau, the average family of three spends 33 percent of its budget on housing (about $13,000 a year). By being creative, it is possible to cut this expense considerably. Under some circumstances, you can cut it in half.

For one thing, if you're willing to relocate to a low-cost neighborhood in your town, to another area in your state, or to another state entirely, your house payment or rent can usually be trimmed. Because many people do not see moving away from family and friends as an option, there are a number of cost-cutting strategies available that don't involve abandoning your hometown. Low-cost rentals, government subsidies, and alternative housing strategies can reduce your outlays dramatically. We'll discuss these later in this chapter.

Home prices vary widely mostly because of construction costs and wages, and supply and demand for housing. When local wages are low, housing costs will probably be moderate; otherwise, residents can't afford to buy. A house that sells for $625,000 in one part of California can be duplicated in another part of the state for $165,000, or in Georgia for $65,000. (Now, don't turn your nose up; Georgia has some delightful communities for retirement.) A house that rents for $1,150 a month in one city can have counterparts in equally nice neighborhoods in smaller towns for $550, a potential savings of $600 a month. That extra $600 will buy groceries every month, with enough left over to pay the electric bill and maybe a set of tires for the car!

Relocating to a low-cost community in some distant part of your state in order to find reasonable housing may not appeal to you. After all, you love your hometown. Your grandchildren live nearby, and your lifetime friends and beloved neighbors live here. Why leave the community if it isn't necessary? You don't have to leave—you can stay in the same community—but you may have to leave your *neighborhood* in order to cut back your housing outgo. By relocating just a few miles away, in a low-cost neighborhood or in a more rural location, away from city property taxes, your house payments or rent could be considerably lower. An alternative, the reverse mortgage tactic, will be discussed later in this book.

Sacred Home Ownership

Let's examine some common beliefs about home ownership and see if they're still valid on your retirement agenda. Most readers who will be retiring in this new millennium entered adulthood during an era of relatively low-cost real estate. Buying a house was easy. Until the late 1970s, when inflation began pushing real estate prices above the clouds, anyone with a few hundred dollars in savings could buy a home. Monthly payments were often less than rent. Home ownership became so common that it was taken for granted. Most of us grew up with the conviction that it just didn't make sense not to own your own home.

For many of these people, the thought of selling their home and becoming rootless is unthinkable. Of course, home ownership was important during our working years because interest and property assessments were tax deductible. These deductions made your house payments affordable. After all, a decrease in your taxes is the same as an increase in your paycheck. However, once you retire with a low income, you'll be paying little or no income tax, so property taxes and interest don't matter.

Many of us who bought homes thirty or forty years ago take it for granted that property appreciation will continue on indefinitely. Maybe it will. At least we can be confident that prices will increase in tandem with inflation, which would maintain your home equity. Yet we must recognize that, at the time of writing, our economy appears somewhat uncertain. Any increase in long-term unemployment would mean that some people will have trouble with high mortgage payments, which could lead to distress sales, which could have a negative effect on the real estate market.

There's always the possibility that real estate will reach another long-term plateau, with prices neither rising nor falling. Should this happen, prospects for property appreciation would be dim. Another factor: Never before have we had such widespread speculation in real estate, with investors buying for nothing down and interest-only loans, confident that next year they'll make a profit.

On the other hand (there's always a third hand somewhere, isn't there?), appreciation could continue far into the future, as a way of keeping up with inflation. There's no way of telling the future. It will have to be your call, depending on your individual situation.

In any event, many retirement-age people cling to the conviction that owning a home is essential for stability and safety. They would rather cut back drastically on their budgets than lose the feeling of permanence and security that home ownership provides. This is fine for those who can afford to live where they are currently living upon retirement. They have enough income that their lifestyles won't change appreciably when they no longer have weekly paychecks. Still others, even though they may be financially strapped, feel that staying in their homes is worth it. After all, the grandkids live nearby, their neighbors are close friends, and they enjoy living where they are.

However, you may find it worthwhile to examine your attitudes toward home ownership and see if alternatives might be worth exploring. Each case is different.

Costs of Home Ownership

An impressive number of couples approaching retirement today own their homes outright. That's not surprising, given the fact that the original purchase price was low compared with today's value, and the mortgage was paid off in affordable monthly payments the equivalent of rent. But the value of the homes kept going up with inflation and increasing demand. Many home owners who are retiring or thinking of making changes in their lifestyles have huge investments in home equity. They probably paid less than $50,000 for that first home. Then over the years they sold or traded homes an average of three times. They kept "moving up" as they bought something better with each move. Depending upon the part of the country where you live, your paid-for home could be worth from $150,000 to more than $500,000. Yet many would never consider selling their homes, taking down a healthy profit, and using the money to finance a new, downsized budget and a more comfortable lifestyle.

"After all, our house is paid for—we'll live rent-free," you might insist. "I may have to pinch pennies from time to time, that's true, but at least I'll always have a roof over my head."

While it is comforting to own your home outright, you can't realistically figure that you'll be living there "rent-free." Look at it this way: A business considers its store, office, or factory to be a capital investment. Your home is exactly the same type of investment. Let's suppose that your home is worth $275,000. That's your capital investment. If that $275,000 equity were placed in a safe, interest-producing investment (say, earning 5 percent interest), your income would be $13,750 a year. When you figure it that way, the actual cost of living in your own home is $1,145 a month plus taxes, insurance, and upkeep, which could add another $2,500 a year. (Depending upon the state and locality where you live, you may have to double that figure.) This brings the cost of a "rent-free" home to $1,400 a month, or $16,800 a year.

Now, suppose you were to sell your home, invest the proceeds, then lease your neighbor's place for $1,000 a month and allow the neighbor/landlord to pay taxes, insurance, and repairs. Your rent would come to $12,000 a year. You would be ahead more than $4,800 a year. Instead of paying for real estate taxes, insurance, and upkeep, you could use that money for travel or upgrading your automobile. Finally, you would have an additional $275,000 in tangible wealth, quickly available in cash should you need it. Should your home be worth $500,000, the figures are even more impressive.

Equity Appreciation

Before you run outside and stick a FOR SALE sign in the front yard, you'll need to do a lot of math to make sure you're doing the right thing. (I'm always worried that readers take my suggestions to heart without analyzing their situations thoroughly.) Home ownership is usually a built-in hedge against inflation. During periods of inflation, your equity (capital investment) will be growing because the value of the home increases as the value of the dollar decreases. This can be especially significant in regions where real estate is appreciating rapidly, in parts of California, Connecticut, Florida, or other states with unusual real estate activity. Below is a chart showing activity in various parts of the country and the percentages of gain or loss (mostly gain). As you can see, appreciation is sometimes way over what the equity would earn in high-yield investments.

Rates of Appreciation

Low

Beaumont, TX	-6.5%	Cedar Rapids, IA	-1.5%
Canton, OH	-4.5%	Greenville, SC	0.3%
Syracuse, NY	-2.6%	Pasco, WA	1.6%

Average

Milwaukee, WI	9.1%	Toledo, OH	9.1%
Okla. City, OK	9.3%	Springfield, IL	10.4%
Green Bay, WI	10.3%	Albuquerque, NM	11.2%

High

Norfolk, VA	22%	Sacramento, CA	27%
Phoenix, AZ	25%	Las Vegas, NV	29%
Honolulu, HI	26%	Bradenton, FL	46%

(2004–2005 from National Association of Realtors®)

As you can see from the chart, even in locations with average appreciation, your home equity at the beginning of 2006 would have been worth much more than an equal value invested in stocks or CDs. Of course, you do understand that this appreciation is not something that is guaranteed to continue year after year, don't you? Traditionally, real estate appreciation happens in unpredictable spurts, trending upward, but with long periods of flat price increases and occasionally, in some markets, falling prices. The question is, how long will this increase in real estate prices continue? (Don't ask me. I've been predicting the collapse of the California real estate market for the last thirty years! Some day, I may be right.)

Recently I've been looking over what "financial experts" have to say about real estate's future as an investment. I get the feeling that the experts aren't too much better at guessing the future than I am. Some are optimistic, others pessimistic. One thing all agree on is: No trend is forever. Where they don't agree is when the trend will change, and whether the trend will be leveling off, moving downward, or continuing upward to follow expected inflationary trends in the economy. You're going to have to make your own guesses as to what's going to happen to prices. As far as I'm concerned, it's a crapshoot.

If it comes down to the point to where you cannot make a decision, but would like to upgrade your income without selling your home, here is an interesting alternative a friend of ours took. On a year or more lease, she rents her lovely home (paid for) in an exclusive suburban development to executives who are temporarily stationed in the nearby city. Then, for herself, she rents a small, inexpensive apartment in a convenient part of town, just right for a single woman. She uses the house expenses as a write-off against her rental income. She figures she is covering all bases: gaining if appreciation continues, yet earning a tidy monthly income no matter what happens. In effect, she is renting out the many thousands of dollars of equity in the house.

The question finally boils down to whether you can afford to watch your home equity grow, with a chance that it might level off or drop should there be a "bubble burst" in the market, or whether to put your equity to better use in maintaining your lifestyle. Making a decision to pull down equity is not easy. The decision shouldn't be made until all factors are considered and you have consulted a reputable financial adviser.

There are several advantages that come with owning property. As mentioned, property ownership is a hedge against inflation. Should the economy go into an inflationary spiral as it did in the 1970s, property values will follow. Another benefit is that you can often "homestead" your residence in the event of a lawsuit or personal bankruptcy.

Inexpensive Home Ownership

Some people absolutely cannot bear the thought of not owning the home they live in. A castle that belongs to you alone—even a small castle—is more than a luxury; it's a necessity, a feeling of dignity and security. Having to sell the homestead wouldn't be as much of a hardship if they could replace their current home with a less expensive place, with low monthly payments. A good place to begin your search is with the U.S. Department of Housing and Urban Development (HUD).

HUD is in the business of helping folks purchase homes, assisting them with federal mortgage programs, and selling homes, especially to low-income families. If HUD can't help you with a home purchase, they might be able to help you find some low-cost public housing or privately owned subsidized housing. The department wears many hats.

Repossession sales often go through HUD. When someone with a HUD-insured mortgage cannot meet the payments, the lender forecloses on the home. HUD then pays off the mortgage and assumes ownership of the property. The home is then offered for sale, usually priced at the low end of the market so it will sell quickly. You can make a bid (below the asking price) during an "offer period." At the end of the offer period, the offers are opened and the highest bid is accepted. If the home isn't sold during the offer period, you can submit a bid on any business day.

These homes are sold by HUD "as is," without warranty. The agency cannot pay to correct any problems or to spiff up the place. This means that HUD's asking price takes into account that the buyer will probably have to invest work and maybe some money to bring the house up to standard. In some cases, HUD will offer special incentives to make a sale. It might make adjustments in the asking price because the property needs upgrading, or it may offer an allowance for moving expenses or a bonus for closing the sale early.

HUD makes it easy to find out what is available and how to go about buying a home through its Housing Counseling Clearinghouse (HCC), which operates a toll-free, twenty-four-hour automated voice response system that provides home owners and home buyers with referrals to local housing counseling agencies. The number is (800) 569–4287. The Web site is www.hud.gov/offices.

When an economic downturn hits an area, you might find many homes on the verge of foreclosure. The possibility here is finding a home about to be foreclosed, with an assumable loan. Sometimes the owners owe more on the home than it would sell for. In this case, they are happy to find someone to take the home off their hands just to protect their credit. When homes aren't selling, lenders and government agencies will sometimes let you take over a foreclosure with no down payment if your credit is good.

Check Your Credit Before Applying!

Before making an offer on a HUD property, it's a good idea to check your credit status by ordering copies of your credit report from one of the three largest national credit bureaus. The good news is a federal law enacted last year requires each of the three nationwide credit reporting agencies (Equifax, Experian, and TransUnion) to provide you with a free copy of your credit report, upon request, once every twelve months. Information on how to obtain this free report can be found on the Federal Trade Commission's Web site at www.ftc.gov/bcp/conline/pubs/credit/freereports.htm, or you can call (877) 322–8228 and request the Annual Credit Report Request Form.

Another reason for a credit report: If you are considering moving to a new hometown for a new beginning, such as a job change, retirement, or perhaps going into business for yourself, you should make sure you have a clean credit report. You might need financing for a car or to rent a home in your new hometown. You may need credit to purchase equipment to start a business in your new location. Suddenly discovering that you have a bad credit rating—even though it isn't your fault—can be traumatic and time-consuming to say the least.

But how could this be? You've always paid your bills on time. Never defaulted on a loan. Credit cards are paid off in full every month, right? None of that matters because you could be the unwitting victim of an innocent mistake. This is more common than you might think. According to a study by the U.S. Public Interest Research Group, almost 80 percent of credit reports have errors, and 25 percent have mistakes serious enough for you to be denied credit, loans, and housing.

Honest errors can happen in several ways, but the most common is when a lender accidentally transposes a single digit on a loan application or on a purchase agreement, thus reporting *you* as the borrower to the credit-reporting company. (They don't see a name, only a Social Security number.) You'll never know about this as long as the borrower makes regular payments on the loan. Should the borrower be slow making payments or have to be threatened from time to time, you still won't know about it, yet the lender forwards the complaints to the credit-reporting agency. Black marks begin smudging your credit rating. You still don't know. Later on, when you apply for a mortgage on your new home, try to buy an automobile on credit, or rent a home in your new hometown, you could find yourself being refused. This can be cleared up, of course, but not without a lot of hassle. Best check out your credit ratings *before* you need credit. And it doesn't cost you anything.

Before applying for a loan, you can improve your chances of getting a loan or being accepted by taking the following actions:

- Pay off as much as possible on your credit cards and other high-interest loans. The less you owe, the more likely it is that lenders will approve your loan.

- Don't make a major purchase, such as a car, on credit unless you have little other credit debt. Lenders will be most interested in borrowers who have the lowest debt.

- Contact creditors who have filed negative reports on you. Something as small as a $5.00 balance on a bill you thought you'd paid off or canceled can result in a bad mark. Send a written request, asking the creditor to remove the unfavorable mark from your record and to send a report to you. This could take up to ninety days.

- Contact the credit bureau if a creditor has mistakenly or unfairly given you a bad mark. Document the facts and write a letter to be attached to the offending entry in your file.

Why Not Rent?

If, after analyzing your situation, you find you would be better off using your home equity as a cash investment, you might consider renting as an alternative to home ownership. One benefit of renting is that the landlord—not you or your spouse—is responsible for painting the house or repairing tornado damage. You won't be paying $300 a month in property taxes, either.

Another happy thought is the knowledge that you don't *have* to live there. When your lease is up, you are perfectly free to look for a better place. Since you aren't tied to a particular locality, you can move someplace where rents are even less. For example, an apartment that rents for $635 a month in Chico, California, couldn't be duplicated in a comparable San Francisco neighborhood for less than $1,535 a month (according to figures from HUD).

Another argument against renting I often hear is, "Paying rent is like pouring money down a rat hole—no tax breaks." Yes, there was a time in your life when that was true. When you were earning good wages, your high property taxes and interest payments brought you a nice income tax refund at the end of the year. But when you have little income from which to deduct taxes and interest, it's a different scenario. Because the IRS grants a $500,000 tax deduction for a couple selling their home ($250,000 for an individual), you'll probably keep all of your profits, tax-free, provided the home you're selling has been your primary residence for at least two of the previous five years.

What are the disadvantages of renting? For someone who's always owned a home, there's a vague feeling of insecurity. Also, when you're renting a house, you never know if the owner is going to put it up for sale, and you'll have to move. When you were younger, moving was no big deal, but as you grow older, the chore looms larger and more distasteful. The bottom line is undeniable: You lose the sense of security that comes with home ownership. On the other hand, when the roof springs a leak, you place a call to the landlord and let him worry about it instead of calling roofers, hoping for an estimate under $10,000!

To sum up: Home ownership, even though monthly payments are high, clearly makes sense for a young couple whose earning power will probably grow over the years. As time goes by, they pay off the loan with larger paychecks, with dollars that will shrink in value with inflation. They are building for the future, just as you did at their age. But before you enter an expensive, long-term commitment to build equity for the future, you might want to consider whether it wouldn't be better to invest your money in your retirement rather than in some nebulous future thirty years down the line. Maybe this is that future you waited for. Will you be able to enjoy your money as much thirty years from now as you can today? How old will you be then? In short, don't automatically fall for the "money down a rat hole" line. Figure out the financial advantages for yourselves realistically, with an eye on today, not thirty years in the future.

Rental Assistance

For those who absolutely cannot afford conventional rents, some special federal government programs sometimes come to the rescue. One program, known as *Section 8,* is titled the Housing Choice Voucher Program, designed to provide rental assistance for very low-income families, the elderly, and the disabled. The purpose is to subsidize rents for decent, safe, and sanitary housing in the private market. Because rental assistance is provided on behalf of the family or individual, you are free to find and lease privately owned housing, whether they be single-family homes, town houses, or apartments. This means you're not necessarily limited to units located in housing projects, which can sometimes be dangerous as well as dreary.

A caveat about the following information: The rules and regulations are in place at the time of writing, but you must be aware that given the way Congress is fiddling with the rules and laws—believe me, not in your favor—there's a good chance conditions will have tightened up by the time you get ready to apply for benefits. Also, federal subsidies on a large number of housing units set aside for low-income tenants nationwide are expiring. Once these subsidies expire, owners are free to exit the federal and state programs to take advantage of the trend toward rising rents, which are typically far higher than government-subsidized rents.

To qualify, renters need to show certain income and asset limitations. Of course, once you qualify, you still have to find a landlord who is willing to participate in the Section 8 program, and the rent must fall within the limits set by the federal government. Sometimes that can be difficult, particularly in communities and neighborhoods where rentals are scarce. The landlord gets assurance that HUD will take care of unusual wear and tear of the property and guarantee the rent should the tenant skip out.

Renters have the security of never having to pay more than 30 percent of their income for rent. HUD has a formula for fair rents in various communities and pays the difference. The formula for average rents for various parts of the country can be found at www.huduser.org/datasets/fmr.html (the Web site is a little confusing, but before long you'll figure it out).

Sometimes another rental assistance approach is taken: The qualifying applicant is given a coupon or voucher that's worth the difference between 30 percent of the tenant's income and the market rental value of the apartment. The landlord doesn't have to agree to the Section 8 Housing Program to participate in the Housing Voucher Program. This plan is also administered by your local housing authority.

The program is funded by HUD, but it is administered locally, usually by a county or city housing agency. When you qualify and are issued a rental voucher, you are responsible for finding and selecting a suitable rental unit of your choice. This could be your current rental residence. Rental units must meet minimum standards of health and safety, and they could be inspected by the housing authority before being approved. A rental subsidy is paid directly to the landlord by the housing authority. You then pay the difference between the actual rent charged by the landlord and the amount subsidized by the program.

Eligibility for rental assistance is determined by the housing authority based on the total annual gross income and family size and is limited to U.S. citizens and specified categories of noncitizens who have eligible immigration status. In general, the family's income may not exceed 30 to 50 percent of the median income for the county or metropolitan area in which the family chooses to live. This figure can vary widely, depending on the part of the country where you live. For example some localities in Florida allow a maximum income of $7,800 for a couple, whereas Connecticut sets the limit at $21,000.

Once the housing authority determines that you are eligible, your name goes on a waiting list. When your name reaches the top of the waiting list, the housing authority contacts you and issues a rental voucher. Depending on circumstances, you could get immediate assistance.

When selecting applicants from the waiting list, preferences are given to those who are homeless or living in substandard housing, paying more than 50 percent of the family's income for rent, or involuntarily displaced. Those who qualify for these preferences will move ahead of others on the list. Each local housing authority has the discretion to change the rules to reflect the needs of its particular community.

Contrary to stereotype, public housing tenants aren't restricted to welfare recipients and single moms with kids. Retired and disabled households without children account for 40 percent of all public housing residents. And, contrary to popular belief, the primary source of income for more than two-thirds of public housing residents comes from wages, Social Security, and pensions—not welfare.

In some communities, many more people apply than there are openings for low-rental units. So if your local HUD-sponsored facility has a long wait, you might check around with other communities. A friend of ours, Alice W., qualified for low-cost housing, but when she applied in the popular Pacific Coast town where she was living, she was informed that it would be at least six years before her name could possibly come up for a HUD-subsidized apartment. Then she discovered a small town in a beautiful Sierra Nevada location with a waiting list of only a few months. She moved there, intending to rent until something opened up. However, because she could legitimately plead hardship—with an exceptionally low income and resources well below the allowable amount—Alice was awarded a one-bedroom apartment. Her rent equals 27 percent of her net monthly income. After deductions and allowances—according to a complicated formula—her rent comes to about $70 per month.

Nonprofit Subsidized Housing

Nonprofit housing is often owned and managed by private nonprofit groups such as churches, ethno-cultural communities, and sometimes local governments. This type of housing can use private funding as well as government subsidies to support a rent-geared-to-income program for low-income tenants.

One of the nation's largest nonprofit providers of subsidized retirement facilities, the Retirement Housing Foundation, operates more than 145 retirement communities. They range in size from a twelve-unit home for the developmentally disabled to a 1,000-unit apartment complex in the heart of Los Angeles. This is the largest subsidized retirement community for the elderly and persons with disabilities in the country. It's a member of the Human Service Ministries of the United Church of Christ. All units are HUD approved, and the tenants' rents are partly subsidized by HUD. In other, non-HUD–subsidized units, residents pay a deposit and competitive rents, although these are somewhat lower than conventional commercial rents because of the HUD low-interest mortgages.

For information, contact the Retirement Housing Foundation, 5150 East Pacific Coast Highway, #600, Long Beach, CA 90804; (310) 597–5541. Their Web site is www.rhf.org. Another large provider is National Church Residences, 2335 Northbank, Columbus, OH 43220; (614) 451–2151; www.ncr.org.

Work Exchange

One option for staying where you are, yet cutting your housing expense to zero, is to work as property managers. It's entirely possible to enjoy free rent plus a small salary in exchange for your services as property managers. Example: An apartment complex in our hometown was recently advertising for a married couple to take over management in return for a small salary ($800 a month) plus a two-bedroom apartment and utilities. The smaller the property, the fewer your obligations and responsibilities will be, and of course, the less the pay. Often you can find an absentee owner of a six- or eight-unit apartment complex who is delighted to offer a nice reduction in rent for someone to watch over things, to call the plumber when necessary, to collect rent checks and deposit them, and generally solve problems.

Another situation offered in our local newspaper's classified section was management of a mobile home park in return for free housing (presumably connected with the office), medical benefits, a modest monthly salary, plus two weeks' vacation. The downside to this job is the obligation to keep the office open forty-four hours a week. Not exactly retirement, but the housing expense is affordable!

Sharing Housing

One way to reduce your monthly housing outlay—without moving away from your hometown—is through house sharing. In Europe the concept of more than one family to a home is traditional, as it used to be in the United States in the early half of the last century. During the Depression, people thought nothing of families doubling up to share expenses. A large house can easily accommodate many more people than usually live there. After World War II, a tremendous housing boom made homes readily available and cheap. It then became almost obligatory for every family to own its own little piece of real estate. Shared housing and double-family living became a thing of the past.

Today, however, with real estate priced out of reach for many, the concept of house sharing is returning to the American scene. For those who are retired and who don't own a home, or for those who can no longer afford the burdens of home ownership, the notion of house sharing can be very practical. If you own a large house that is empty now that the children are out on their own, sharing with another retired couple is one way to cut costs and have income at the same time. If you have three bedrooms, maybe two couples can share with you.

Group living turns out to be an efficient as well as convenient way to cut living costs. This is particularly true in some of the more desirable but expensive locations. "We really wanted to live in Pacific Heights," said one couple, who couldn't afford the rent in this spiffy San Francisco neighborhood. "But we'd have to pay at least $2,500 a month for rent and utilities. That just wasn't in the cards. We found another couple and a single lady to go in with us on a spacious home, and we've cut our share of rent and utility expense to about $900 a month, yet we live in an elegant neighborhood."

Shared housing is not just for retirement-age people. Many arrangements include multigenerational "families," in which young, middle-aged, and elderly people live as one cooperative unit. Others are organized according to sex; women often prefer to live with other women rather than have disruptive menfolk dirtying up the house. A typical home sharer could be a senior citizen, a person with disabilities, a formerly homeless person, a single parent, a recuperating patient, or simply a person wishing to share his or her life with others. For these people, shared housing offers companionship, security, mutual support, and much more.

Obviously, in order to make a success of one of these situations, the group's members must be compatible. This isn't the place for someone who is rigid, closed-minded, or doesn't enjoy being around people. Making the decision to try a shared-housing lifestyle requires that you not only investigate the situation very thoroughly but also objectively analyze your own personality.

Ask yourself some questions: Do noise and confusion disturb me? Would pets bother me? Would I be terribly upset if someone weren't as neat as I am? What if a living companion left underwear hanging on the shower curtain? If these things bother you, or if you are notorious for the offenses mentioned above, you should think things over carefully before making a decision. In any event, see if you can't do a month's trial stay to make sure everyone is like-minded and compatible.

There are other considerations. Will the space be adequate? Besides the bedroom, how much of the house will be yours? Will you have room for your hobbies? Also, how are decisions made in the house? In other words, is it a democracy or is someone in charge—perhaps the owner or the original tenant? Neither arrangement is inherently preferable, but you need to know how the system works in advance. If the person in charge is strict but fair, and if everyone knows where the boundaries are and precisely what the responsibilities are, there should be few problems. But if that person is a tyrant, you may be better off elsewhere. On the other hand, a democratic management—with each resident politicking, lobbying, and arguing heatedly over each and every excruciating detail of life in the house—can be just as bad. A happy medium is always the best path.

There should be sharing of work responsibilities, chores, and perhaps cooking. Often housemates take turns cooking supper, giving the others a welcome break. "There are ten of us living in our house," said one lady as she detailed her experiences in shared housing. "Each of us is responsible for preparing three dinners every month and for cleaning up afterward. That means that except for our three chore days, we have dinner waiting for us every night. We can watch the evening news or read a novel and relax before and after dinner. The dinners are excellent, too, because we cook our favorite meals, and each person tries to outdo the others!"

Further questions: Will you be close to shopping and transportation? If you have an auto, will you have a parking space? You also need to decide the kind of house partners you'd like to live with. Some groups behave like small, extended families, while others are more formal, with relationships on a neighborly rather than familial level. Note, too, that a larger group gives more of an opportunity to choose friends and to spread expenses over a larger base.

Sometimes a shared housing unit can be large, from 20 to 200 units operated as a commercial enterprise. This is called congregate housing. This arrangement is suitable for those in good health who may need assistance in everyday chores, cooking, housekeeping, and shopping, or those who don't want to be bothered with any of the above. The living quarters are small, usually with a tiny kitchen, and there is a group dining room where residents can take meals if they wish. Cooking and cleaning are done by staff. Sometimes these units are federally subsidized and available only to low-income, elderly applicants.

How do you find these situations? The most common source is the classified section of your daily newspaper. The number of "housemates wanted" advertisements grows in direct proportion to increases in housing costs. There are also private and nonprofit agencies that specialize in placing individuals in shared housing. Your telephone book's yellow pages will put you in touch with these agencies. A great resource is the Eldercare Locator, a nationwide toll-free service that helps older adults and their caregivers find local services. The U.S. Administration on Aging has incorporated this service since 1991. For the nearest source of help, call the toll-free Eldercare Locator service at (800) 677–1116, Monday through Friday, 9:00 A.M. to 8:00 P.M. Eastern time. Online, contact www.eldercare.gov/default.asp or www.nationalsharedhousing.org.

Renting Rooms in Your Home

You may feel that sharing your home with strangers might take away too much of your autonomy, flexibility, and privacy. After all, the word *share* implies a certain amount of equality among the group, and you may feel more comfortable just renting part of your home rather than sharing. This way, you make the rules and set the boundaries of exactly which privileges your paying guests may be entitled to. Many of the same concerns about sharing your home will apply to renting out a room. You must feel prepared physically and emotionally to welcome nonfamily members into your home and be willing to accept some inconvenience in return for the extra income.

Desirable renters tend to be senior citizens, serious college students, and young professionals who do not want the expense and bother of renting and furnishing an apartment. When selecting a tenant, you must consider whether you would prefer someone who might keep you company on a social basis or someone who will live privately, who will come and go as unobtrusively as possible, and whose lifestyle will not infringe on yours.

Depending on your desires, you can develop a set of "house rules" that outline which behaviors are acceptable and which are unsatisfactory. The rules should clearly cover behaviors such as smoking, drinking, and guests. How often are guests allowed, which parts of the house are off limits to guests, and are overnight privileges allowed? Your renter should have a clear understanding of whether cooking and kitchen privileges are included in the rent, and details concerning space in the refrigerator, cleaning up, and when the kitchen will be available. Other house rules should cover laundry privileges, bathroom policies, use of telephone, a security deposit, and a fixed date for the rent to be paid. It isn't a bad idea to put your house rules in writing and ask the renter to sign in acknowledgment.

It doesn't happen often, but occasionally an unscrupulous con man will answer your newspaper classified ad and try to pull some scam on you. It's recommended that you not give out your exact address (especially if you live alone) until you have confidence that everything is on the up-and-up. In your phone interview, explain your house rules, find out where the applicant is employed or where he or she goes to school, and find out why he or she wants to rent your room. If you live alone, make sure you have someone else with you when you conduct the face-to-face interview. Of course, get landlord and employer references, as well as the applicant's driver's license number and Social Security number. You cannot be too careful in your selection process. After all, it *is* your house, and you are doing someone a huge favor by sharing part of it. Some communities have a professional agency that goes through this process for you for a fee. Check your yellow pages for organizations such as Elder Help or call your local AARP chapter for assistance.

Intentional Community Housing

There is a growing movement toward planned, or "intentional," communities. Though sometimes these are small, family-type affairs, many are larger groups, more like clubs, where people with common interests band together to forge new lifestyles and to share expenses and experiences. The intentional community differs from ordinary shared housing in that there is usually a common goal or special shared beliefs among the participants. They think of themselves as "members" rather than simply "neighbors." For a complete listing of interesting locations, look for a book in your library called *Communities Directory: A Guide to Intentional Communities and Cooperative Living* (Fellowship for Intentional, August 2005). The book contains information on 600 intentional communities as well as 100 overseas locations. A Web site with detailed information can be found at www.ic.org and an online newsletter at www.communities.ic.org.

A few myths need to be dispelled about the concept of intentional communities. The common belief is that this concept, which started in the '60s, disappeared in the '70s with the end of the hippie era. The fact is, many of those communities survived and evolved into more conventional living arrangements. Many new ones have formed since then, as a significant new wave of interest in intentional communities has grown over the last decade.

Another belief is that they are mostly "communes," operating with a common treasury and sharing ownership of property. Or else that they center around a particular religion or spiritual practice. Some do, of course, but most have the goal of sharing resources and creating an extended family environment. Usually they are people wanting to share their lives with others who hold similar values. Ecological concerns are a prevalent theme of many intentional communities. Some of these experiments are outgrowths of communities started during the "hippie" era. Others are more modern in origin. You'll find communities for women only, for couples, or for mixed and intergenerational members. Some communities are religiously oriented, sometimes receiving funds from a church. You'll find all spectrums of religious beliefs represented in intentional communities, from conservative Baptists to broad-minded Unitarians. We know of one community that combines lesbian feminists who are interested in witchcraft and Buddhism! About 35 percent of intentional communities are explicitly religious or spiritual in nature, so if this isn't your cup of tea, inquire before wasting your time.

Most intentional communities are owned by members. They sometimes provide free room and board in return for a specified amount of work in tasks ranging from cooking and gardening to teaching and housekeeping. Other groups require a stipend or at least a sharing of expenses. Some charge a monthly fee and also require work in exchange for residence and seminars. Some facilities are located on farms, others in forest or desert settings, while still others are urban collectives. About 65 percent of these communities are self-governed by democratic means, with decisions made by some form of consensus or voting. However, a few communities (mostly religious groups) have strict hierarchical or authoritarian rules, so it would be worthwhile to investigate before joining.

Be aware that new communities are continually in the process of formation and may never get off the ground. So be cautious about investing time and money in a mere pipe dream. Many do not actively solicit new members, so don't think you can simply drop in and take up residence. First, you need to contact the group to see if there are any openings and if your interests coincide.

One point to keep in mind: Just because an organization offers inexpensive living doesn't mean you will be happy there. One community listing sounded all right to me until it described member residents as generally having "undecided sexual propensities." (Can't quite figure out how I would fit in.) Another group, still in the process of forming, plans on building an under-the-ocean village where you will be surrounded by the "awesome beauty of the sea." Right.

Whatever You Decide On for Your Housing Needs, Investigate Before Moving In

In any kind of shared or cooperative living situation, certain conditions must be thoroughly understood. Ideally, there will be a contract, especially if you will be renting from a private or public entity rather than just informal sharing. If you are going to have to put up any money, here are some things you need to know.

How much, if any, of the entrance fee is refundable? Are there additional expenses besides the monthly fees? Should you die, will your heirs receive a portion of your entrance fee or deposit? Suppose you are unable to pay the monthly fee; is any financial assistance available? Are there any controls on how much fees can go up? Under what conditions can the arrangement be terminated by either side? Usually there's a three-month trial period, so you should have the right to cancel and get a refund of your entrance fee. Nonrefundable entrance fees should be avoided. You might want to check with the Better Business Bureau to see if there have been complaints against the facility and whether it is in good financial shape.

Older retirees might be interested in an American Association of Homes for the Aging publication, *The Consumer's Directory of Continuing Care Retirement Communities*, which lists more than 300 continuing-care retirement communities. Your library should have a copy. For information on shared housing, contact the National Shared Housing Resource Center at (802) 862–2727; www.nationalsharedhousing.org, or write to AARP Fulfillment, 601 East Street NW, Washington, DC 20049. Another source of information is the National Consumers League, 1701 K Street NW, Suite 1200, Washington, DC 20006; (202) 835–3323; www.natlconsumersleague.org.

chapter three

Transportation, Energy, and Taxes

Next to housing, the largest budget item in most households is transportation. Americans typically spend more on their automobiles than they do for food on the table and clothing combined. According to recent surveys, the average two-car American family spends around $7,600 a year for transportation. That's more than $600 a month, about half of an average couple's Social Security check!

Obviously, lower-income households are hit harder because owning one or two cars eats up a higher percentage of the family income than more affluent folks. Obviously, transportation is an obligatory expense to get to and from work, home, school, and shopping. Yet the Bureau of Labor Statistics does not include the cost of transportation as one of the basic necessities, along with food, apparel, and housing. In my opinion, this is intended to make the official inflation rate look lower than it really is.

Back in the 1970s the average family spent one dollar out of every ten on transportation. Spending kept increasing until by 1984, automobiles gobbled one dollar out of every five. Costs leveled off in the 1990s—those good old days, when we lived in a world of peace and plenty and the price of crude oil was $12.00 a barrel. Gasoline averaged $1.20 a gallon. Automobiles kept getting bigger every year, with SUVs crowding parking spaces all over the country. Who cared? Gasoline was affordable.

How different today! At this writing, a barrel of crude oil is hovering in the range of $70.00 a barrel. Yesterday I paid $3.51 a gallon for gasoline to power our 20-mile-per-gallon gas hog. Instead of one dollar out of five that we spent on getting around in the 1990s, we are approaching one dollar out of four! At that rate, before long it will cost more to drive your car than to pay the mortgage. In my opinion, it isn't going to get any better and could possibly get worse. Experts predict that the era of cheap gasoline is behind us.

So if you are looking for a way to trim your expenses, transportation costs offer a good place to start. Actually, you could slice from 18 to 23 percent of your budget simply by getting rid of your automobiles. Easily said, not so easily done. Most people are highly dependent on a car—they live too far from shopping, and if they work, it's almost certain they have to drive to the job every day. If husband and wife both work, that usually means two cars. Unless you live in one of those few cities with good public transportation, there's no alternative way to get to your job, to the supermarket, or to run errands.

For those who will be relocating upon retirement, this is something to think about: When looking for housing, if at all possible, locate somewhere within walking distance to shopping, a library, restaurants, and other favorite places. It's nice to be out in the country, but you'll be doubly dependent on an auto and probably will need two of them. At our California home, my wife and I happen to live within walking distance of two grocery stores, the library, post office, and several really nice restaurants. We didn't plan it that way; it just happened the house we bought was so located. Sometimes a week will go by and the only time we start our station wagon is for heavy shopping at the supermarket.

Trimming Automobile Costs

Budget experts suggest the following to take control of your transportation costs:

Get rid of that second car. So you have to drive your husband to work and thus rack up twice the miles for that trip? You save by paying for only one insurance policy, one license, personal property taxes, interest on a loan, and other expenses involved in car ownership.

Pay cash for your car if at all possible. Car payments gouge heavily into the budget. By the time you finally get the car paid off, it invariably needs to be replaced. So you go into debt again to buy another set of wheels. Remember that a new car loses thousands of dollars in value the moment you drive it from the showroom. If you are financing, many of your monthly payments will go to pay off that depreciation. Instead, look around for a reliable used car that's in good shape, one at a price that you can afford to buy for cash. You'll save on insurance costs, since you aren't obligated to purchase as much high-cost collision insurance on a $6,000 car as you would on a $20,000 model. The savings in insurance premiums will more than pay for an occasional fender bender. Also, a crumpled fender doesn't look nearly as bad on an older model Honda as on a pristine new Jaguar.

Better yet, get rid of both cars and save. If you've found a nice neighborhood within walking distance of most places you go every day, you'll have made a good start. You say you can't possibly do without a car? You can't carry all those groceries home from the supermarket after your regular Saturday shopping trips? How about an occasional weekend trip to the lake, or to the big city to visit friends, or to take in a big-league baseball game and dinner?

Okay, for that once-a-week shopping trip, walk to the supermarket, then call a cab for the return trip—$5.00 dollars or less. That's $20.00 for a month's shopping. For that trip to the lake or big city, rent a car from Avis, Hertz, or whoever offers the cheapest auto rentals. In many locations, particularly near big cities, compact autos can often be rented for as little as $20.00 or $30.00 a day. In smaller towns, between $35.00 to $50.00 a day. So let's suppose you spend $50.00 a month on taxis, $100.00 a month for a weekend car rental—that's $150.00 a month compared with $600.00 that the average family spends. That's a savings of $400.00—enough to pay the grocery bills and have plenty left over to go out for dinner every week. Sure, take a taxi!

If you relocate, look for a city with good public transit. This can make a difference. Portland, Oregon, for example, has 15 percent cost of transportation compared with Houston with 21 percent (2003 statistics). This is simply due to efficient public transportation. I'm not saying that moving to Portland and saving 5 or 10 percent on your transportation costs will solve your budget problems. But with good public transit, you won't miss your automobile nearly as much, should you decide to break your love affair with gas-guzzling iron monsters.

Trimming Utility Bills

Utility costs, the second big category of potential savings, also differ from place to place. Moving to a warmer climate, where real estate sells for a fraction of what you're used to and where cold-weather heating costs don't gobble up your spare cash, will give your budget a real boost. Like the cost of gasoline, utility savings were much more dramatic a few short years ago, before the costs of natural gas, diesel fuel, and electricity began their steep increase. As long as crude oil hovers around $70 a barrel, this means bad news for those who need to keep warm in the winter and cool in the summer. It is good news, however, for oil companies, who are recording record profits. In 2005 Exxon Mobil Corp. recorded the highest quarterly profit ever for a U.S. company: $10.7 billion. It's a simple case of supply and demand. They supply the gasoline, and they demand an arm and a leg.

Nevertheless, since electricity and natural gas bills can vary from 27 percent below average in some communities to 47 percent above average in other places, those who will relocate will have another way to control expenses. (See the chart below, and note the relationship between cost of living and utility costs.) The biggest energy hog—heating your home—obviously varies with the climate.

Your electric and heating-fuel expenditures can dwarf your grocery bills when you stave off cold weather with an energy-gobbling furnace half the year and then fight stifling summer weather with an air conditioner for half the year. Bills of $275 a month for heating and $175 a month for air-conditioning are common in many locations. We've visited

Cost of Living and Utility Rates
(Percent of National Averages for Selected Cities)

Town	Cost of Living	Housing	Utilities	Health Care	Groceries
Cedar City, UT	90%	73%	84%	85%	103%
Ashland, OH	91	74	115	93	102
Aiken, SC	91	74	92	97	105
Clarksville, TN	86	75	81	92	88
Hot Springs, AR	87	77	92	86	95
Dothan, AL	90	77	87	81	99
Panama City, FL	96	81	90	99	104
Klamath Falls, OR	98	82	99	106	112
Corpus Christi, TX	89	82	100	90	80
Providence, RI	128	168	127	108	116
San Diego, CA	143	219	95	120	117
Honolulu, HI	161	240	142	113	153
Boston, MA	152	241	118	119	112
San Jose, CA	171	279	117	119	116

NOTE: The relationship between cost of living, utilities, and housing costs (rent and median prices of homes). Data from latest available ACCRA Cost of Living Index.

places in Wyoming and Montana where monthly heating bills of $350 to $400 are normal in winter. Ironically, people living in sunny California were receiving very low utility bills until the state deregulated the industry a few years ago. Now they are paying dearly. Fortunately, most of the state isn't plagued by frozen winters.

You can cut utility bills by a third by moving to a section of the country where you can live without air-conditioning. And if you go someplace where you never need an air conditioner and seldom need to turn on a furnace, you'll save even more. (You'll find such places along the Pacific Coast from northern California to reaches of British Columbia.) We've interviewed folks who cut their average utility bills from $250 a month to $65 simply by moving to a mild climate. That means $185 a month left over to help with bills or for luxuries.

Home Energy Assistance Program

Everybody can't move to a mild climate to avoid high heating bills in the winter. In fact, most people don't want to move away. If you choose to stay put in your hometown—as the majority of retirees do—there are ways of cutting utilities without pulling up stakes and leaving the kids and grandchildren. Fortunately, several assistance programs are out there to help low-income home owners and renters cut energy costs. A federal effort you should know about is the Home Energy Assistance Program (HEAP), which comes to the rescue of low-income people who face unaffordable energy bills.

However, the HEAP program is continually under attack by Congress in its zeal to increase the size of their pork barrel *piñatas* by reducing amounts spent on poor and needy. Not long ago they had to beat a retreat when state and local officials lobbied against drastic cuts in the Home Energy Assistance Program, especially during the winter of 2005–2006, when fuel oil costs hit all-time highs. The government was embarrassed when Venezuela offered to supply heating oil at half price to poor people in the United States.

Although in some states HEAP assistance is limited to heating expenses, in other states HEAP also helps with lighting and cooking costs. As a renter, even if heating is included in the rent payments, you may still be eligible for reimbursement. The more liberal states allow HEAP funds to pay for maintenance and repair of heating equipment. Sometimes HEAP assistance will even pay for weatherizing your home or apartment. In many areas, your local utility company gets into the act, helping you maximize your energy efficiency through weather stripping and insulating water heaters as a free service.

While you're at it, inquire about energy- and utility-company discounts for low-income families; it's worthwhile to check this out. Put your bid in early in the year; there's often a limit on the amount of relief available. If you use oil for heating, ask whether there's an oil buyer's cooperative in your area. Sometimes residents band together to cut fuel costs through group purchasing power.

To qualify for HEAP, you must file an application with your local department of social services or public welfare. Regulations for qualifying vary from state to state. Ohio, for example, requires that you meet the following criteria: a household of one person, a three-month income of no more than $4,187; a couple, less than $5,613; three persons, less than $7,039; and no more than $8,465 for a household of four. Remember, you should be prepared to prove that you are truly needy. This will be no problem if you already qualify for food stamps or receive welfare or Supplemental Security Income (SSI). In any event, remember to apply for assistance as early in the year as permitted, because the federal funds for HEAP are limited; once they've been allocated, no more help is available. For information about HEAP, contact your local office of public welfare or social services department.

Recognizing that cold weather hits low-income families hardest, many utility companies join with state and local governments to conduct energy audits and weatherization assistance. Experts will survey your home at no charge and show you how to save money on heating bills. Low-interest or interest-free loans are then available for you to follow through with recommendations—things like adding insulation to critical parts of the house and weatherizing doors and windows.

The Weatherization Assistance Program enables low-income families to permanently reduce their energy bills by making their homes more energy efficient. It is this country's longest running, and perhaps most successful, energy efficiency program. During the last twenty-seven years, the U.S. Department of Energy's Weatherization Assistance Program has provided weatherization services to more than five million low-income families. By reducing the energy bills of low-income families, weatherization reduces dependency on public assistance and liberates these funds for spending on more pressing family issues. On average, weatherization reduces heating bills by 31 percent and reduces energy bills by hundreds of dollars per year.

Eligibility rules and the scope of help vary from locality to locality, but generally preference is given to home owners or renters with homes built before a certain year. Eligibility for these audit and weatherization programs usually doesn't depend on income. To find out about programs in your area, call your state public service commission or contact the Department of Energy, Division of Weatherization Assistance, 1000 Independence Avenue SW, Washington, DC 20585; (202) 586–2207; www .eere.energy.gov/weatherization.

Another way of cutting heating costs is to live in an apartment or condominium complex instead of individual housing. Because the living quarters have less exposed outside wall surface and because costs are shared between living units, you'll usually find lower heating and cooling bills. Utilities are often included in the rent. Although you pay indirectly through rent, the landlord assumes the problem of insulation and getting the best rates in order to keep his rents competitive.

Taxes and Your Budget
Property Taxes

For those who rent, real estate taxes will not have a huge impact. Your landlord pays them for you. But for those who insist on home ownership yet need to live on a tight budget, taxes can be an item to be reckoned with. You have only two ways to reduce real estate taxes: Either move to a less-expensive home or move to a low-tax area. Moving doesn't necessarily mean moving out of the state or even out of the vicinity where you live. In most states you'll often find dramatic differences in property tax rates in neighboring communities, sometimes in the same county. Each state has its own unique tax structure, and each county, township, and city adds its own assessments to create a bewildering patchwork of rates throughout the nation.

Choosing the right tax niche is where you could save enough to cover your monthly grocery bills and then some. I recently interviewed friends who live in a San Francisco suburb and were ecstatic about the future retirement home they purchased in Fairhope, Alabama (a popular retirement community near the city of Mobile and just a few miles from the

Gulf Coast beaches). They fell in love with the town while vacationing in the area and visiting friends. Almost on impulse, they came up with a small down payment and became owners of a beautiful $89,000 home almost the same size as their $350,000 California home. (Of course, $350,000 doesn't buy much near San Francisco!) Since the Fairhope home was rented and the rent almost covers their mortgage payments, the transaction was painless. They will be building equity until full retirement. The interesting part of the story is that taxes on their California home were a little more than $4,000 ($333 a month), but their taxes on their future retirement home will be about $450 a year. (That's only $37 a month!) This $3,550 in saved taxes can cover the cost of a yearly vacation in Costa Rica or a Caribbean cruise.

Another example of how property taxes can determine where to relocate is the case of a friend and his wife who owned a lovely home on Long Island. His bedridden mother—who lived overseas—needed intensive care yet refused to move into a nursing home. So my friend gave up his business and moved to Germany to help his mother. After an extended period of time, his mother passed away and they were free to return to Long Island. Here is what he says:

"My lack of income forced us to move out of Long Island, mostly because our property taxes had gone up an amazing amount. Even with our senior discount, they were more than $10,000 a year. So we moved to Lewes, Delaware—a booming area with property taxes even for a $400,000 home on a three-quarter wooded acre only about $1,100, and

Property Tax Burden by State
(1/lowest burden; 50/highest burden)

1. Alaska	7. Florida	13. Nevada
2. New Hampshire	8. Texas	14. Colorado
3. Delaware	9. North Dakota	15. Oregon
4. Tennessee	10. Missouri	16. Pennsylvania
5. Alabama	11. Oklahoma	17. Virginia
6. South Dakota	12. Montana	18. South Carolina

(continued)

Property Tax Burden by State (continued)
(1/lowest burden; 50/highest burden)

19. Massachusetts	30. Arizona	41. Minnesota
20. Georgia	31. California	42. Utah
21. Illinois	32. Kentucky	43. Nebraska
22. New Mexico	33. Indiana	44. Ohio
23. North Carolina	34. Maryland	45. Vermont
24. Idaho	35. Louisiana	46. Wisconsin
25. Mississippi	36. Kansas	47. Rhode Island
26. Iowa	37. New Jersey	48. Hawaii
27. Washington	38. West Virginia	49. New York
28. Wyoming	39. Connecticut	50. Maine
29. Michigan	40. Arkansas	

senior exemptions reduce taxes further. Homeowner and car insurance, as well as electricity, is half that of what we paid in Long Island. No sales taxes in Delaware either! Yet we are near the ocean and fairly close to New York City, Philadelphia, Baltimore, and Washington D.C."

The previous table takes into consideration all federal, state, and local taxes. Property taxes are variable, depending on many individual conditions and changing so much between communities even in the same county, so it's impossible to quote property taxes state by state with any precision. Your assessments will vary depending on the following:

- Are you a veteran?
- Do you have a low income?
- Are you over sixty-five or disabled?
- Is your house undervalued or overvalued?
- Does your community have unusual bond debts?

State and Local Income Taxes

Don't get the idea that moving to a no-income-tax state will guarantee a lower overall tax bill, unless you have an exceptionally high income. (In which case, you wouldn't be reading about retirement on a budget!) The bottom line is state and local governments have to get money somehow. States that have no income tax use other methods to make up the shortfall. Property taxes, sales taxes, high automobile license fees, and other fees will always find their way into the state treasury. Some states collect no sales taxes, then boost property taxes to make up the differences. In the long run, other taxes are adjusted to compensate the state treasury.

Texas, Nevada, Florida, Washington, South Dakota, Wyoming, and Alaska collect no state income tax, and Tennessee and New Hampshire tax interest and dividends only. But if you are retiring with a modest or tax-exempt income, what difference does this make? Unless you have a substantial taxable income, state and local income taxes should be among the least of your concerns.

chapter four

Tax Investments

Let's talk about the money you've invested by paying Social Security taxes to the government all these years. This is money that could be returned to you in one of three ways: Social Security, Social Security Disability, or (for those who are very short of funds) Supplementary Security Income (SSI).

Don't for a moment think of these monthly checks as "charity." Currently, for every dollar you earn, you pay 7.65 cents to Social Security, and your employer matches that with money that otherwise would have gone into your paycheck. That's $15.30 out of every hundred dollars you earned. You've invested these tax dollars over your lifetime, money deducted from your paycheck every week, for a good cause. Your money has gone to help others before you. Now it's your turn.

You've also invested many thousands of dollars into another nest egg: your home mortgage. In this chapter, we'll investigate ways to draw down money from the equity in your home. The money is just sitting there, fattening your net worth but not doing anything for your lifestyle. This locked-up money could help finance your retirement if you could only get at it. This route must be approached with caution. As we shall see, a few potholes could make it an unsafe road for the unwary.

Social Security

Social Security is the key to retirement for the vast majority of workers in our country. Without it, retirement would be impossible for many of them. Two-thirds of today's retirees depend on Social Security benefits for more than half of their monthly income. For millions of retired Americans, that's all there is. Without Social Security, an incalculable number would be forced to continue working until they dropped dead or until their employers decided to replace them with younger employees.

A campaign to privatize this most successful and valued social program has been under way for two decades now. Stockbrokers, insurance companies, and bankers (who stand to make a handsome profit if Social Security is converted to individual investment accounts) have pulled out all the stops to influence public opinion. They've spent millions in an effort to persuade younger Americans that Social Security is going bankrupt and to convince middle-aged Americans that they'd be richer if the money went into the stock market. They would change the monthly payments from being based on how much you paid in to how good you are at beating the stock market. (If you don't do any better than me, we will both be in trouble.)

This is what Alan Greenspan, former chairman of the Federal Reserve Board, thinks of the Wall Street plan: "Investing Social Security assets in equities is largely a zero-sum game," Greenspan said. "Only an increase in national saving or an increase in efficiency with which we use our savings can help us meet the retirement requirements of the coming years."

Attacks against Social Security are not new. Since its very conception in the 1930s, Social Security has been under attack by those who believe that people should save and make investments for their own retirement. (Many cannot, and that's why the program came about.) Fortunately, despite continuing efforts by powerful politicians to weaken and even eliminate Social Security, the program survives. These attacks are extremely shortsighted. If Social Security is scuttled, millions of elderly would plunge below the already-low poverty line. The country's economy would suffer irreparable damage, and the extra load on social services would overload the welfare system to the point of disaster. So rejoice that we have Social Security, and keep a jaundiced eye on any politician who wants to trash it—and on those who keep saying the system is "bankrupt."

Well, is Social Security bankrupt? Of course not. According to the Social Security trustees, the plan is completely funded for at least the next thirty years. In any event, it is absurd to label as "bankrupt" a program that is secure for at least the next third of a century. Moreover, given Social Security's importance in protecting millions of Americans from poverty, such a label is irresponsible.

Listening to the propaganda would make one think that the Social Security Administration is running out of money and will soon stop sending out checks. Nothing could be further from the truth. The fact is that Social Security is one of the few sectors of government that runs at a surplus. It takes in billions of dollars a year more than it pays out. In fact, if Social Security were removed from the budget, the $400 billion deficit estimated for 2006 would have doubled. If the government would simply stop spending the annual Social Security surplus on other programs to reduce the deficit, the interest on the debt to the Social Security funds would support the program forever. When we were running a $290 billion deficit, Congress managed to find $300 billion to bail out the savings and loan institutions and doled out billions in aid to foreign countries. Don't worry: They'll find the money to fix Social Security or the voters will find a new Congress.

Social Security Eligibility

Qualifying for Social Security benefits is straightforward. You need to have earned a minimum amount of money for a minimum number of quarters and paid Social Security taxes on these earnings. The minimum number of quarters needed depends on your age, and the minimum amount of wages depends on the years worked. Before 1977, you needed to earn at least $50 in one three-month period to count that as a quarter. Beginning with 1978, you needed to earn $250, and the amount has increased each year. Currently, earnings of $830 in at least one three-month period are required. The more money you earn, the higher your checks will be. If you work for yourself and have been paying self-employment tax, you should be able to qualify for benefits.

Generally, anyone who has worked for ten years or more will qualify. Figuring out how much your check will be is not so straightforward. You'll have to ask the Social Security Administration to assist you. The local office can help you make a request for a Personal Earnings and Benefit

Estimate Statement. Or you can call the Social Security Administration at (800) 772–1213 and request the form. This can be ordered online at www.ssa.gov/online/ssa-7004.html.

When you receive your statement, make sure that all of your employers and all of your earnings are included. It's always possible that mistakes have been made. It's wise to check this from time to time, even if you are a long way from retirement, just to make sure you're being credited properly. After all, benefits are based on the highest of the last thirty-five years' earnings, so missing a year's worth of earnings might cause a reduction in benefits of $10 to $15 per month. The form will ask you to make an estimate of your average earnings between now and retirement. Just put down your current earnings. That way you'll receive an estimate in today's dollars, which gives you a better idea of what your retirement picture will look like. Your Personal Earnings and Benefit Estimate Statement will also show you how much you would earn, in today's dollars, if you retired early.

Retirement at What Age?

Normal retirement is at age sixty-five, at which time you'll receive a "full benefit" for your time worked. The earliest you can retire is age sixty-two, but your monthly benefits will be reduced by 20 percent. For example, if you would receive $960 a month at age sixty-five, at age sixty-two you'd be entitled to $768 a month. For each year you wait to retire after age sixty-five, you'll get an additional 4.5 percent added to your benefits. Therefore, if you wait until age seventy to retire, your check would be $1,176 per month.

Those who were born after 1937 will find their checks shorted for early retirement and won't get full retirement credits until they reach the age of sixty-seven, instead of sixty-five. That's one of the ways Congress is dealing with the crisis that could face the plan down the road. That change could very well alienate folks who are rapidly reaching retirement age, so there's a possibility Congress will soon face some angry voters who are just realizing that they are being shortchanged.

So when do you retire? You can retire at any time between age sixty-two and full retirement age. However, if you were born during or after

1937, your benefits will be reduced a fraction of a percent for each month before your full retirement age. Let's suppose that you expect to collect $1,500 a month at age sixty-six and three months. But you elect to take retirement at age sixty-two. The chart below shows your monthly check will be 26.66 percent less by retiring early. That would be $1,100 a month, instead of the $1,500 if you worked another four years and three months before retiring. But on the other hand, you would have collected $39,600 by not waiting. You'll be ahead of your coworker who waits until sixty-six to retire, and you'll stay ahead until she catches up with you at age seventy-seven. From then on, she will be ahead. As a general rule, early retirement will give you about the same total Social Security benefits over your lifetime, but in smaller amounts to take into account the longer period you will receive them.

Key to Retirement Benefits

Year of Birth	Age of Full Retirement	Percent of Reduction
1937	65 years	20.00
1938	65 + 2 mos.	20.83
1939	65 + 4 mos.	21.67
1940	65 + 6 mos.	22.50
1941	65 + 8 mos.	23.33
1942	65 + 10 mos.	24.17
1943–1954	66 years	25.00
1955	66 + 2 mos.	25.84
1956	66 + 4 mos.	26.66
1957	66 + 6 mos.	27.50
1958	66 + 8 mos.	28.33
1959	66 + 10 mos.	29.17
1960	67 years	30.00

For many, the decision about when to collect Social Security is difficult. Obviously, if you plan on working after retirement and earning lots
of money, you're going to have to give money back to the government.
Remember, if you are under sixty-five, you're allowed to earn only
$11,520 before you start paying back one dollar for every two earned.
However, if you can work part time without going over the limit, you
should come out ahead. Another possibility is waiting until the age of full
retirement to retire—this adds three more higher-income years to your
record and gives you a slightly higher benefit check. But you'll miss out
on three years of retirement. Decisions, decisions!

Workers who hang onto their jobs after reaching the age of full retirement not only earn more credits but can draw their Social Security benefits and continue working. Also, don't forget that the amount of your
benefits increases with each year worked after full retirement age. For
example, if you were sixty-five in 2006, for each year you work up until
the age of seventy, you'll gain a 4.5 percent increase in your benefit check.
For five years of work, your $1,219 benefit would grow to $1,494, an extra
$274 a month. On the other hand, had you retired at sixty-five, you would
have drawn $73,140 by the time you reached the age of seventy. More
decisions!

Social Security Disability

If you are disabled or blind, you don't have to be sixty-two or older to draw
Social Security. A doctor must certify that you are "totally and permanently
disabled for a period of not less than one year." No matter what your age,
you will draw benefits at the same rate as a person who is sixty-five years
old, who has earned the same amount of credits as you have. These benefits are paid regardless of your financial situation or how much other
income you have each month. After two years on disability, you are also
entitled to apply for Medicare, just as if you were sixty-five years old.

To encourage you to return to work once you have recovered suffi-
ciently, the government permits you to work on a trial basis, for a limited
amount of time, without penalty. That is, you receive your disability payments and your salary for this period.

However, be aware that obtaining disability status is not easy, particularly if your disability is the least bit marginal. Because so many people have faked disabilities in the past, the Social Security Administration takes a hard look at each case and will disallow all but the most obvious disabilities. From time to time they crack down, routinely turning down obviously valid claims and forcing legitimate applicants to appeal the decisions.

To qualify for disability you must prove that you have a severe physical or mental impairment (or combination of the two) and will be unable to do any "substantial gainful activity" for a year or more. Where difficulty most often arises is in interpreting the term "substantial gainful activity." When a close relative of mine applied for Social Security Disability and was turned down, a caseworker explained it to me this way: "Let's suppose a stockbroker who earns $150,000 a year receives a brain injury and is no longer able to work as a broker. If he were capable of working as a dishwasher, then he could not be considered disabled under our rules. The fact that dishwasher jobs aren't available doesn't enter into the matter. We can only consider the question, 'Is the applicant *capable* of working?'"

The key to qualifying for disability is to have a reputable doctor, and preferably more than one doctor, willing to testify that you have "severe physical impairment that prevents you from doing substantial gainful activity for a year or more." Often, when you apply to a Social Security office for disability, a caseworker will offer to get the medical evidence for you, ostensibly to save you the trouble and expense of going to a doctor yourself. From personal experience, I can advise you to get your own evidence from your own doctor! To avoid approving the claim, caseworkers have been known to take affidavits from doctors who are sympathetic to the government's side—doctors who know next to nothing about your case—and then ignore your personal physician who could testify that you are disabled. To be fair, because there are so many frivolous claims of disability being made, it's not surprising that many genuinely disabled people have to go through the appeal process.

If you feel that you are truly disabled and your application for Social Security Disability is turned down, by all means appeal the decision. Well over half of disallowed applicants win on appeal. You don't need an attorney for an appeal, but should you decide that you want one, get a lawyer who works on contingency (if you get nothing, he or she gets nothing).

For More Information

If you would like more information about Social Security programs, you can order any of the following publications by calling (800) 772–1213. The publications can be found online at www.ssa.gov/pubs/10024.html.

- Understanding Social Security (Publication No. 05-10024)
- Retirement Benefits (Publication No. 05-10035)
- Survivors Benefits (Publication No. 05-10084)
- Disability Benefits (Publication No. 05-10029)
- Medicare (Publication No. 05-10043)

People who are deaf or hard of hearing may call a toll-free TTY number, (800) 325–0778, between 7:00 A.M. and 7:00 P.M. on business days.

Are You Missing a Pension?

Many people have pensions coming and don't realize it. Happily, there is a government agency working to locate "missing people" who are eligible for defined-benefit pensions (pensions that assure a fixed benefit) but are not receiving them.

Some are spouses of deceased workers who are entitled to some part of his or her pension but don't realize it. Others know they earned a pension but assume it's lost because their employer went bankrupt. Still others are victimized when companies facing financial difficulties deliberately misappropriate the pension funds in an effort to bail out.

The Pension Benefit Guaranty Corporation is a federal agency that insures the private pensions of forty-one million workers and takes over when a private pension plan is terminated without sufficient money to pay the promised pensions. The agency director says, "Our central mission is to make sure everybody who's owed a pension gets one." The agency is currently paying benefits to about 160,000 retirees, and they're finding an additional 1,000 "lost" retirees each year.

If you can't locate a former employer who promised a pension, or if you believe your employer may have switched or terminated your defined-benefit plan, you may contact the Pension Benefit Guaranty Corporation for help. The address is PBGC Administration, Review and Technical Assistance Division, 1200 K Street NW, Washington, DC 20005; www .pbgc.gov.

Another source of retirement income you may overlook: Social Security benefits based on your ex-spouse's earning records. This is particularly important in the case of divorced women, who typically qualify for much lower Social Security benefits than their higher-paid ex-husbands.

You are eligible for benefits based on your ex-spouse's records, even if he is not retired, if you fulfill the following requirements:

- You are age sixty-two or older.
- You were married to your ex-spouse for at least ten years, and the divorce is at least two years old.
- You haven't remarried, or you remarried someone who is receiving Social Security benefits as a widower, widow, parent, or disabled child.

Your monthly check will be the same as if your earning records were the same as your spouse's. Of course, if you earned more than your spouse, forget it. He may qualify on *your* schedule!

Supplementary Security Income

If your monthly income is exceptionally low and you aren't eligible for Social Security or Social Security Disability, Supplementary Security Income (SSI) can come to your rescue. SSI is a federal program administered by the Social Security Administration but does not use Social Security funds.

To qualify for SSI, you must be sixty-five or older or disabled or blind, and you must have little or no income. It's important to note that SSI isn't just for the elderly; it can be paid at any age as long as the applicant meets the disabled or blind standards. Blind doesn't necessarily mean totally blind; very poor vision will sometimes qualify you. Disabled doesn't mean confined to a wheelchair, either. If doctors agree that you have a physical or mental problem that keeps you from working and that is expected to last at least a year or to result in death, you may qualify. The rules are similar to Social Security Disability.

The financial qualifications vary from state to state. For example, in New York State, if you are older than sixty-five, blind, or disabled, the maximum monthly income allowable income in 2006 for a person living alone is $690. If you are a couple living alone and in New York State, the maximum monthly income allowable in 2006 is $1,008. The basic SSI check is $530 for a single person and $796 a month for a couple. Some states add money to that amount. In addition, folks who qualify for SSI usually also qualify for Medicaid and food stamps.

Some items of income don't count against you, including, for example, the first $65 of your earnings every month; food stamps; food, clothing, or shelter provided by private, nonprofit organizations; and most home-energy assistance. There are other exemptions that your local welfare office will explain to you. You also cannot have assets that exceed $2,000 for singles or $3,000 for couples. Some assets are exempt; these will be explained to you when you apply.

Contact your local Social Security office, or go to the Web site www.ssa.gov/notices/supplemental-security-income.

Drawing on Your Mortgage Equity

There is a way of cashing in on your mortgage investment without selling your home: a "reverse mortgage." The idea of a reverse mortgage started in California, where highly inflated property values shelter huge sums of untouchable equities. As properties increase in value and equity, the idea becomes ever more popular. Many couples who bought their homes thirty years ago for $45,000 are still living in the same home, but it's paid for and it's worth $450,000. That's wonderful; you made 1,000 percent profit, but what good does that do you if love your home and aren't interested in selling and moving away?

When retirement rolls around, unless your income is adequate, you could be "house poor." Some decisions need to be made. You could sell the house and pull down the equity for retirement. But then where do you live? You could take out an equity loan, but then you'd be back to making monthly mortgage payments. Should you move to a less expensive but less desirable neighborhood? Or do you move to a lower-cost part of the country altogether? If you like your neighborhood and love your home, it might not make sense to sell and move away.

An alternative for those with huge equities is to take the value built up in their homes and turn it into a reliable monthly income through a reverse mortgage. Instead of paying a monthly installment payment to the bank, the bank sends *you* a monthly check, adding that amount to the total debt, or mortgage, against your home. These payments aren't taxable income, and they do not affect your Social Security benefits in any way.

Before we go any further, let us understand that there is an enormous difference between a reverse mortgage and the potentially dangerous *equity loan*. With an equity loan, you are gambling that the real estate market will continue to boom, or that it will at least stay on an even keel, so that later on, you can sell the house and bank an even greater amount of equity. Should you take out large equity loans on the house and the market goes *down*, you could end up owing more money on the house than it's worth. You might have to borrow money to pay off the loan just to *give* the house away! It's a gamble.

A reverse mortgage promises you a stipulated monthly payment based on four factors: the value of your house, where you live, current interest rates, and your age. For an estimate of what size loan you might qualify for, go online to Reverse Vision (reversevision.com), or consult your local HUD office. The cost of the loan and the annual percentage rate applied against your equity also affect the cash payment. Your life expectancy enters into the equation, as well. That is, the largest cash amounts usually go to older borrowers who live in homes of higher values.

Typically, a reverse mortgage loan requires no repayment for as long as you live in your home. But the loan must be repaid in full—along with accumulated interest and any other charges—when you sell the home or move away permanently or when the last living borrower dies. As you receive monthly repayments, the amount you owe grows larger; therefore, the amount of money that you or your heirs will receive upon selling the house and paying off the loan correspondingly shrinks. Of course, if local real estate prices increase the value of the house, there may well be more cash for you or your heirs.

Because you continue to own your home, you are still responsible for property taxes, insurance, and repairs. If you don't fulfill these responsibilities, the loan could become due and payable in full.

To qualify for a reverse mortgage, you must be at least sixty-two, and the home must be your principal place of residence—where you spend the majority of each year. Also, you must own your home outright or have a low mortgage balance that can be paid off at the closing with proceeds from the reverse loan. You are further required to receive consumer information from HUD-approved counseling sources prior to obtaining the loan. You can contact the Housing Counseling Clearinghouse at (800) 569–4287 to obtain the name and telephone number of a HUD-approved counseling agency and a list of Federal Housing Administration (FHA)-approved lenders within your area. You can visit their Web site at www.hud.gov/offices.

Lenders usually accept only single-family, one-unit dwellings for reverse mortgages. However, some will accept two- to four-unit owner-occupied dwellings as long as all owners are borrowers. Some condominiums and manufactured homes may also qualify. Mobile homes and cooperatives are not eligible for reverse mortgages. The home must be in reasonable condition and must meet HUD minimum property standards. In some cases, home repairs can be made after the closing of a reverse mortgage. An FHA mortgage requires a hefty insurance premium that protects the lender in case the value of the house declines.

Be careful, though—a reverse mortgage isn't a simple solution. You'll need to be quick with your calculator and analyze all possible scenarios. Before taking such a big step, you should discuss your plans thoroughly with family members, your attorney, or other trusted advisers. Essentially, there are three kinds of reverse mortgage loans:

- A "tenure plan," which pays a fixed monthly cash advance for as long as you live in your home. You can stay until you die, the home is then sold, the bank takes its money, and the remainder, if any, goes to your heirs. By the way, this mortgage bears a compound interest rate, with interest being charged on accumulated unpaid interest.

- A "term plan," which pays a fixed monthly cash advance for a specific time period. The cash advances stop when the term ends, but you are not required to repay the loan until you die, sell your home, or move permanently away. Short-term mortgages are practical if you plan to live in your home for five or six years and then move to a retirement community. You can then sell the house, pay off the loan, and have something left over for your new lifestyle.

- A "line-of-credit plan," which lets you decide when to draw advances and how much of your home equity to use. Interest accumulates only on the money you draw.

The difference between regular home-equity loans and reverse mortgages is that home-equity loans usually require proof of a certain amount of income and require installment payments over a specified length of time, usually ten or fifteen years. With a reverse mortgage, lending institutions are secured by a first trust deed on the home, so they don't care about your income. They're protected because a typical reverse mortgage loan pays out considerably less than the market value of the house. When the borrower moves or dies, whichever comes first, the house is sold and the mortgage is paid off with the proceeds of the sale. Interest on the reverse mortgage is debited from the equity.

As in any financial transaction of this complexity, you'll find lenders all too willing to take advantage of our ignorance. They may come up with outrageous calculations based on unrealistic life expectancies, or they may try to saddle the home owner with high interest rates that quickly eat up the equity. In some cases, the borrower finds his home drained of value, with zero equity, by the time the agreed-upon term is up. This can be serious; you'll have no equity in your home to pay for your spouse's nursing home care, or your care, and nothing to leave your grandkids.

Don't let anyone talk you into signing a "service" agreement to help you get a reverse mortgage. You can get all the help you need for little or no cost from a HUD-approved housing counseling agency or your nearest

HUD office. Your out-of-pocket expenses should be no more than the cost of an appraisal (maybe $300 or $400) and a credit report (about $50). Another trap is a clause that the lending institution is entitled to 50 percent of any appreciation in your property over the term of the loan. Don't go for this. Before you agree to pay a fee for a simple referral, call (800) 569–4287, toll-free, for the name and location of a HUD-approved housing counseling agency near you.

If a reverse mortgage sounds like the answer for your situation, take steps to protect yourself and learn how to shop for a reverse mortgage. First, request the free forty-seven-page booklet *Homemade Money* by mailing a self-addressed postcard to AARP Home Equity Information Center, 601 E Street NW, Washington, DC 20049. Better yet, if you have Internet access, go to www.aarp.org and search for *Homemade Money,* and you won't have to wait for the booklet to come by mail. It's right there. Also there's an AARP Web site on reverse mortgages at www.aarp.org/money/revmort.

Wait! Before you start signing papers for a reverse mortgage, you need to realize this is a big step, and you need to take a close look at all your options before making such a major financial decision. Let's review your alternatives to see if you can find a less costly or better way to meet your needs.

Selling your home and buying a less-expensive home. If there is a possibility that you might consider selling and moving anytime soon, you need to think twice before taking out a reverse mortgage. These loans are expensive when repaid within a few years after closing because of substantial start-up costs, mortgage insurance, and "risk-pooling" fees. You pay these fees to guarantee that you can stay in your home for as long as you need to. But if you end up selling a couple of years after closing, you will be paying for a guarantee you won't need.

To decide whether to sell, you need to compare the cash you can get from the sale with the cost and maintenance of buying a newer but less expensive home. Also, how much money will be left over after you buy the new home, and how much income will you derive from that investment?

Selling your home and moving to a rental or apartment. Will you be satisfied living in a rental after all those years as a home owner? Again, how much money will be left over from the sale of your home, and can it be put into a safe investment?

Renting your home and using the rent money for living expenses. This can work in an area where the rental potential is high, yet property isn't moving very quickly. You would need the option of low-cost rentals not too far away or would need to be moving to another part of the country. This way, you can hold onto your equity until the home can be sold.

For more information about insuring a reverse mortgage or to find a reverse mortgage lender in your area, search through the HUD's Web site (www.hud.gov) or call the FHA at (800) 732–6643. The FHA can also refer you to a HUD-approved independent counselor who can check the terms of a reverse mortgage, analyze your financial situation, and advise you about whether to proceed. The counselor can also give you a list of HUD-approved lenders.

Single-Purpose Loan. Single-purpose loans, when available, are granted for one specified purpose, for example, to repair your home or to pay your property taxes. These loans are the lowest-cost reverse mortgages you will find, and they are usually offered by state or local government agencies. Thus your dealings with the lender will be straightforward, with no hidden catch phrases.

Deferred Payment Loan. A variation of this plan is a deferred payment loan (DPL), which also can be used for repairing or improving your home or paying back taxes. This type of public sector reverse mortgage provides a one-time, lump-sum advance. Some agencies forgive part or all of the loan if you live in your home for a certain length of time after taking out the loan. If you find and qualify for one of these "forgivable" loans, you'll probably have more equity left at the end of the loan than you started out with.

Property Tax Deferral Loan. A final option, available from some state and local government agencies, is a property tax deferral (PTD) loan. This is a reverse mortgage that pays your property taxes with yearly loan advances. No repayment is required for as long as you live in your home. Like other reverse mortgages, PTD loans are generally paid off from the proceeds of the sale of your home. This is a solution for those living in exceptionally high-tax areas, where taxes can eat up most of your Social Security income.

Single-purpose loans, DPLs, and PTDs aren't available everywhere and may be difficult to find. You'll need to query your city or county department of housing or community development agency. Eligibility criteria will vary from program to program, and loans are limited to home owners with low or moderate incomes. Many lenders place a limit on a home's value or lend only in defined areas. Some have a minimum borrower age or a disability requirement. Sometimes community agencies that do not offer single-purpose or deferred loans offer other low-cost home repair programs with affordable monthly payments.

Other Ways to Tap Equity

More conventional ways to spend some of your home equity are refinancing your home, taking out a second mortgage, or taking out a home equity line of credit. But remember that all three of these strategies require that you make monthly installment payments on your loan. And because the loan is secured by your home, you could face foreclosure if you can't make the payments for any reason. If you're on a restricted budget, you may rightly be hesitant to do this. You are also responsible for loan fees and for points charged by the lender. As mentioned earlier, this is a strategy I do not recommend without a great deal of thought and calculation.

A more creative way of drawing your equity and staying put in your home is through a "sale leaseback." The idea is this: You sell your home to an individual for a substantial down payment and monthly installment payments over the term of the mortgage. In return, you receive a lease for the term of the mortgage. Your lease payments will be much less than the house payments you will be receiving because the purchaser will be paying interest on the loan.

Normally this type of sale leaseback transaction is done between parent and adult offspring. Let's suppose you sell your house to your daughter. She knows she will be getting the property anyway, but in the meantime, she can be taking deductions on interest, taxes, property maintenance, and depreciation. These breaks, along with the rent you pay, make it painless for her to help you because it won't cost her any money. (In order to do this, the sale price of the home should be at a fair market value, and your rent should be a fair market rent.) Should you die before the mortgage runs out, she will inherit the property and the mortgage is moot. By that time there's probably been appreciation, so your daughter will make money on the deal.

Another way to work this is to have your daughter take out a conventional loan through a bank to purchase the property. In this case, you would receive all the proceeds from the sale and can use this money to invest in a safe, income-producing investment to help out with retirement expenses.

You'll need a family lawyer to make out the papers and ensure that both parties are protected. You'll want to be sure you have a lifetime lease with full rights to share the house with whomever you please. The contract must have a clause requiring subsequent buyers to honor that lifetime lease. You'll also want a rent-control clause that limits rent increases to the cost-of-living index, as well as a clause that makes the buyer responsible for taxes, insurance, and repairs.

chapter five

Now It's Your Turn!

All your working life you've paid federal income tax and probably state income tax, as well. Maybe you've even been nicked for city or county income taxes. If you own property, you don't have to be told that you've paid a wagonload of dollars to city, county, and state governments over the years. If you didn't own property and just rented a house or apartment all your life, don't feel smug and think that you've avoided paying property taxes. Actually, you've graciously included taxes in your monthly rent payments. The landlord simply paid the taxes for you out of your rent money and took a tax deduction for his trouble. When his taxes went up, so did your rent.

Now, to this amount add the state, county, and city sales taxes you've paid over your lifetime, as well as miscellaneous hidden taxes and fees, and you begin to get an idea of how much money you've paid to keep your government solvent. You'll never know for sure because every time you buy something from the store, the cost of the manufacturer's taxes—corporation taxes, sales taxes, property taxes, import duties, payroll taxes, and who knows what else—are passed along to you as part of the purchase price.

You've wondered what the heck they do with all this money, right? (If you haven't, you must have an exceptionally high pain threshold.) We often hear politicians taking cheap shots at food stamps, Medicare, Social Security, and other programs as being wasteful. If you listen carefully to their solutions, you'll find that we could solve all our budget problems simply by cutting back on programs that help the elderly, the needy, and the unfortunate, while decreasing taxes for the well-to-do. Congress doesn't hesitate to spend our money to bail out wealthy corporations, bankroll foreign dictators, and provide ever-increasing benefits for its members. They take our surplus Social Security money and spend it on current budget items to reduce the deficit and then advocate cutting back on benefits and cost-of-living increases for retirees because "we can't afford it."

Although an enormous amount of tax money is wasted, we have to recognize that most of our tax money is more or less spent prudently. Without police and fire protection, highways, libraries, schools, and health services, our lives would be very different. Without Medicare, Social Security, and other programs for senior citizens, prospects for retirement would be very grim. Not all tax money is spent on boondoggles. This brings us to the focus of this chapter: What government and private services are out there for senior citizens and how do you get your share?

"Wait a minute," I hear you saying, "some of those services sound like charity, like welfare. Charity is for losers, not for me!" Well, perhaps some of this sounds like charity, but the cold fact is that you have paid for these services all your life. You've paid through taxes, club dues, United Way contributions, and money in the Sunday collection plate. All these years you've subsidized tasty meals at the local senior-citizen center, paid for card tables and bridge prizes to entertain retirees. You've contributed for home care and Meals-on-Wheels for invalids. If you don't participate when it's your turn, it's like investing money for an insurance policy and failing to make a claim when you most need it. Now *that's* being a loser!

It is of utmost importance that those forced to retire on limited budgets participate in these worthwhile services for senior citizens. It makes retirement on a budget much easier.

Food Stamps

The food stamp program is one of the tax-funded services designed to help low-income citizens. Yet many folks look down their noses at food stamps. They feel as if food stamps are a form of panhandling or charity. One reason for this negative impression of food stamps is the continual target of political opportunists who see this as a way to increase their popularity with middle-class voters. Some politicians love to suggest that food stamp recipients are guilty of crimes or immoral conduct when they receive stamps from the government and then use them to buy food for the table. They link food stamps with welfare.

The fact is, the funding for food stamps comes from the Department of Agriculture and has nothing whatsoever to do with welfare, which is financed largely by property taxes. These same Department of Agriculture funds go to wealthy farmers who receive payments for raising certain crops and for not growing others. Huge corporate farms collect millions of dollars of Department of Agriculture money in the form of crop insurance and assistance of all kinds. At one point, dairy farmers received millions to slaughter milk cows so the government could cut down on the amount of surplus milk it has to buy from farmers in order to keep prices up. Until recently, these same funds were used to pay lavish subsidies to gentlemen farmers who grow tobacco for cigarettes and chewing tobacco.

We rarely hear criticism of Agriculture Department subsidies for the wealthy. But we hear plenty about "welfare queens" who drive Cadillacs and buy groceries with food stamps. Well, it turns out that if a person owns an automobile that's worth more than $4,700, any value over that is counted against the food stamp applicant as cash assets, which affects eligibility. So don't be upset when some out-of-work housewife happens to drive a beat-up old Caddy to the supermarket to buy food for the family table!

Food stamp eligibility requirements change with the consumer price index. According to the latest available regulations, the rules go something like this: For folks older than sixty, a single person can have no more than $905 a month in gross income, and a couple no more than $1,219 per month. Gross income includes all sources of income, including Social Security payments. If you have enough expenses to deduct from your gross income figure and if your net worth is low enough, you may qualify for food stamps.

You are allowed a standard deduction, plus 20 percent of the family's gross income, child or dependent care, and certain medical expenses. You can also take a deduction for a combination of rent or mortgage, utilities, taxes, and insurance that totals more than 50 percent of your income after other deductions have been subtracted (up to a maximum of $250).

After all this figuring, you can qualify for food stamps only if your net income is less than $798 for one person or $1,070 for a couple. Can we agree that if a couple has less than $1,070 net income a month, including their Social Security benefits, they deserve all the help they can get? (Remember, this money comes from the same funds that pay farmers for not growing crops.)

But just a low income may not qualify you for assistance. You must prove that you have no more than $3,000 in allowable assets ($2,000 for those younger than sixty and not handicapped).

A home is not counted as a cash asset, but an automobile is, as noted above, if it is worth more than $4,700. The excess value over $4,700 is counted against the $3,000 in allowable assets. Licensed vehicles are not counted if they are used more than 50 percent of the time for income-producing purposes or if they're needed for long-distance travel for work (other than a daily commute), to transport a physically disabled household member, or to carry most of the household's fuel or water. Your reportable assets include money you have in savings or checking accounts, money market funds, certificates of deposit (CDs), credit-union savings plans, Christmas clubs, cash in hand, stocks, bonds, mutual funds, and the cash value of any collection (stamp or coin collection or other collectible that's worth money). It's noteworthy that a motor home or a travel trailer is not considered an asset when valued over $4,700—as long as you live in it! Then it's considered your residence and doesn't count against food stamp eligibility. But you have to live in your rig for more than half the year.

The amount of food stamps you receive depends on your income and assets. The formula is rather complicated. At one time, a one-person household could receive up to $152 in food stamps per month; a two-person household will receive up to $278. (This can change and probably has by the time this book is published.) To apply for food stamps, be prepared to show lots of proof to the food stamp office. Besides your personal identification, you'll need Social Security numbers for everyone in your household, bank books, pay stubs, payroll check receipts, and copies of checks or benefit statements from your Social Security, pension, SSI, or any other earned or unearned income. Never lie or withhold information! Everything is checked against other government records; you could lose your benefits for a long time if you give false information. The thirty-day (maximum) wait for your food stamps starts the day you fill out your application and sign it. You don't need all the information or all the documents on your first visit; you don't even need to have your formal interview the first day. The important thing is to get the process started. Insist upon signing and dating your application the very first day!

Emergency food stamps are available from your county human services, welfare, or social-services department. If you have no place to live or if you have less than $150 monthly gross income and no more than $100 in ready cash, you may be able to get emergency food stamps in three days or less. If your rent and utilities for the coming month are more than your income and the cash you have on hand or in the bank, you can ask for emergency food stamps. The department must act by the third calendar day. Migrant farmworkers, homeless individuals and families, and persons whose shelter and utility costs exceed their income have additional exemptions that may qualify them for action by the third day. If you feel that you have not received a fair shake or if you have been denied food stamps, you have the right to request a fair hearing. Contact your legal services office or other community group that has trained advocates for help.

If you are not receiving food stamps, feel fortunate that your income is large enough that you don't qualify, but please don't look down on those who are not so fortunate. If you must be angry with someone, take it out on wealthy agribusinesses that lobby Congress and the Department of Agriculture for more cash payments for not growing food. Should you qualify, by all means, demand your rights. You've always paid your share, and now it's your turn to benefit.

Senior-Citizen Services

Some communities have highly successful programs that can make a world of difference in people's lives. For many retired folks, a well-run senior center is their focal point, a place to enjoy free medical services and nutritious meals, as well as social activities and a host of other free benefits. Senior-citizen centers help make budget retirement possible.

The surprising thing about these community services is that so few retirees take full advantage of them. Recently, when doing research at a particularly attractive senior center, we asked the director what she considered to be her biggest problem. She replied, "Getting the news out that we exist! Folks just have no idea of what we offer. We send out mailings, and we ask our people to spread the word among their low-income neighbors. Many of our services are free, some have a nominal cost, others have a sliding fee, according to the ability to pay. Some items are limited to lower-income folks, but most are available to everyone. We just can't seem to spread the news!"

She then began listing the things senior citizens are entitled to in her area and the surrounding region, most of them just for the asking:

- Adopt-a-senior programs provide social and transportation assistance for those who are socially or geographically isolated and need assistance to meet daily living needs.

- Adult day care programs provide volunteers to visit the homes of full-time caregivers to provide respite care and assistance as needed. This service is a lifesaver for a spouse who is tied down while taking care of his or her invalid partner. It provides the caregiver a chance to go shopping or to enjoy a movie or some outside recreation without having to worry about the partner.

- Adult family homes offer room and board in a licensed residential environment for seniors who require some assistance with daily living tasks. This is also an option for single persons who are unable or unwilling to enter a nursing home.

- Adult protective services investigate elder abuse, neglect, exploitation, and abandonment, and provide short-term emergency support to adults in need of protection.

- Advocacy programs provide assistance for low-income seniors to cut through red tape. They receive help with forms, applications, and appeals, plus advice on how to handle government bureaucracy.

- Alzheimer's support groups provide counseling, information, and support for families. This service is very important for those frustrated by an inability to get help.

- Blind or impaired-vision services offer assistance to the blind of all ages. "Talking books" are featured as a part of this program.

- Chore and in-home care services provide assistance with household tasks, shopping, meal preparation, personal care, and transportation to medical appointments. Sliding fees make this service affordable and help keep folks out of expensive health-care institutions.

- Clothing banks provide suitable clothing for senior citizens. Donations come from the closets of well-off members of the community, so the quality of the clothing is very good.

- Companion programs provide social contact and support for elderly persons who show signs of confusion or weakness.

- Dental care is available to low-income seniors at reduced costs.

- Educational opportunities include classes that are available to seniors free or for a nominal fee. Course offerings include not only classes in traditional subjects but also classes in aerobics, art, health and nutrition, water exercise, and driver's education.

- Employment programs especially for seniors provide on-the-job training, part-time employment, and job-search assistance.

- Energy assistance programs inform seniors about utility discounts and rebates to which they are entitled and administer a federally funded program designed to assist low-income households during the winter months. These programs help pay heating bills and assist homebound seniors in completing applications.

- Financial assistance counseling is available for seniors dealing with Medicaid, Social Security, and other financial-assistance programs for folks who are on low incomes or are elderly, disabled, or blind.

- Food banks provide food to elderly folks in need or in emergency situations. Some of the food comes from government surplus commodities, some from donations by local businesses, and the rest from community funds. USDA food surplus and donated food are distributed to needy low-income people.

- Food stamp assistance offers help to low-income seniors who need help obtaining food stamps.

- Guardianship programs provide advocacy services for those who are no longer able to make decisions or access essential services for themselves.

- Health care services include immunizations; screenings for diabetes, hearing loss, and blood pressure; tuberculosis clinics; and low-cost programs for foot care. Financial assistance is available for those who need hearing aids.

- Home-delivered meals are provided by the famous Meals-on-Wheels program for homebound seniors older than sixty. A donation of $1.50 per meal is suggested, but only if the person can afford it. Care is taken not to embarrass those who cannot pay. In addition, the senior center provides lunch at noon, Monday through Friday.

- Home health care is available from skilled nurses and physical therapists who visit the home. Costs are covered by Medicare, Medicaid, private insurance, or on a sliding-fee scale for low-income people.

- Hospice programs enable terminally ill patients to stay in their own homes, and they provide education and emotional support both for the patient and the patient's family.

- Legal services are provided to older persons regarding their civil rights, benefits, and entitlements. There are reduced fees for simple wills and community property agreements. Free civil legal services provided by volunteer attorneys are available to eligible low-income clients. Child custody, criminal, or litigation cases are not usually accepted.

- Low-rent housing in this particular town includes more than 300 units, ranging from efficiencies to small houses, that are managed by the county housing authority. Residency is limited to low-income adults aged sixty-two or older or senior couples, at least one of whom is sixty-two or older. There is currently a waiting list for vacancies, but mortgage assistance is also available.

- Medical equipment is available for loan to eligible individuals.

- Recreational opportunities include arts and crafts, card games, senior dances, and an almost unlimited number of recreational programs.

- Rent assistance is available in emergencies to help low-income elderly when an eviction notice has been served and when all other state and local resources have been exhausted.

- Telephone reassurance programs provide volunteers who talk with homebound seniors at prearranged times daily. This service helps many invalids live independently and gives them confidence that someone in the community cares about their well-being. There are no fees for this service.

- Transportation door-to-door is available for eligible seniors. Volunteers provide transportation to shopping, libraries, doctors' offices, therapy sessions, hospitals, and other places. There are also regular van and bus services available.

- Travel clubs for seniors provide day trips, overnight getaways, and longer excursions at very low cost.

Volunteering

The most successful and energetic senior-citizen centers all seem to have one thing in common—a large number of volunteers. Folks at centers with high levels of service don't just sit back and wait for things to happen or for the government to do something for them; they get out and *make* things happen! Their enthusiasm is catching. It spreads to local officials and to local citizens and businesses, bringing everybody into the act.

They get involved in local politics and let their voices and needs be known. Politicians listen when voters speak!

The best way to help yourself in a senior-citizen center is to volunteer in helping others. By volunteering, you gain a deeper sense of self-respect and well-being, and you build up a store of gratitude and goodwill that may well be repaid someday—when you need it most. Somewhere down the line, when you need help, you'll feel free to call in your debts.

Volunteer jobs have a way of developing into paid positions. You will widen your network of friends. And, finally, you'll know that you aren't receiving charity because you are giving just as much as you are receiving.

Finding Services

Where are these senior-citizen services located? Depending on the community, you can locate senior services at senior-citizen centers, community or civic centers, the local park district, colleges and universities, the YMCA or YMHA, YWCA or YWHA, and churches and synagogues. Your telephone book's yellow pages are a good place to start. Sometimes your town's city hall or county offices can help you locate senior services.

The Eldercare Locator is a good source, no matter where you live. Eldercare Locator is a public service of the Administration on Aging, U.S. Department of Health and Human Services, and was created for the purpose of locating local support resources for aging Americans. Anyone can call the Eldercare Locator on the toll-free number, (800) 677–1116, Monday through Friday, 9:00 A.M. to 11:00 P.M., Eastern time. Be ready to provide your county and city name or zip code, as well as a brief description of the problem. If you are unsure about what kind of service is best for your situation, Eldercare's staff can direct you to a source that can answer your questions. The Web site is www.eldercare.gov/Eldercare/Public/Home.asp

You can get information on how to locate a wide variety of services, such as housing alternatives, meals, home care, transportation, recreation, social activities, legal assistance, and other community services. The Eldercare Locator can also direct you to an office of the Senior Community Service Employment Program, if there's one in your area. This program helps low-income persons over age fifty-five find part-time work in community service. Often there's a job-training program involved for those who want to find employment in the private sector.

All Centers Are Not Equal!

The senior-citizen programs listed above are splendid examples of a community in action, providing quality services for its retired and elderly citizens. But be aware that these services are not available everywhere. Before making a decision about where to retire, I recommend that you pay a visit to the local senior-citizen center. Talk to the director and staff and see what is provided and the spirit in which it is offered.

During our research, we were continually surprised at the wide differences between senior centers in the towns we visited around the country. In some places the level of interest and quality of services were excellent—in others, next to nothing was available. The lesson is simple: Not all senior-citizen centers are equal.

For example, one center we visited served free coffee and doughnuts in the morning, while arts and crafts programs were getting under way. Daily meals were delicious and tastefully served, with cooking done on premises by a staff of paid senior-citizen workers. At least ten rooms were devoted to activities, including a library, a conference room, and exercise rooms. Enthusiastic senior citizens worked on volunteer or self-help programs while city, county, and federal government funds paved the way for success.

Another center, in a town of similar size, consisted of nothing more than a small room furnished with a few shabby card tables. The door was open for just a few hours every afternoon, mostly for poker games. As for meals, we were told that two churches served lunch—one day a week each—as did the local Elks Club and Lions Club, making a total of four meals during the week. Nothing was provided by the center itself; you had to go to the club or church to be served. In addition, an automobile was required to get to the meals, which had the unmistakable aroma of charity. Instead of enthusiastic, caring staff members, we found a senior-center manager who resented our taking up her time with an interview.

If, God forbid, you have health problems, volunteer in-home care workers may be available to perform household tasks necessary to keep you in a clean, safe environment. They will prepare meals, vacuum, change linens, do laundry, mop floors, and clean sinks. In addition, they may well be able to provide transportation and escorting to all types of medical services when public transit isn't available, and they may even do shopping and run errands when necessary. In-home care programs mean being able to remain at home during convalescence instead of being forced into expensive care facilities not covered by Medicare. These in-home care programs are funded by federal, state, and local taxes. Most of these programs aren't limited to low-income senior citizens, by the way. Folks at all income ranges are eligible, although higher-income individuals are sometimes required to contribute toward the service cost based on a sliding-fee scale.

An additional benefit, of particular interest to senior citizens who are in need of part-time work, is that the paid in-home care employees are often senior citizens themselves.

chapter six

Medical Care USA

This is the most difficult chapter of the entire book to write. The situation of medical care in the United States is bad and getting worse every year. For many who will be retiring in the next couple of years, Medicare and Medicaid will come to the rescue as far as health care coverage goes. But I suspect that many readers of this book are well below the age of Medicare, which won't be available until they hit the magic age of sixty-five. For those hoping to retire on a tight budget, and who are looking for advice about health care, I'm afraid that the best I can do is to explain the situation and prepare you to face the fact that you may well be without health care unless you can come up with large insurance premiums. And insurance premiums keep getting higher, having increased some 73 percent since 2000, according to a government report by the director of the National Economical Council. As insurance company lobbyists gain influence, Congress becomes less interested in any restrictions on the health insurance industry.

The quality and access to medical care isn't only a problem of the poor; every year it affects more of those working at fairly good paying jobs. The days of health insurance being the norm are in the past, as employers eliminate this perk because of rising costs. Actually, 41 percent of workers with incomes between $20,000 and $40,000 a year did not have health insurance in 2006. Of employees making less than $20,000 a year, 53 percent were uninsured. When these workers drop out of the work-

Health Insurance . . . Did You Know . . .

- Most people at age sixty-five are eligible for federal health insurance provided through Medicare.

- Eighteen percent of workers at companies with 50 to 200 employees and 33 percent working for larger firms get some medical coverage from their employers. The rest are uninsured—Kaiser Hospital Foundation.

- A typical retirement budget includes about $425 a month per person to cover Medicare premiums, supplemental insurance, deductibles, and prescription drug insurance. For a couple, that amounts to $10,200 a year, currently.

- Twelve years ago, those joining Medicare at age sixty-five were paying Medicare supplemental premiums of about $900 a year for a good policy. Today, they'll pay $2,700 for the same plan. A 76 percent increase!—Kaiser Family Foundation.

place, either for retirement or lack of work, you can be sure the employers aren't going to provide coverage for retirement as was the tradition in the past.

If you do retire before being eligible for Medicare and cannot afford medical insurance, you are joining a large group of uninsured Americans: a number nearing 50 million! Of course, should you be poor—I mean *really* poor—you could be eligible for Medicaid or other welfare-based programs. Medical debt has become a growing problem even among people with insurance, with deductible expenses steadily increasing. A Harvard University study released last year found that almost half of those who filed for bankruptcy in five states, including California, cited illness and medical bills as a major reason, even though more than 75 percent were covered by insurance at the onset of illness. Those without insurance are more likely to visit a hospital medical emergency department.

They have no other choice. About 35 percent of uninsured adults with a chronic condition go to an emergency room, sometimes staying overnight in a hospital, compared with 16 percent of insured Americans with a chronic condition.

Thank Heavens for Medicare!

Over the years, Medicare has saved millions of elderly couples from disastrous poverty. Instead of having to save every possible dime of their retirement funds to prepare for that "last medical emergency," they were free to spend extra money on whatever they felt like, thus providing a tremendous boost to the economy as well as their quality of life. How many cruise ships do you suppose would be sailing the high seas were it not for senior citizens and honeymooners?

Medicare was originally designed to be the first step toward universal health care. The goal was a health system such as those almost all modern countries in the world enjoy—where health care is considered a human right. Somewhere along the line, this idea was sidetracked, or maybe better said, *hijacked* by insurance and pharmaceutical lobbyists in Washington. Congress has been routinely amenable to handouts and gifts from wealthy lobbyists, allowing the lobbyists to attend committee hearings and virtually write the bills. But universal health care has never been on the table.

Ironically today, the percentage of our nonretired population without health insurance is even greater than it was when Medicare was enacted forty years ago. In addition, most people who can afford health insurance face ever increasing out-of-pocket expenses and limited access to medical care. As far as I know, the United States and Communist China are the only two major countries that deny health coverage to all citizens.

Medicare Eligibility

Below are the current ways you can become covered by Medicare and Medicaid. Remember that the rules change from time to time, and they will vary from one state to another. Be sure to obtain up-to-date information before applying.

First, how do you qualify for Medicare? Three conditions make you automatically eligible:

1. When you reach the age of sixty-five and are receiving Social Security retirement benefits or railroad retirement benefits, you are automatically entitled to Medicare.

2. When you turn sixty-five and your spouse is receiving Social Security, or you turn sixty-five and your deceased spouse had worked enough quarters to qualify, you are also automatically eligible.

3. At any age after you have been eligible for Social Security Disability payments for twenty-four months you automatically qualify. Note that the twenty-four-month waiting period begins the date you were disabled, not when you first started receiving disability checks.

If you fall into one of these three "automatic eligibility" groups, you will be enrolled in the Part A Medicare program without filing an application or paying a premium. Part A benefits cover hospitalization, skilled nursing facility services, home-health-care services, and hospice care.

Three other groups are entitled to enroll voluntarily in the Part A Medicare program by filing an application:

1. If you are age sixty-five or older and would be eligible for Social Security but are not drawing benefits—that is, you're still working or are not ready to retire for any reason—you can voluntarily enroll in Medicare and not pay any premium.

2. At any age if you, your spouse, or any of your dependents has permanent kidney failure, that individual is also eligible for Part A Medicare without premiums, starting from the third month of dialysis or from the first month if you participate in a self-dialysis program.

3. Anyone older than sixty-five who doesn't qualify for Social Security benefits can enroll and pay a premium for the Part A coverage. However, this coverage is fairly expensive; you might be better off with a private plan.

NOTE: If you don't fall into one of the "automatically qualified" categories, you must take it upon yourself to enroll. Even though you automatically qualify, don't wait for the government to act. To make sure you are protected when you retire, apply for Medicare three months before your sixty-fifth birthday. That way you'll be covered the month you turn sixty-five. If you don't enroll within three months after your birthday, you can enroll later, during the first three months of each year, but any premiums you pay will be 10 percent higher for each twelve-month period that elapses after the time you first could have enrolled.

Medicare Part A and Part B

Basic Medicare comes in two segments: Part A and Part B. The first part covers you while in the hospital; the second part takes care of you outside the hospital. When you qualify for Medicare, you are automatically covered for hospitalization, Part A. The second part of Medicare, Part B, is the outpatient portion of Medicare and is optional. This is the part that pays doctor bills, medicines, and items of that nature. To make sure you receive all benefits possible, sign up for Part B as well as Part A. This is *your* responsibility! They'll deduct the premium from your Social Security check, but it's worth it.

Again, when you qualify for Medicare, you automatically receive Part A benefits, which help cover hospitalization, skilled nursing facility services, home-health-care services, and hospice care. This coverage is financed by the payroll taxes you've paid during your working life, both before and after you become eligible for benefits. There's a deductible of about $800 for each benefit period and a co-payment of around $200 per day for the sixty-first through the ninetieth day of your stay in the medical facility.

Part B is called *Supplementary Medical Insurance*—it helps cover the costs of physician and outpatient services. While Part B coverage is optional, 95 percent of those eligible choose to participate in Part B. When you become entitled to Medicare, you will be asked if you wish to enroll in Part B or to decline it. If you decline Part B and choose to join later, your premiums will be higher. Part B is financed partly by your monthly premiums and partly by general revenues of the federal government. Generally, after a deductible, Part B takes care of 80 percent of doctor bills, outpatient hospital services (such as emergency room visits), diagnostic tests, ambulatory surgery, laboratory services, and pap smears. It also pays 80 percent of approved charges for occupational and speech therapy services and durable medical equipment and supplies. Items not covered are things like eyeglasses, hearing aids, dentures, or routine physical exams.

It's important to remember that you must apply for Part B. It isn't automatic. Part B pays all approved charges for medically necessary home health care. The catch here is what Medicare considers to be approved and what it does not approve. For this reason many doctors are refusing to accept Medicare patients—the government keeps reducing the amount of fees they believe doctors should receive. You are cautioned to inquire about this should you decide to move to another community. You might find there are few doctors willing to accept your Part B plan.

Something you need to pay attention to is whether a hospital "participates" in Medicare. Participating hospitals are under contract with the government to accept Medicare reimbursement. Most hospitals do participate in Medicare, but you should confirm this with hospital admissions or the administrative office. With few exceptions, Medicare insurance does not cover care in foreign hospitals.

Even though you are covered by Medicare, you have to continually and carefully analyze Medicare coverage and options. Make decisions about what is in your best interest by keeping abreast of rule changes. The rules change from time to time, with deductibles and limits continually going up with inflation and the whims of Congress. Therefore, you might want to order a copy of *The Medicare Handbook,* Publication #HCFA 10050, from the U.S. Department of Health and Human Services, 6325 Security Boulevard, Baltimore, MD 21207. Or order it online free at www.medicare.gov/publications/pubs/pdf/10050.pdf. Also, AARP can supply you with information on the nearest Medicare/Medicaid Assistance Program. Write or call AARP at 601 E Street NW, Washington, DC 20049; (202) 434–2277. Be sure to order the free booklet, *Guide to Health Insurance for People with Medicare.* Web site: www.aarp.org/bulletin/yourhealth.

Medicare Part C

Insurance lobbyists didn't waste time convincing Congress that money could be saved by moving retirees out of the regular Medicare program—which is funded by the government—into private insurance plans known as *Health Maintenance Organizations*—or HMOs. (These are "private" insurance plans, even though they receive funding through federal tax money.) It works this way: Medicare turns over your financial entitlement to the HMO and has no further obligation. Private enterprise is in charge from then on. Since the bottom line is profit, the HMO insurance company gets to decide whether the treatment your doctor prescribes for you is necessary. In other words, the insurance underwriters make decisions that can affect your health, life, or death, overruling your personal doctor. You may have to go to court and let a judge use his medical expertise to decide what the doctor can do.

This is not to imply that all HMOs are devious or that ordinary Medicare is a better choice. Most health-care organizations offer perfectly satisfactory care with very low costs. Actually, we belong to an HMO, and although the policy is somewhat expensive and without prescription benefits, the quality of care and services are superb. The philosophy of my HMO is to cut costs by encouraging preventive care and healthy living, rather than cutting back on care. The lesson is that you have a duty to investigate local HMOs before dumping traditional Medicare. Should an HMO plan find your area too expensive, they can simply drop the plan and leave patients scrambling to find someone else to insure them!

Part D: Prescription Drug Plan

The final hijacking of Medicare by high-powered Washington lobbyists came in 2006 with the enactment of Medicare Part D, the *Prescription Drug Plan,* which subsidizes prescription drugs for the disabled and for people sixty-five and older. This was a brilliant coup by lobbyists and their congressional stooges—a multibillion-dollar windfall for insurance companies and drug manufacturers. Congress could have simply added prescription drug coverage to Medicare and saved a lot of money plus making it unnecessary to shop forty or more insurance companies to find one willing to cover your particular prescriptions. (The companies also have the right to drop prescription coverage for unprofitable products.)

As one political observer wrote: "Enacted after midnight, the drug bill contained hundreds and hundreds of pages unintelligible to anyone but lobbyists." The legislation enriched pharmaceutical and insurance companies, giving them a virtual gold mine, while senior citizens and taxpayers got the shaft. The bill guaranteed that drug companies could set whatever prices they wanted for their prescriptions and that insurance companies would be guaranteed their own handsome share of profits.

The new prescription plan didn't score well with the public, either, mostly because of its complexity, expense, and no control over prescription prices. Even though 86 percent of America's seniors take prescription drugs on a regular basis, at least three million low-income seniors who could benefit the most from the program failed to sign up before the May 15 deadline. The most common complaints were that people thought the cost was too high and the plans were too confusing and impossible to decipher.

Low-income Medicare seniors have been eligible for subsidies on prescriptions, but now an asset test disqualifies singles with $11,500 or more in savings and couples with $23,000 or more. They might no longer qualify for subsidies despite low incomes.

Most medical professionals say not signing up for the plan would be a mistake. Even though you do not take prescription drugs today, who knows what might happen down the road? For refusal, there is a monthly penalty of 1 percent per month increase in premiums. The lesson here is to sift through the hundreds of plans offered and try to find one that will best fit your needs and, most importantly, will cover your type of prescription drugs. Companies are being picky as to what they will cover—naturally they want to maximize profits.

Actually, depending on circumstances, many people will benefit from the new plan, especially those who have exceptionally high prescription costs, who are prescribed generic drugs, and those who completely understand the program. The number of plans is bewildering, as is the list of drugs each particular plan will cover. So if you haven't signed up, you need to analyze your situation carefully and choose something.

The Doughnut Hole

For example, if you have high drug costs, you may consider a plan that offers additional coverage until you spend $3,600 out-of-pocket. In most plans, once your costs reach an initial coverage limit of $2,250, you pay the next $2,850 in pharmacy bills yourself, after which Medicare pays 95 percent of all further drug expenses. This is called the coverage gap, or the "doughnut hole." Some plans offer partial coverage during the gap.

Before deciding on a particular insurer or insurance plan, be sure to make sure your pharmacy or a pharmacy convenient to you will accept the plan. You might visit the pharmacy with a list of medications. Also, some plans may offer a mail-order program that will allow you to have drugs sent directly to your home. Consider all of your options to find the most cost-effective and convenient way to have your prescriptions filled.

To be perfectly honest, I am like millions of others who can't make up their minds about the plans. My wife and I have a philosophy of refusing to take drugs designed "to keep us healthy," which I'm convinced most people are doing. But there just could come a day when we actually need to treat a problem that requires prescription drugs to regain our health. So, after consulting with three doctors who belong to our bridge club, they convinced us that we should make a decision to buy coverage. They mentioned a well-known insurance company (Humana) that offers policies beginning at $5.41 a month. The other choices with this particular plan were $11.25 a month and $51.00 a month. At only $5.41 a month, what did we have to lose? The first $250 in costs would be on us, and after that, we pay 25 percent of the cost of prescriptions.

So we made that plan our decision. We feel it's unlikely we'll ever collect (we haven't spent $250 on prescriptions between us over the past ten years), yet should we *need* prescriptions, we would be covered. Those who have regular and expensive prescription needs probably should make other choices. If you are still confused (I know I am), you are advised to call (800) MEDICARE, or go online to www.medicare.gov, or to consult with AARP, go to www.aarp.org/bulletin/medicare. From what I hear, AARP would be your best bet for information. Good luck.

Medicare Strategies

- If you are retiring early (or about to be laid off) and you are covered by a company health policy, try to make arrangements for continued insurance coverage (if you can afford it). This is especially important should you or a family member have an "existing condition" that could make it impossible to find a company willing to insure you. A federal law known as COBRA guarantees the right to continue on your company health plan for up to eighteen months at your own expense. (Web site: www.dol.gov/ebsa/faqs/faq_consumer_cobra.html)

- In some cases, your spouse and children are also eligible for COBRA coverage, sometimes for as long as three years. However, individual plans that you buy on your own, rather than through work or an association, are not subject to COBRA laws. If you have used up your COBRA benefits and attempt to buy new coverage within sixty-three days, you are eligible for a policy regardless of any health problems you have.

- Use generic drugs and don't demand the latest drug you see advertised on TV or in a magazine. Some medical experts caution against using new drugs that haven't been on the market long enough for the side effects to become known.

- If you're in a low-income bracket, be sure to investigate state programs that help patients pay for drugs.

- If you're eligible for Medicare and have trouble paying the Part B premium and the coinsurance, see if you are eligible for the Medicare subsidy programs that can help pay these costs. Your state insurance counseling program will tell you how to apply.

- If you are eligible for health care through Veterans Affairs, look into it. It may be a way to get coverage for prescription drugs. Also, the VA's electronic medical record system is said to improve the quality of patient care.

- If you do not qualify for Medicare and have too much income for Medicaid, you might consider relocating to a place where medical costs are not so high. The chart below illustrates differences in health-care costs.

Health-Care Costs (Percent of National Average)

Lower Costs		Higher Costs	
Dothan, AL	81.4	Fort Lauderdale, FL	115.5
Youngstown, OH	82.8	New London, CT	115.7
Cedar City, UT	85.3	Pasco, WA	116.4
Tupelo, MS	85.8	Miami, FL	116.5
Burlington, IA	86.1	Framingham, MA	117.3
Hot Springs, AR	86.3	Gastonia, NC	112.9
Manhattan, KS	87.8	Reno, NV	113.1
St. George, UT	88.5	Hartford, CT	117.9
Holland, MI	89.6	San Jose, CA	118.6
Corpus Christi, TX	90.1	Olympia, WA	119.0
Columbia, MO	90.5	Stamford, CT	119.1
St. Petersburg, FL	92.7	Corvallis, OR	120.2
Glens Falls, NY	93.2	San Diego, CA	120.2

Medigap Insurance

As you can see, Medicare has some big gaps, holes that can deplete savings accounts in a hurry. Most people purchase additional coverage if they can afford it. This supplemental insurance is known as "Medigap," and it is supposed to cover some or all of your extra medical costs. Medigap policies come in the form of Medicare supplements and major medical policies sold by private insurance companies.

Be very careful when purchasing Medigap coverage. This has been a fertile field for con artists working for unscrupulous insurance companies. They pressure clients into buying more insurance than is needed or policies that don't pay off as advertised. Don't let a fast-talking salesman scare you into a policy that isn't right for you. One comprehensive Medigap policy is all you need. Some low-income people don't need Medigap at all. However, be sure that the policy you buy to supplement your Medicare coverage does exactly that. Policies that pay only for hospitalization or for a specific disease are not substitutes for comprehensive health insurance. Premiums may be small, but so are the benefits.

Follow these recommendations when you are buying extra insurance:

- Choose from reputable companies and do comparison shopping. There can be big differences between one company and another.

- Resist pressure to buy and don't let anyone sell you more than one Medigap policy. Ask friends and your doctor for advice. You needn't change policies if you are satisfied with the one you have.

- Don't buy a policy by mail, at least not before checking with your state's department of insurance or consumer protection agency.

- If you aren't satisfied with your new Medigap policy, by law you have thirty days to demand a full refund. If they give you a hard time, call your state department of insurance.

- Medigap benefits are divided into two categories: core benefits and optional benefits. According to the law, only ten standard plans can be sold, and every insurer that sells Medigap insurance must also offer the basic plan.

The basic Medigap plan includes:

- Coverage of Medicare Part A coinsurance expenses for hospitalization to the extent not covered by Medicare from the sixty-first day through the ninetieth day in any Medicare benefit period

- Coverage of the Medicare Part A coinsurance amount during use of Medicare's sixty lifetime nonrenewable hospital inpatient reserve days

- Upon exhaustion of all Medicare hospital inpatient-care coverage, including the lifetime reserve days, coverage of the 100 percent Medicare-Part-A-eligible expenses for hospitalization subject to a lifetime maximum benefit of an additional 365 inpatient hospital days

- Coverage for the reasonable cost of the first three pints of blood unless replaced in accordance with federal regulations

- Coverage for the coinsurance (generally 20 percent of the approved amount; 50 percent of approved charges for outpatient mental health services) of Medicare-eligible expenses under Part B regardless of hospital confinement, after the Medicare Part B deductible is met

In addition to the core package of benefits that Medigap insurers are required to offer, there are other packages of benefits that companies can sell. They include various combinations of the following benefits: lower deductibles, skilled nursing facility care, medical emergencies in foreign countries, at-home recovery benefits with paid visits by health aids, preventive medical care, and other benefits.

Medicaid: The Second-Level Safety Net

Of course, not all retired people qualify for Medicare. Many retire before the eligible age of sixty-five. Others haven't paid enough into the system to be eligible for Medicare. A growing number aren't retired at all; they've been forced into unemployment because of downsizing, job outsourcing to India, or companies going bankrupt. These workers have years to go without insurance, before Medicare kicks in. This last group is among those who might be reading this book.

For the large number of low-income people who live on the edge of poverty, who cannot afford medical insurance, and who do not qualify for Medicare, there's a substitute health program called Medicaid. This is a joint federal-state medical-assistance program that squeaked through Congress along with Medicare. Medicaid (called Medi-Cal in California) provides health benefits to people who are blind, age sixty-five or over, disabled, or have very low incomes, yet are not eligible for Medicare. To qualify, they meet certain strict financial eligibility requirements.

When your income is low enough, you have a chance to get in on Medicaid insurance, a second-level safety net. This is not guaranteed because first you must fulfill various requirements of individual state governments. The requirements become more strict as funding is reduced. For those who have no medical coverage yet are unfortunate to have too much income to qualify for Medicaid, they are out of luck. How much is too much income? In Texas a family of four with an income of $1,000 a month would be covered only if medical expenses were at least $692 a month. Not very generous, I'd say. Other states are more helpful.

Medicaid is constantly under attack by cost-conscious Congressmen who are eagerly seeking additional funds for favorite pork-barrel projects. Under the latest Medicaid rule, which went into effect July 2006, you must show either a birth certificate and a driver's license, or else a U.S. passport, and thus prove you are a citizen. Never mind that many low-income people have no birth certificates (especially older people who were born at home, in the country, or Native Americans who were born on reservations). Even if poor people have birth certificates, without a car, how could they have a driver's license? How many poor people are likely to have traveled overseas and therefore have passports? Patients in nursing homes, Alzheimer's wards, and mentally confused poor are not exempt. They could legally be tossed out on the street. From three to five million low-income citizens on Medicaid could find their coverage at risk, and new applicants face being turned down or denied care until they can obtain documents.

My recommendation: Send away for a birth certificate and save an old driver's license, just in case you need to qualify for this last-ditch medical safety net. The benefit in all of this (according to Congress) is that the Congressional Budget Office estimates the new rules will save the federal government $220 million over five years. Not much of a saving when compared with the $300 million a day the Iraq War was costing in early 2007.

Long-Term Care

It isn't only the indigent and elderly infirm who need to be aware of the Medicaid program. Even those who think of themselves as financially comfortable should know about steps they can take to protect themselves and shelter their life savings in the event they or their spouse require long-term care. The reason is the largest hole in Medicare's safety net is nursing-home care. Because Medicare was designed to cover "skilled" medical care, it won't pay for "unskilled" or "custodial" care. Furthermore, Medicare covers the costs of skilled care in a nursing home only if the patient enters after hospitalization. Yet, it's these unskilled and custodial services that disabled patients desperately need—things like dressing, bathing, and cooking. Expenses for at-home care that are not covered by Medicare can easily exceed $2,000 a month, and nursing care can cost $3,000 to $5,000 a month. It doesn't take long for your life savings to disappear. This is where Medicaid becomes essential. Medicaid has become the major provider of long-term care for older Americans.

Some elderly deliberately get rid of their assets, dispersing them to children, in order to qualify for Medicaid should they need nursing care. But be aware that federal and state governments have been tightening the screws on eligibility to avoid some of these efforts, not without some justification. At one time it was possible for affluent seniors to "give away" their money and property to children and claim to be indigent. While trying to seal this gap, the remedy has hurt those who truly need the help. It isn't nearly as easy as it used to be. Check with local senior services and legal aid groups about state and local restrictions and how to qualify for long-term care.

Who Is Eligible for Medicaid?

Medicaid eligibility is complicated. Because Medicaid is both a state and a federally administered program, each state interprets and applies the rules differently. Unless you fall into the class of very poor, you may need expert help in figuring out whether you are eligible for Medicaid. Even if you don't appear to qualify, the experts may be able to show you how you can be covered. They can also tell you how to appeal an unfavorable decision.

In general, three categories of individuals may qualify for Medicaid. The first category includes aged, blind, or disabled people who are receiving federal Supplemental Security Income (SSI) payments. They automatically qualify for Medicaid assistance. Some states, however, place additional restrictions on SSI recipients. If you live in Connecticut, Hawaii, Illinois, Indiana, Minnesota, Missouri, Nebraska, New Hampshire, North Carolina, North Dakota, Ohio, Oklahoma, Utah, or Virginia, check with your local social-services office for limitations.

The second category includes individuals who are on Medicare but who are financially unable to pay the premiums, deductibles, and co-payments. All states are supposed to pay for Medicaid coverage in these circumstances, provided the recipient qualifies under the Medicaid limits. But you have to request payment. We'll discuss this at greater length below.

The third category includes the medically needy—aged, blind, or disabled patients—who have income in excess of the Medicaid limits but not enough income to pay their medical bills. However, many states won't pay if an applicant receives as little as a dime above the Medicaid income limits. The states that do not provide Medicaid coverage to "medically needy" applicants are Alabama, Alaska, Arizona, Arkansas, Colorado, Delaware, Florida, Idaho, Iowa, Kansas, Louisiana, Mississippi, Nevada, New Jersey, New Mexico, Oklahoma, Oregon, South Dakota, Texas, and Wyoming. In the states not listed, recipients must "spend down" their excess income on medical bills; Medicaid benefits kick in when the recipient's income falls below Medicaid income limits.

Qualifying for Medicaid

You must apply for Medicaid in the state where you live at your local Medicaid office. You can check with your local Social Security office or call Medicare at (800) 633–4227 to find the location of the Medicaid office, or if you have Internet access, go to the Web site at www.cms.hhs.gov. Some states also let you apply on the Internet, by telephone, or at locations in your community.

In many states, if you are eligible for Supplemental Security Income (SSI), you are automatically eligible for Medicaid. To get Medicaid benefits by applying for SSI, call the Social Security Administration at (800) 772–1213.

Actually, the whole matter of Medicaid income limits is so complicated that those who are on the verge of qualifying are urged to consult the local Medicare/Medicaid Assistance Program office. To find the office nearest you, contact AARP, 601 E Street NW, Washington, DC 20049; (888) OUR–AARP; www.aarp.org/states/; or contact your local Social Security office.

You are usually required to present the following documents when you apply:

- Proof of who you are (such as a birth certificate)
- A photo ID, such as a driver's license or passport
- Proof of where you live (such as a lease or utility bills)
- Proof of your income (such as pay stubs or a letter from Social Security)
- Proof of what you own (such as bank account statements and car registration)
- Your medical bills

Medicaid Resource Limits

Another complicated matter that may require expert help is determining whether your assets are near or over the limits. The amount of cash and property you can possess varies with individual state regulations. Depending on the state, you generally are permitted to hold cash and property not to exceed $2,000 to $4,000 for a single person and $3,000 to $6,000 for a married couple.

Items that do not count against your eligibility are:

- Your home, which must be your primary residence
- Your household goods and personal effects
- An automobile up to a value of $4,500

- Life insurance with a face value of up to $1,500

- A cemetery lot and $1,500 for burial expenses

- Income-producing property, such as land you use to grow food for personal use

These exempt resources are subject to some conditions that may or may not be to your benefit, depending on how you handle your affairs. For example, your home is exempt, even if you move out of it, as long as it remains occupied by your spouse or if you plan to return home after your illness. Yet sometimes state Medicaid officials add a qualification: that you realistically will be able to return.

Several strategies exist for qualifying for both Medicaid and SSI— maneuvers for bringing assets and income down that sound devious yet are perfectly legal. You'll probably need a Medicaid legal practitioner or an attorney who specializes in Medicaid before you take any such steps. Your senior-citizen center or local bar association can refer you to such a specialist. If you're entitled to it, go for it; your taxes paid for it.

Dual Eligibles

Those covered by Medicare yet have incomes low enough to qualify may qualify for dual coverage, with Medicaid paying some of the bills not covered by Medicare. These individuals are known as "dual eligibles." Services that are covered by both programs will be paid first by Medicare and the difference by Medicaid, up to the individual state's payment limit. Medicaid also covers additional services such as nursing facility care beyond the one-hundred-day limit covered by Medicare, prescription drugs, eyeglasses, and hearing aids.

Limited Medicaid benefits are also available to pay for out-of-pocket Medicare cost-sharing expenses for certain other Medicare beneficiaries. The Medicaid program will assume their Medicare payment liability if they qualify. The qualification requirements are up to the state, and the formulas are quite complicated. But if you have low income, it's worth checking out.

Free Medicare?

More than two million Medicare beneficiaries are paying too much for their Part B premiums. They don't take advantage of some benefits intended for low-income retirees, usually because state governments keep these benefits quiet and so save money by not fulfilling their obligations under law.

You should know that Congress enacted a Qualified Medicare Beneficiary program (QMB), which requires states, through their Medicaid programs, to pay Part B premiums for financially needy individuals who are on Medicare but who cannot pay the premiums, deductibles, and co-payments because of low income. The earnings limit is a little more than $1,100 a month for a single person (with assets under $4,000) and around $1,600 for a couple (with assets under $6,000). In some cases the states will pay for co-payments and deductibles. That is, if a patient qualifies, he or she isn't billed for some or all of the excluded charges. However, if you don't apply for this assistance, the state won't pay. The state government has no way of knowing your economic situation unless you speak up.

There are other Medicare and Medicaid benefits that accrue to very low-income patients. If you are in this category, you should inquire at the Medicaid office of your local department of human welfare or social services. The local senior-citizen center can supply you with directions. Should you have problems getting information, check in the phone book in the government section and look for the local office of your state or local agency on aging. For a pamphlet describing eligibility, an application, and other detailed information, send a self-addressed, stamped envelope to Families USA, 1334 G Street NW, Washington, DC 20005; www.familiesusa.org.

Discount Health Care in Mexico

No discussion of low-cost medical care is complete without mentioning what's happening along the borders of the United States and Mexico. Medical, dental, and optical practitioners are luring patients with cut-rate services and low-cost prescription drugs. It could be argued that the quality of the medical and dental care may not be up to U.S. or Canadian standards. I'm in no position to judge something like this. I can only observe that the prescription drugs come from the same manufacturers who sell on this side of the border. Also, most patients return enthusiastic about their treatment. And there's no question that the fees are affordable.

Almost all "border towns" have a steady stream of Americans crossing the border to patronize medical services on the Mexican side. A dramatic example of this is found in the Mexican border town of Los Algodones ("the cotton fields"). For several years this quiet community has been drawing thousands of people from all over the United States and Canada to take advantage of unbelievably low-cost dental, medical, and optical care. You'll find $135 root canals, discount eyeglasses, and hormone pills selling for a fraction of the cost charged on this side of the Mexican border. Los Algodones is also popular with those seeking alternative medical treatments that aren't available on this side of the border, especially restricted cancer drugs such as laetrile.

Discount medical care is nothing new in Mexican border towns. But nowhere else has medicine taken over the economy as it has in Los Algodones. Doctors and dentists are big business here. Although the town has fewer than 10,000 residents, you'll find fifty dentist offices, fifteen doctors' offices, almost thirty pharmacies, twenty optical shops, and many related businesses. On the other hand, you'll find only ten restaurants. Thousands of visitors cross the border every single month of the year, looking for low-cost medical care. The fierce competition for patients and customers helps keep costs down.

At the time of writing, Advair, a popular drug for asthma, sells in Mexico for about one-half the cost in U.S. pharmacies. You can pay about $45 for a month's supply instead of the $90 you would fork over on the American side. Not long ago, a friend said she found Ciprofloxacin, a powerful

Drug Bus?

Tour bus companies based in Arizona take advantage of the proximity to Mexico to shuttle thousands of seniors each year to buy prescription drugs, charging about $30 to $40 for a daylong trip.

antibiotic, selling for 31 cents per tablet, compared with $4.00 per pill in the United States.

Why so cheap? The Mexican government successfully controls prescription drug prices to prevent unfair profit-taking. On the other hand, it's no secret that Washington, D.C. lobbyists work hard and successfully to protect the interests of the pharmaceutical companies. So be aware that at times, there are discussions of preventing or stopping this practice of shopping for medications across the Rio Grande. As far as I know, people aren't being hassled when returning with their prescriptions at this point in time. However, I believe that it would be wise not to purchase in massive quantities—that is, more than a couple of months' supply—and carry an old prescription when purchasing a controlled type of drug.

Mexican Dental Care

Dentistry is especially popular with visitors. Because neither Medicare nor Canada's government-sponsored health system covers dental care, many patients journey to Los Algodones in search of affordable dentures, root canals, bridges, and implants. People claim they save two-thirds of normal dental bills by having their teeth fixed in Mexico. Eyeglasses, frames, and contact lenses are well crafted, supposedly using materials identical to those used in the States but at drastically reduced prices. Because Los Algodones is only a short drive from Yuma, Arizona, it isn't even absolutely necessary to stay there overnight.

How does the quality of care stack up against the care you'll find north of the border? As you might guess, U.S. dentists caution that low-cost dentistry could be accompanied by substandard care, and of course it's difficult to lodge a complaint within Mexico. And naturally, U.S. medical doctors abhor the unconventional treatments for everything from cancer to arthritis that attract visitors from all over the country, particularly those who are searching for cures to "incurable" problems. In short, the American medical and dental establishments discourage patronage of professionals on the Mexican side of the border.

As an uninformed layman, I'm obviously not qualified to make judgments about the quality of care served up in Los Algodones or the advisability of going there. My only observation is that we've interviewed many people who see doctors and dentists across the border, and they've enthusiastically endorsed the treatment and products they receive. We may simply have missed folks who have had bad experiences.

Understand, the people we interviewed are low-income retirees who are not covered by private dental plans; some are not even covered by Medicare. They have two options: either Mexican dental and medical care at one-third the regular cost or no treatment at all. For some folks, places like Mexican border towns are their only option.

Across the Canadian Border

For years, folks living in the northernmost part of the United States have been aware of the bargain prices for prescription drugs in Canada. People make regular bus trips to save 25 to 50 percent and more on lifesaving drugs. Now a new twist has cropped up: Internet prescription sales. More than eighty Web sites provide this service. A recent article in the *AARP Bulletin* profiled a Maryland Social Security recipient who used to spend a third of her monthly check on medications at the cheapest pharmacy she could find. Then she discovered Canada and began buying over the Internet. Her drug costs dropped to $200 a month from the U.S. price of $550. The yearly savings come to $4,200.

As you can imagine, the pharmaceutical companies are furious about this trend and are lobbying Congress to not only stop Internet sales but also prevent patients from crossing the Canadian border. At this point in time, we don't know how successful they will be. There's an old saying, money talks, and the pharmaceutical corporations (who make billions of dollars in profits every year, enough to pay their CEOs $20 million a year or more in bonuses) have plenty of money to talk loudly.

AARP recommends that if you use the Internet for your prescriptions, make sure you are dealing with a legitimate pharmacy. This would be one that has—besides an e-mail address—a postal mailing address and a telephone number so that patients can talk to a pharmacist, and will prominently display its license number and name of the authority that granted the license. Be skeptical of a Web site that says prescriptions aren't necessary.

chapter seven

Working and Retirement

Work begins the day we enter kindergarten. That's when our on-the-job training begins (without pay, of course). We quickly learn that we have a solid obligation to get up every morning—whether we want to or not—and that we must appear at a certain place at a certain time. We discover that we have a "boss" (the teacher), and we must please the boss if life is going to be tolerable. Until each long, wearisome school day draws to a merciful close, teachers and administrators direct our souls, control our lives, and limit our leisure time. I'm convinced that the fifth grade is the longest period of time ever measured. (Fifth-grade recess may be the shortest time span ever measured.)

By the time we finally finish school and enter the job market, we've learned our lessons well. Get up every day, go somewhere, perform work we may or may not enjoy, and be rewarded with a weekly paycheck instead of a report card. Weekends off, plus a two-week vacation, are the only respite from the grinding schedule. To miss a day's work means losing a day's pay—a serious blow to many budgets—so we go to work even though we feel terrible. Missing too many days' work could mean losing a job—a disaster.

This process, started in kindergarten, is relentlessly reinforced through the next sixty years of our lives. We often suffer from a mental hang-up called the "work ethic." To have a job is good. Not to have a job is bad. To lose a job is ruinous. Only hobos and criminals live without working at jobs.

Then one day—willingly or not—you stumble into retirement. You no longer have a job, someone to boss you, or a place to be every day at a specified hour or else. You can get up when you please, take a nap when you please, and you don't have to please anyone who doesn't please you.

For some people, retirement is wonderful. It's the goal they've worked for and anticipated since that first day in kindergarten. School's out! Recess and vacation from now on! When you wake up in the morning, you can roll over and go back to sleep if you jolly well feel like it!

But for others, retirement is a terrible shock. They feel there's something wicked or evil about not having a job. When one of these unfortunate individuals wakes up in the morning without a job to go to, a feeling of guilt sets in. "Something is terribly wrong here," the person thinks. "I should be working, suffering, making money."

This guilty feeling is why many folks refuse to retire, even though they work at jobs they dislike. Others, when forced into retirement, insist on finding full-time or part-time jobs even when they don't need the money. What a tragic waste of a lifetime's goal.

Retirement doesn't necessarily mean the end of a person's working career. On the contrary, retirement means the opportunity to do what you *want* to do rather than what you *have* to do. You now have the time to write a book, join an acting group, become a fishing guide, or turn your hobby into a profitable occupation. No law says you have to suffer while making money.

This may be the time to take up a new hobby, to explore an unlimited range of options. Learn to feel sorry for those who feel forced to work instead of feeling guilty for not being with them.

For those who need to be "doing something" but who can get by without extra income, our recommendation is volunteer work. As a volunteer, you will not only be doing something meaningful and worthwhile but will also meet other volunteers in your community, widen your network of friends, and lay the groundwork for later years when you may need volunteers to help you. You'll also be deeply appreciated for whatever you contribute. We'll discuss volunteer work later.

Expensive Jobs

On the other hand, many retirees truly need extra earnings to supplement their Social Security and other income. Part-time or full-time jobs can mean the difference between bare survival and a comfortable retirement. Yet sometimes the income earned can be costly—in several ways.

One condition that can make a job uneconomical is the government's policy about working while drawing Social Security. To discourage retirees from earning money, the government reduces benefits when you earn more than a certain amount. Fortunately, in 2000, they stopped reducing benefits for those older than sixty-five who work. Before, you had to wait until you were seventy-five to work and collect full Social Security benefits. As of 2006, if you are under sixty-five, you are permitted to earn $12,000 a year ($1,000 a month); after that you'll be penalized one dollar for every two dollars you earn over that amount. So if you happen to find a job making from $20,000 and up and are under sixty-five, you will forfeit your Social Security checks. Once you reach the age of full retirement, of course, you can earn as much as you like.

Let's take the case of Roger, a commercial printer who lost his $20-an-hour job because desktop publishing put his employer out of business. He was sixty-two years old, so Roger applied for Social Security and was entitled to $1,200 a month (amounting to $14,400 a year or $276 a week). Finding he needed more income, he looked for a job. The best job he could find paid $10 an hour ($400 a week). *Better than nothing,* he thought.

At the end of the year, however, he discovered that he had to repay $4,400 of his Social Security money because at $10.00 an hour he was earning too much! For full-time employment, Roger was only entitled to make $6.25 an hour without penalty; that's just a little more than minimum wage. In other words, Roger worked more than thirteen weeks for nothing—just to make up for the money deducted from his Social Security! To add insult to injury, he had to pay income tax on the excess that he earned over the allowable amount. He immediately started looking for a part-time job!

One interesting way around the above dilemma is something known as *flex retirement,* an idea that seems to be catching on with some companies. You might inquire of your employer if the company might be interested in this arrangement. If you are a valuable worker with difficult-to-replace skills, you just might come to an agreement. You might even maintain some medical benefits, if you are a good negotiator.

It works like this: Your employer hates to see you leave because he needs your experience and job skills. Therefore he might be willing to hire you on a part-time basis, perhaps to train newcomers or to cover busy periods to fill unexpected rush jobs or vacancies, yet step aside when not needed. The understanding would be that you would only work as many hours as permissible under the Social Security rules. This is a great way to break into retirement less abruptly, earn extra income, and still have plenty of time to enjoy the benefits of retirement.

Good Jobs and High Prices

Part-time work is, of course, one solution for a shoestring budget. The problem is that competition for these jobs can be fierce and the pay can be minimal. This creates a dilemma: Where part-time jobs are plentiful and pay is good, you'll often find that the cost of living is impossible. A booming economy brings high rents, higher living costs, and high wages. It doesn't make sense to retire where living costs are exorbitant in order to find a good-paying part-time job that will only help pay the extra expenses of retiring in a costly area! You're right back where you started.

We have a friend who lived in a small apartment in Monterey, California. Her rent was $800 a month, but it wasn't a fancy place—it was just in a nice neighborhood near the ocean. The high cost of living in Monterey really wouldn't permit her to live on Social Security. She found a part-time job in a bookstore that paid $6.25 an hour ($448 a month clear) for working five afternoons a week. When she decided to move to a smaller town in a low-cost area on the Oregon coast, she found an equally nice apartment for $350 a month. Part-time jobs there paid about $5.15 an hour, but no jobs were available. At first she was disappointed—until she realized that the $450 she saved in rent made up for the $448 she had been earning at her bookstore job. In other words, she had been going to work five afternoons a week just to pay higher rent! Now she devotes her time to satisfying volunteer work in the community and takes classes in oil painting at the local community college.

Finding Retirement Jobs

Some retirees have lifetime job skills that make it relatively easy to find part-time work. Although you might no longer have the strength and stamina to handle some of the tougher jobs, your experience and good judgment might qualify you for consulting or supervisory work. Perhaps you have a skill that is in demand for vacation fill-ins or emergency work in case of an employee's illness. Nurses, secretaries, bookkeepers, and others with specialized or professional work backgrounds find themselves in demand for these temporary positions. For example, I have a brother—a retired veterinarian—who likes to work but not on a regular basis. It turns out that many small veterinary offices are one-doctor clinics, so taking a vacation is out of the question unless another vet can fill in. This works out perfectly for my brother, who schedules his vacations well in advance and limits the number of weeks he works to those he chooses. In other words, he decides when the veterinarian can go on vacation.

Not everybody has high levels of competency at a trade or profession, and many skills have been replaced by computers. Yet most jobs in offices and businesses do not require high-tech or professional skills. A pleasant personality and a willingness to be on the job when needed are the basic requirements. Temporary employment agencies can be the job solution. The yellow pages of your telephone directory will list temporary employment firms, such as Manpower or Kelly Services (used to be Kelly Girls, remember?). These firms nearly always need temporary or seasonal workers and can usually be depended on to find you a job when you need a job or are willing to take temporary employment. Some employment agencies actually specialize in finding work for older workers, being aware that many employers prefer to hire a dependable, mature worker, someone with experience in the workplace as well as in life.

These temporary jobs have a way of turning into regular gigs when an employer is pleased with a worker's performance. A nice thing about these situations: It's understood from the beginning that the work is temporary. You aren't embarrassed when you quit because you are under age sixty-five and you've earned as much as Social Security permits. Or maybe you and your husband want to hop into your RV and toodle off to Mexico for the winter. You'll find another temp job when you return, maybe working for the same company.

Another way to find work is to inquire at your local senior-citizen center. They can direct you to a Senior Citizen Council office (if it isn't in the center itself) where the staff works at placing senior citizens in both permanent and temporary jobs. Of course, the newspaper's help-wanted classified pages carry employment opportunities, but many employers are looking for full-time workers. Of course, that could be exactly what you are looking for. By placing your own ad in the "situation wanted" column, you can put forward your own unique qualifications, job requirements, and preferences. If you have special skills that might be attractive to a particular group of employers, the telephone book will provide a list of companies to whom you can send résumés. As a final resort, there's always the state employment bureau or human development department—whatever it calls itself in your area. There, however, you are often competing with younger unemployed workers who are looking for jobs while collecting temporary unemployment benefits.

Employment Opportunities

The U.S. Department of Labor sponsors a program known as the Senior Community Service Employment Program (SCSEP), which is utilized by most states. The purpose is to assist low-income persons age fifty-five or older who have limited employment prospects. Through this program, older workers have access to the SCSEP services as well as other employment assistance available through the One-Stop Career Centers of the workforce investment system. In addition to providing community services and part-time work-based training, the program has a goal of placing into unsubsidized jobs the number of participants equal to 30 percent of the authorized positions. Program participants work an average of twenty hours a week and are paid federal, state, or local minimum wages or the prevailing wage. Applicants are placed in a wide variety of community service activities at nonprofit and public facilities, including day-care centers, senior centers, schools, and hospitals. It is intended that these community service experiences serve as a bridge to other employment positions that are not supported with federal funds.

To qualify, participants must be at least age fifty-five, with a family income of no more than 25 percent over the federal poverty level. Enrollment priority is given to persons over age sixty, veterans, and qualified spouses of veterans. Preference is also given to eligible individuals who have the greatest economic need. To find out if this program is active in your community, contact the Administration on Aging's Eldercare Locator at (800) 677–1116 or go to the Web site www.eldercare.gov. Another resource is the National Council on Aging, 409 Third Street SW, Suite 200, Washington, DC 20024; www.ncoa.org.

Yet another resource can be found at your local American Association of Retired Persons (AARP) office; they often offer career counseling and support a program called Workers' Equity Initiative. AARP has a computer database of employers who need older workers. They can also advise you of your rights under the federal Age Discrimination Act. If you are interested, you might request AARP's free publications, *How to Stay Employable: A Guide for the Mid-life and Older Worker* and *Working Options—How to Plan Your Job Search, Your Work Life*. Contact AARP Fulfillment, 601 E Street NW, Washington, DC 20049; www.aarp.org.

For the outgoing personality, one of the easiest part-time jobs to land is commission sales work. The reason is obvious: Many employers pay no salaries or benefits until you sell something. Automobile agencies typically have half a dozen salespersons lounging about in hopes that a buyer will happen along. Real estate offices can afford to have large staffs because they don't pay wages. Often, the new salesperson is obligated to spend some time each week taking care of the office (at no pay) in addition to sales work. The upside is that while you are manning the desk you can pick up leads for listings. Even though it is either "feast or famine," the potential earnings for an effective salesperson can be quite high.

The fact is, many sales positions offer little in the way of wages; employees earn the bulk of their income from commissions. If you are successful, these jobs make good part-time occupations and sometimes pay well. The nice part about these jobs is that you needn't invest in any capital except for a few dressy outfits. The downside is that when things aren't selling, you not only get nothing for your time, but it can also be boring. Before you consider investing any money in a sales business, please check very, very carefully; the overwhelming majority of these "money-making opportunities" are scams.

Snowbirds Follow the Weather

People usually think of retirement as a time to travel, to go south for the winter and north for the summer, to enjoy the seashore, breathe fresh mountain air, and live the good life. However, when retirement rolls around, and people find they must exist on a tight budget, travel plans often evaporate. "Too expensive," you say. "It's tough enough getting by without quitting my part-time job to spend a winter in Florida or a summer in Wyoming."

Here's the good news: A large subculture of retirees does quite well chasing good weather. They enjoy the best seasons in places where others pay big money for vacationing, yet they do it on a budget. How? By working. They call themselves "snowbirds." These happy-go-lucky travelers flock south at the first sign of frost, then migrate north when sultry summer weather sets in. Not all snowbirds work; some just like to be on permanent vacation. Many live in RVs during their travels, using their vehicles as mobile living quarters. Others accept living accommodations such as a small house or apartment as part of their part-time salary. How do they find jobs while following good weather? It's easier than you might think. Seasonal jobs are plentiful; the more popular the vacation spot, the more work is available. We have friends who spend each summer in beautiful Yosemite Valley, working in a tourist gift shop and restaurant. Living accommodations are part of the pay package.

Any time a seasonal migration of tourists descends on a popular tourist area, temporary employees are suddenly in great demand. Business is alive and booming after the doldrums of the off-season. Motels are full, restaurants are busy, services and stores are pushed to the limit. The area's entire economy is positively affected. Businesses of all types need temporary help, especially workers who understand that their jobs cease when the tourists and snowbirds go home.

Almost every business in a resort area needs extra help to handle the increased tourist traffic. From gift shops to garages, restaurants to recycling centers, almost every business needs temporary help. RV mechanics and repairmen can write their own agendas when thousands of RVs are in town. Temporary jobs in RV parks, motels, and campgrounds are available for assistant managers, clerical staff, housekeepers, and groundskeepers. Ski instructors are needed in mountain resorts for the winter, and fishing guides are needed for the summer.

Understand that many of these jobs offer little in the way of salaries, but most provide accommodations and benefits for a limited number of hours worked. Many snowbirds are happy to put in four hours a day cleaning rooms or mowing lawns in exchange for a vacation in a desirable resort. Those jobs that do pay money in addition to benefits often require full-time work, which many people don't need or don't want, preferring instead to have time off to enjoy their surroundings.

It's true that retirees who own RVs have the advantage here because they bring their own housing. They typically receive free hookups and utilities, cable TV, and free laundry as part of their compensation. One of the advantages of RV travel is the ability to take your home with you to the job site. This opens many new work opportunities.

But those without RVs aren't left out of the snowbird picture, not by any means. Many businesses maintain special facilities to house temporary employees. Motels often reserve one of the units for temps or know of inexpensive housing that can be reserved for the season. Some snowbirds, those who return season after season, make arrangements for renting a house or apartment early, before the rush starts and rents begin to climb into the tourist range.

Seasonal work situations are not confined to tourist resorts. Christmas tree lots love to have commissioned salespeople who can park their RVs in the middle of the merchandise and watch over it at night. Other retirees work as salespeople, following trade shows or shopping-mall promotions, manning booths and selling items to the public. Many of these traveling jobs are best suited for RVers; the work would be impractical if you had to stay in hotels and eat in expensive restaurants.

See our chapter on RVs and retirement for more information on seasonal jobs in national or state parks and private campgrounds. Many positions are volunteer and don't pay any cash salaries. The joy of spending a glorious vacation in a natural wonderland (in many cases *free*) is pay enough for some folks.

Finding Snowbird Jobs

At the same time snowbirds are looking for paid or volunteer jobs, employers are seeking workers who are looking for temporary or full-time positions. An excellent publication known as *Workamper News* brings everyone together. *Workamper News* began a few years ago as an eight-page newsletter to inform RV travelers of both volunteer and salaried jobs available to them. The first issues carried about thirty-five job announcements. Today, the publication has grown to sixty-four pages and averages more than fifty pages of listings representing thousands of job openings.

Although the publication was originally directed toward RV owners (and still is to a large extent), the publication lists jobs of all descriptions for people with or without their own housing. The publication has been used by a wide variety of public and private enterprises with great success. The publishers try to weed out phony get-rich-quick schemes, so most of the help-wanted ads are legitimate. Each listing includes information on the job location, duties, benefits, and how and where to apply.

If you have special skills or work situations in mind, you might make your needs known through your own advertisement. The newsletter provides situations-wanted ads (first thirty words free) and a résumé referral system. Résumés from active job seekers are maintained on file and are scanned for those that meet an employer's requirements, based on skills, geographic location, and benefits and length of employment desired.

A new feature, *Workamper Hotline*, provides twenty-four-hour access to jobs from coast to coast via a voice-mail message and ads posted on the *Workamper News* Web site, www.workamper.com. The hotline is updated weekly. Job seekers call and hear the voice-mail message or check the Web site, then contact employers directly concerning job vacancies.

Help Wanted

Here are some typical job opportunities from a recent issue of *Workamper News*:

Campgrounds & RV Parks (commercial & government)

Activity director/entertainer	Relief manager
Camp host	Membership sales
Assistant manager	Naturalist/interpreter
Manager	Contract gate attendant
Off-season caretaker	Volunteer park attendant
Maintenance supervisor	Camp host coordinator

Theme Parks/Amusement Parks/Tourist Attractions/Circuses/Carnivals

Retail salesperson	Ticket office worker
Ride operator	Actor/performer
Tram driver	Musician
Security officer	Groundskeeper
Waiter/waitress	Petting zoo attendant

Dude Ranches/Outdoor Outfitters/Lodges/Cabins/Motels/Retreats

River guide	Reservations/front desk attendant
Canoe livery driver	Housekeeping supervisor
Wrangler	Security
Cooks	Grounds supervisor
Waiter/waitress	Housekeeper
Livestock tender	

(continued)

Help Wanted (continued)

Motorsports

Usher	Concessions worker
Ticket stubber	Souvenir salesperson
Parking attendant	Campground attendant
Campground manager	

Business & Income Opportunities

RV park snack bar operator	Souvenir/award salesperson
Campground owner/operator	Power tool distributor
Map salesperson	Aerial photo salesperson
Forwarding/message service salesperson	

Career Opportunities

Director of education	Park management team
General manager	Assistant manager
Operations manager	Bookkeeper

Other

RV delivery driver	Gift shop clerk
Utility inspector	Golf course attendant
Campground inspector	Tour guide
Park map salesperson	RV technician
Field rep	RV salesperson
Kiosk salesperson	Estate/property sitter
Airport attendant	

According to the publishers of *Workamper News*, Greg and Debbie Robus, there are often more jobs than people to fill them. They also maintain a complete bookstore with books on retirement, work-travel, how to find jobs, and so forth. One popular book they recommend is *Road Work: The Ultimate RVing Adventure* by Arline Chandler. Others include *The Back Door Guide to Short-Term Job Adventures* by Michael Landes and *Travel While You Work* by Kay and Joe Peterson.

The address for subscriptions to *Workamper News* is 709 West Searcy Street, Heber Springs, AR 72543-3761; www.workamper.com. For a free brochure, call (800) 446–5627. A year's subscription is $25.

Underground Economy

The Internal Revenue Service is understandably concerned about what it calls the "underground economy." Throughout the country, folks are dealing with each other in cash transactions—or trading goods and services that amount to income—yet they neglect to report these transactions on their income tax forms.

For example, if you do housework for someone in exchange for reduced rent, you are expected to report the rent as wage income, while the landlord reports your labor as rental income. If you sell items at a flea market, you are supposed to report your profits. I don't know if it's ever happened, but that's the way it's *supposed* to be. Without a "paper trail" of transactions, and because individual amounts are relatively insignificant, the IRS finds it almost impossible to track these small-time tax evaders. The IRS seems genuinely surprised and indignant at these transgressions, and it estimates that if everyone paid income tax on all their earnings there would be additional billions pouring into our national coffers every year. (On the other hand, if the wealthy were limited in their loopholes, the amount of additional revenue would be even more staggering.)

But the law is the law, and if you deal in cash transactions, you need to bear in mind that at some date in the future you could face an audit by the IRS. So keep receipts, just in case. Unless you earn a lot of money, chances are you'll pay very little tax anyway.

Arts and Crafts

Now that you are retired, you'll have more time to spend on your favorite hobby. When your pastime involves arts and crafts, you may be able to turn it into cash, selling your wares at local craft shows, fairs, flea markets, and by consignment to gift shops. If you have a product that is unique and of high quality, you might find it accepted at a national craft consignment shop. Arts and crafts shows are big business in many parts of the country, and some retirees make a good living this way. I interviewed Jean O'Connor and her husband, Dwan, a Clarksville, Tennessee, couple who devote much of their spare time to their hobby-business. They travel to craft fairs in several Southern states as far away as Florida, selling all the handicrafts they can make.

"Our best time of the year is fall," Jean said, "from Labor Day until the first week in December. The closer to Christmas, the better the sales of lower priced items. Anything priced $10 or less sells like hotcakes." Jean specializes in tole-painted objects—shelves, bread boxes, wall plaques, and other small items. "Dwan works with the band saw, and I do the painting," she explained. "From January on through to August, we build our inventory, and then we go on the road."

Their net profit averages between $1,000 to $1,500 per weekend, although some of the more successful sellers can take in as much as $15,000 at one of the larger craft fairs, where as many as 40,000 visitors browse the shows. However, getting a booth at one of these high-volume shows requires exceptionally good products (you need to submit good-quality slides and samples of your work), a substantial fee for the selling space, and a long time spent on the waiting list. Jean described one show in Ann Arbor, Michigan, that's reputed to have a waiting list several years long.

To locate these arts and crafts shows, pick up a copy of *Sunshine Artists USA,* a magazine that bills itself as "the Voice of the Nation's Artists and Craftsmen," listing 10,000 arts and crafts shows in the United States. Write to *Sunshine Artists USA,* 1700 Sunset Drive, Longwood, FL 32750; www.sunshineartist.com.

Free Flea Market Enterprise

Looking for an inexpensive way to start your own retail business? Check out your local flea market or swap meet. It's a start-up-on-a-shoestring opportunity and a fun way to potentially earn a substantial income. Currently there are an estimated 2,500 to 3,000 weekly flea markets around the country, with around $5 billion in annual sales. Flea market vendors even have their own organization and Web site, the National Flea Market Association (www.fleamarkets.org). A valuable Web page that shows exact locations of flea markets across the nation can be found at www.flea marketguide.com.

The president of the flea market association, Chuck Pretto, says, "The first step is to research your local flea market. Shop the market to get a feel for the customers, the booth design/setup and the kinds of products that sell well, paying special attention to vendors in your same category. Determine who your competition is, and then you can make your offering a bit different or a bit better." Occasionally, those starting out with flea market sales discover they've found a niche and branch out into more conventional retail outlets for their products.

Several years ago, when I first met my friends Jack and Marie, they were the epitome of early-day "yuppies." Jack had just graduated from a university with a degree in business. Marie was making money hand over fist from a direct-sales enterprise she had started. Clearly, this couple was headed for the top. And that's exactly where they went. Unfortunately, a few years before retirement, a series of accidents and some bad investments seriously diminished their financial portfolio. But not their drive to succeed. Although far from poverty-stricken, Jack and Marie wanted to earn money and decided to use their business knowledge to do it.

"The problem was," said Marie, "we didn't have the 'seed money' necessary to get into a substantial business. Besides, we were retired; we wanted to control our time and not be slaves to business hours. Since we both enjoy meeting the public and selling, we figured that nothing could be more natural for us than working flea markets."

So for the past several years, they've been traveling to flea markets and an occasional craft fair. They pick up merchandise to resell from auctions, distress sales, and wholesalers. Garage sales sometimes provide stock, "but we stop at garage sales only if we happen to be driving past," said Jack. "Most of the time, people want more for their junk than we can sell it for at the flea market!" Classified ads in the local newspaper are another source of merchandise, especially when a family is moving away and is anxious to get rid of everything.

What's required to become an entrepreneur in the flea market business? You'll need a van large enough to carry your inventory, some folding tables, and a canvas awning to keep off sunshine and rain. And, of course, you'll need to fill your van with interesting items for sale. Most cities and states require a vendor's license, and most flea market managers are happy to provide all the information needed to get started. Fees and terms of participation vary by locations. Generally booth rentals range from $10 to $100 per day (the high end is usually for permanent vendors selling new merchandise), and fees are usually payable up front in cash.

House and Pet Sitting

Remember when you used to go on vacation? You'd load the kids and the dogs into the car, lock the front door, and head for the mountains. If you forgot to lock the front door, no big deal. Probably you paid a neighbor's kid a buck or so to mow the lawn while you were away.

That was before the days of mass burglaries, vandalism, and NO PETS ALLOWED signs at your favorite resort. Times have changed. Many people now insist on a "house watcher" when they go on vacation, business trips, or extended visits. Furthermore, they no longer trust the neighbor's kid to watch over things, not as long as he has access to spray paint and a penchant for graffiti (and it's no longer a dollar a lawn). As a result, many vacationers are willing to pay real money to mature adults in exchange for peace of mind. And most don't expect you to do lawns or windows.

One lady we interviewed managed to build her pet-care and home-watching business into a full-time job. She even has to hire help during the busy season. For $30 a day, she makes two trips to each home. She feeds the pets (walks are extra), waters the house plants as needed, changes the lighting to make it appear that the home is occupied, carries in newspapers and mail, and checks the telephone answering machine for important messages. Total time: two half-hour visits each day. Four customers a day constitutes a maximum schedule, for an average of $300 a week in cash. Her business grew by word of mouth, with no outlay for advertising. "I'm afraid that if I put an ad in the yellow pages, I'd have so much business I'd never get back into retirement!"

Some pet sitters specialize in bringing the pets (usually cats) to their own home so they won't be alone in the house. This arrangement saves driving back and forth to the pet owner's home for feeding.

A friend who lives in upscale Monterey, California, managed to work her pet-sitting business into an unusual lifestyle. She rents a tiny studio apartment as her home base, then specializes in house- and pet-sitting in the exclusive Pebble Beach area. She stays in multimillion-dollar digs while the home owners are away (in Europe, Alaska, New Zealand, or wherever super-rich people spend long vacations). Marilyn often has use of the Mercedes or Jaguar to do shopping. She sleeps in the master bedroom, generally lives in luxury, and gets paid for it. In return, she waters the plants, pampers the dogs and cats, and lolls around the swimming pool while she watches over the grounds.

Pet Grooming

This is a business that can be easily conducted in your home with a minimum of capital investment. According to one source, there are around 28,000 pet grooming businesses listed in the yellow pages, yet professional groomers are obviously in demand because there are more than 4,000 dogs and cats for every listed grooming business. Pet lovers spare no expense in caring for their animals, so a competent pet groomer can be assured of steady repeat business. Customers realize that grooming is a necessary luxury and schedule it on a regular basis.

However, pet grooming is one of those skills that is difficult to "learn as you go." You should take a hands-on class if at all possible. An Internet search using Google will yield hundreds of resources, ranging from in-depth professional training in your area to correspondence courses in the skills of pet grooming. A truly in-depth course could run into money, but the more in-depth you go into training, the higher your skills and earning potential. Local community colleges sometimes offer classes where you can learn the fundamentals. Occasionally, pet groomers learn the trade on their own by studying books on the subject and by experimentation. (However, I would recommend that you practice on your dog before you begin accepting customers!)

An interesting Internet source can be found at www.PetGroomer.com with connections to a bulletin board for exchange of information among professionals, an online radio show, information about trade shows, schools, and training, and many how-to-do-it tips.

Child Care

This is another business that can done in the home with little investment. This used to be a traditional way for housewives to earn money—taking care of the neighbors' kids. Today, with so many mothers having to work, the demand is higher than ever before. Without someone to care for the children, a married or single mother is out of the job market.

Unfortunately, right at the peak of the demand, the city, county, and state bureaucracies have made it more complicated. Now you have to be certified and licensed in most communities. This is another area in which local colleges come in handy. Ask if they have child care provider classes that qualify you for a license as a day care provider. The courses usually include preschool activities, pediatric first aid and safety, and basic life support strategies for youngsters. (How in the world did we raise children before the government got involved?) The school can also help with the licensing process.

Licensing laws vary from state to state and provide a baseline of quality below which it is illegal to operate. Before going into child care other than taking care of your neighbors' kids on a casual basis, you should contact your state's child care regulatory agency and see what is required for a professional license. If you don't have an Internet connection, borrow your neighbor's computer and go to www.childcareaware.org/en/licensing or www.sba.gov/library/pubs/mp-29.pdf.

Home Companion

For a single retiree with no resources, an excellent way of making ends meet without spending any of your income is to become a home companion. By watching the classified section of your newspaper or by placing your own ad, you may find a situation with a nice home, good meals, and a small monthly stipend. All you do in return is act as a live-in companion to an elderly or infirm person.

Many people in their declining years fiercely resist entering rest homes for the elderly. They see no reason to leave the comfort of their homes, they want to stay in familiar surroundings, and they neither want nor require round-the-clock nursing attention. This is where the home companion comes in. The home owner needs someone to do the cooking, run errands, do laundry, clean and dust—in short, do light housework as well as provide assistance in getting around when needed. The home companion usually has a private room and run of the house (although some agree to sleep on the living room sofa bed) and often has weekends off as well as several nights out a week, providing the home owner is capable of being alone.

We commonly think of this as woman's work, but single men are in demand as well, particularly when the client is a male who feels intimidated by a female companion. Also, some women prefer to have a man in the house, providing security and not objecting to fixing the garbage disposal when it conks out. We have a friend in Seattle who for several years was a home companion to an elderly college professor. He enjoyed living in a lovely home, attended classes at the local university, and banked most of his Social Security. He earned an associate's degree in computer science and at age sixty-eight was probably the oldest of the graduating class.

Obviously, the drawbacks to a job like this are being restricted to the house for long hours at a time and being responsible for the safety and comfort of the employer. Another disadvantage is low pay. However, the advantage is, your living costs are totally paid, which permits you to build up a nest egg by banking all of your Social Security money. Also, your duties are usually rather light, with little to do other than light housework. This work can be minimized if you ask that a housekeeper visit once a week or so. You'll have plenty of time to read, work on your hobbies, and watch television.

Part-Time Teaching

Teaching is an excellent (although not always lucrative) way to take advantage of your life experience. Throughout the country, courses in trade schools and adult education classrooms are often canceled because instructors are not available. The problem can be especially critical in smaller towns where qualified craftsmen have forsaken the low wages paid in the community to move to better-paying situations in bigger cities. This means that local students are deprived of the opportunity to learn a trade or a skill—one that you may be able to provide.

The essential requirement to be a teacher in these circumstances is not necessarily a college degree but often just a solid knowledge of your craft and the ability to pass your skills on to the students. Even in states and localities where academic qualifications are strict for community colleges and trade schools, adult education instructors seldom have to match the formal requirements demanded of academic instructors.

I once volunteered to work as a teacher's aide in an English for Foreigners section of the local adult education program. I enjoyed it immensely, but when I tried to quit my volunteer position, the school administrators begged me to stay. They insisted on putting me on a paid basis and granting me a lifetime California teaching credential as a bonus. And all I'd really wanted to do was have fun helping foreigners learn to speak our language.

Teaching opportunities are often advertised in the local newspaper classifieds. A phone call to the relevant school department, especially to the adult Education office, will verify whether there are any openings. If nothing's available, they'll surely know where to refer you. Some departments will actually create a class to fit an instructor's skills. If they can locate fifteen or twenty students who are interested in your specialty, the school will receive money from the state to fund the class and pay your salary. It's best to prepare a résumé detailing your work experience and what aspects of this experience you are capable of teaching. If you have some college credits, don't fail to mention them.

Many school districts find themselves faced with a shortage of substitute teachers for regular grade school and high school classes (partly because of the low pay scales for substitutes). If you have at least a bachelor's degree, many schools are eager to put you on their substitute list, even if you have no teaching credentials. Classroom assistant jobs, almost always part time, are possibilities for those with little or no experience. Starting off as a volunteer is an excellent way to break in. Private schools don't always demand approved teaching credentials, and because their regular salaries are often lower, they offer a lot of job opportunities. If you have some formal education and feel qualified to teach a subject, you might consider a part-time position in a private school.

A real bonus is that working in a school situation puts you in contact with the community, creating an ideal situation for meeting new people and making friends. If you're a stranger in town, this is the quickest way to lose that status and become known and appreciated.

Beware of Fancy Advertisements

Magazines are liberally sprinkled with ads urging you to start your own business, with the advertiser offering to help you get started. If you've been around long enough to think about retirement, you've also got the smarts to know that these things are too good to be true. The ads claim that you can make $100 an hour cleaning carpets, selling stationery, or engaging in some other scheme, but you end up paying lots of money for nothing. Don't pin your future on a flowery magazine advertisement assuring you that you can make $100,000 a year in your spare time.

Local newspaper ads can also be phony. I had a friend who answered an ad that offered to set up applicants with a free delivery route business, stocking supermarkets with a nationally known product. He should have known there was something wrong when the company insisted that he buy an expensive delivery van from them—at their price. Next, the company "union" demanded a huge initiation fee. It turned out that the union and company were splitting the initiation fees and down payments on the vans. The new "employees" were laid off when new applicants showed up with enough money to buy a truck and pay union initiation fees. To top it off, the company terminated the job but not the payments on the van. Oh, well, he was able to use the van for camping and eventually drove his money's worth out of it.

Taking Inventory of Your Business Skills

Before you think of starting a home business, you need to examine your own personality, ask yourself some questions, and supply some honest answers. Consider the following questions:

- Are you a self-starter? If you are someone who hates getting up in the morning and getting after business, being your own boss won't be any fun.

- How do you feel about dealing with people? You need to like working with people if you are going to get into your own business. Almost all types of businesses require daily contact with others.

- Can you take responsibility? Are you the type who can forge ahead and get things done, or have you always expected others to do things for you?

- How good an organizer are you? Running a business means being organized. You're going to have to keep books and records and keep your fingers on all the strings.

- Can you make decisions? At every turn in the road, there will be instant choices to be made. If you can't, you're going to be paralyzed. Your business will suffer.

- Can you stick with it? You can't always expect to make money from the very beginning. If you don't encounter instant success, are you going to become discouraged before your enterprise gets the chance to fly?

- How good is your health? Will you truly have the energy to follow through on your business?

If, after assessing your own strengths, you are still assured that you really want to go into business, you might check with your local office of the U.S. Small Business Administration. There are one hundred offices in cities nationwide, offering free counseling, literature, and sometimes financial assistance for starting a business.

For information about where they are and what they offer, call (800) 827–5722; or visit www.sba.gov. Be sure to ask for a copy of SBA's *The Small Business Directory: Publications and Videotapes for Starting and Managing a Successful Small Business*. SBA district offices are listed in the telephone book under "U.S. Government," or call the toll-free number above for the office in your area. The SBA has a Web site at www.sba .gov/starting_business/startup/basics.html.

Volunteer Work

If you don't absolutely have to work to keep bread and beer on the table, why do it? If you feel guilty about not "doing something," or if you get bored hanging around the house, try volunteering. You'll feel good about yourself. A special bonus of volunteer work is that your services will be sincerely appreciated and valued more highly than if you were to work in a fast-food restaurant or some other high-competition, low-pay job, trying to please an employer you don't like in the first place.

Volunteering is also one of the fastest ways of making friends in a community. You'll find yourself rubbing shoulders with genuine people, like-minded folks who want to help others. A dividend is that someday, when you might need help, you will be well-known in the community, and help will be available without asking.

One of the major retiree volunteer organizations is the Retired and Senior Volunteer Program (RSVP), sponsored by the Corporation for National and Community Service. RSVP volunteers provide a variety of community pursuits, helping old and young alike. Services include health care, companionship, security, and education, as well as financial and social services at day-care centers, nursing homes, schools, libraries, crisis centers, courts, and other community locations. RSVP volunteers operate runaway shelters, organize widows' support groups, and offer occupational counseling to first-time criminal offenders. RSVP volunteers are usually paid expenses incurred while volunteering, such as transportation and other out-of-pocket expenses. They also receive accident and liability insurance while on service. For further information on the Senior Corps and the RSVP program, call (800) 424–8867 or visit www.seniorcorps.org.

Another volunteer organization that may fit your needs is the Senior Corps' Senior Companions program. Participants receive a modest tax-free stipend, reimbursement for transportation, meals during service, annual physical examinations, and accident and liability insurance while on duty. In addition to these benefits, the program gives participants the opportunity to share a lifetime of experience with youth and other seniors. Senior Companions must participate in preservice orientation and in training workshops throughout your service.

The program focuses on providing assistance and friendship to elderly individuals who are homebound and, generally, living alone. By taking care of simple chores, providing transportation to medical appointments, and offering contact to the outside world, Senior Companions often provide the services that a frail elderly person needs to live independently. Senior Companions not only assist clients with chores such as paying bills, grocery shopping, and finding transportation to medical appointments, but they also help make the lives of the people they serve less lonely. Senior Companions also provide respite care to relieve live-in caretakers for short periods of time. They usually serve two to four clients through twenty hours of weekly service. Many Senior Companions serve clients for several years and form the most meaningful friendships in their lives.

The goal of Senior Companions is to help the elderly live independently at home for as long as possible. Senior Companions must be sixty years of age or older and meet low-income eligibility requirements. To find out more about the Senior Companions Program, contact your local senior-citizen center or the national Senior Corps office at 1201 New York Avenue NW, Washington, DC 20525; (202) 606–5000; www.senior corps.org.

Enjoy the outdoors? As a U.S. Fish and Wildlife Service volunteer, you could find satisfying work in a nearby wildlife refuge or fish hatchery. Often it's possible to commute to the job site and back each day. Volunteer positions are often available to match your skills, abilities, and preferences. Web site: www.fws.gov/volunteers.

If you don't have to return home every afternoon, you might consider volunteering with the National Forest Service. There you will help maintain and improve the nation's forests and grasslands by doing light construction work, maintenance tasks, or clerical work. Depending on the job, you may reside on-site in a barracks, a mobile home, or conventional government housing. Volunteer positions sometimes have a way of turning into paid employment.

To find out about volunteer programs with the Fish and Wildlife Service, call or write the U.S. Fish and Wildlife Service, 4401 North Fairfax Drive, Arlington, VA 22203; (703) 358–2043. To offer your services as a Forest Service volunteer, call or write the USDA Forest Service, Human Resources Program, P.O. Box 96090, Washington, DC 20090; (703) 235–8834; www.fs.fed.us.

chapter eight

Singles and Retirement

Perhaps you've noticed how ads in retirement publications picture retired couples? Always strikingly handsome, tenderly holding hands as they gaze lovingly upon their new retirement home (or Cadillac, or yacht, or whatever the product the advertisment is pushing). The husband is attired in an expensive Irish-tweed sport coat, and his distinguished, platinum-toned hair sweeps back from an aristocratic forehead. (He's never bald, now is he?) His wife's hairdo discreetly reveals a few silver highlights. (If we didn't know she was retired, we'd assume she was about thirty-seven years old.) This typical retired couple is successful, affluent, and looking forward to a future of golf games, gourmet dinners, and bridge parties as they entertain brilliantly in their fabulous new home.

You don't need someone to tell you that this picture is far from accurate. Besides the fact that few of us men can brag about our aristocratic foreheads, most of us actually look our ages and many are bald as a cue ball. More importantly, some retirees don't have that loving other person to hold hands with. Many people approach retirement alone. They also find themselves far from affluent, with their minds on matters other than bridge and golf games.

What happens when your spouse dies unexpectedly just before your planned retirement date? All those wonderful plans you've made get knocked into that famous cocked hat. What about the homemaker who spends her productive years raising a family, only to find herself divorced once the children are on their own? Where do you go from there? I think I can speak from experience in this matter; my first wife died unexpectedly after many years of marriage, just as we were planning our retirement.

Single retirees face different challenges than married couples do. Their economic and lifestyle strategies must be different, too. If being single is not something new, most people without relationships do fine, at least while they are working. But once they leave the workplace, where most of their friends are, some find themselves faced with unexpected changes of lifestyle. The problem is most severe in the case of single women.

Women and Single Retirement

For every 100 older men in the United States there are 146 older women. This ratio increases with age to a high of 260 women for each 100 men for those eighty-five and older. Only 41 percent of these women are married, compared with 78 percent of the men eighty-five and older. Furthermore, more than half of America's women are on their own by the time they are fifty-five years old—before they reach retirement age. Women who retire at age sixty can expect to live another twenty-five years or so and can expect to have to make do with less, so it's doubly important they plan well for retirement.

Divorced or widowed women who manage to find careers in the workplace often find their social lives revolving around work. But once single women leave the workplace, they find a void that needs to be filled by friends and family. Should a retired woman be short of either, she faces a lonely future.

Women also have fewer options or activities that society considers "acceptable" and with which they feel comfortable. A man can be perfectly happy tent camping and fishing in the woods, wearing the same socks a week at a time. Most retired single women not only feel uncomfortable camping in a flimsy tent but also hate fishing—and dirty socks. A man may think nothing of living just about anywhere, but many women feel apprehensive in all but the most secure situations.

Chances are that she will also be short on retirement funds. It's well known that women earn significantly less than men for equal work, so they end up with lower Social Security payments, company pensions, and savings accounts. Furthermore, because of age discrimination, women are frequently pressured to quit work and draw their pensions or Social Security at the earliest possible age, rather than waiting until maximum benefits are due. Finding part-time work is also more difficult for older women. The result of women's low lifetime earnings is that the typical woman's Social Security checks are often half that of a man who earned good wages all his working life. Single people, both men and women, need different retirement strategies than married couples do to survive on a budget. But single women need miracles.

Single Transitions

One might assume that the transition into retirement is easier for folks who never married or for those who have lived most of their adult lives as single persons. Why should retirement be a traumatic experience? After all, aren't they accustomed to a single life? It might seem that the only thing to do now is to adjust to a lifestyle that doesn't include working every day. That would seem to be an easy adjustment. Yet most find retirement somewhat lonely, particularly if their entire social lives have centered on their jobs. At work they had fellow employees to socialize with, friends to talk with, and companions at lunch. When they stop working, all of that is suddenly gone. Also gone are regular paychecks, medical benefits, and Christmas bonuses. It's a different world out there when you quit work.

For those fortunate enough to have built up a network of friends and acquaintances, leaving this umbrella probably doesn't make much sense. Although you may be living in an expensive area, you might well be better off staying where you are and keeping your friends. This can often be done by cutting back on your most expensive budget item—housing.

But if your friends do come mostly from your business or workplace world, and if you have few nearby family connections, you could find that you have little to lose by going someplace more economical, perhaps a place with a nicer climate. You can then start building a new life, acquiring new friends, and exploring new interests. If you're already living in a high-cost area, moving somewhere more economical might be the ticket to a better life. This is true for both singles and couples.

In many economical retirement locations, particularly in smaller towns, small furnished apartments can often be found for less than $500 a month, including utilities. These apartments are perfectly adequate for a single person trying to get by on a budget. We recall looking at a studio apartment in a small town on Oregon's Rogue River—a delightfully peaceful and pretty place for economical living. The rent was about $425. Shopping was a four-minute walk from the door. A single woman would feel perfectly safe here.

Once settled, you can see how you like the area, make new friends, and begin exploring a new lifestyle. As a new kid on the block, you may find that the best way to begin making new friends and acquaintances is through volunteer work. Go to the local senior-citizen office and apply for work with RSVP or another volunteer program. Within days, you'll start building a new network of friends, and before long you will have more friends than you ever made by working every day. One of our correspondents, a retired man, told us that he makes friends through square dancing. He says, "Just check with the clubs, like the Elks, the Eagles, and the American Legion, as well as with the local chamber of commerce."

Another way of making new friends and acquaintances, for women particularly, is to register with a temporary employment agency. You'll likely be sent to different offices to fill in for absent employees, and you'll come into contact with a wide variety of people from which to make acquaintances. From these you can choose to make friends.

Whether you move or stay put, another good way to enter a new world of friends is to see if there is an American Contract Bridge chapter in your area. Lately they have been sponsoring a series of free "Easy Bridge Lessons" for newcomers in an effort to build up interest in bridge and also increase membership. My wife and I took advantage of this a couple of years ago and have made many friends. My guess is that about 60 percent of the bridge players are single women. 2990 Airways Boulevard, Memphis TN 38116; (901) 332–5586; www.acbl.org.

Shared Housing for Singles

Earlier we discussed the concept of shared housing as an effective way for couples to cut their living expenses. But as a single person, shared housing can dramatically lower your cash flow, at the same time elevating your standard of living. Later on, in the "Traveling Singles" section, we'll talk about the "single supplement" penalty, in which single persons are charged just as much for some things as a couple pays. Hotel rooms, cruise cabins, and house rentals, for example, are doubled for the single person. Monthly rents or house payments are the same, whether one person or a family of ten occupies the domicile.

The possibilities are intriguing. Instead of paying $400 a month for rent and utilities in an ordinary, cheap (perhaps risky) neighborhood, you can join with partners to pool your resources, permitting you to reside in a upscale neighborhood with tranquil and eye-pleasing surroundings. Your lifestyle also benefits from the low crime rates and better police protection typically found in more affluent residential districts.

Instead of a cramped, two-room apartment in the inner city, you could share a lovely suburban home with three or four bedrooms, a gourmet kitchen, a large living room, and a separate TV room, complete with a landscaped patio for barbecues and lounging. You might prefer to share a spacious apartment or condo in an elegant section of town with a private deck and a view of the ocean (or the river or the mountains).

Sharing is definitely not the same as renting a room in a private home. Being a lodger involves little commitment, and you are rarely considered part of the household. You are a stranger, a paying guest in someone else's home. The key to a successful living arrangement is the word *shared*. The ideal situation is one where you and your housemates agree on formal rules and arrangements and form a surrogate family. Sometimes it is wise to get everything in writing, so there can be no misunderstandings. If it happens to be your home you are sharing, rather than a rental, you need to be sure you are protected (and because it's your place, you are entitled to be a little more autocratic).

House sharing is a particularly successful strategy for single or widowed women, when two, three, or four pool their resources to enjoy dignified, comfortable living arrangements without giving up individuality. Having friends living together also provides the security of a support group in emergencies. Should someone in the household become ill or have an accident, having caring friends around could be a lifesaver. Women usually prefer to have other women for house partners, but mixed-gender sharing is also common. This doesn't necessarily have to involve romance or intimacy (assuming that's not what you want), if that is made crystal clear from the beginning. Having a gentleman around the place to fix the roof and change the storm windows can come in handy, while a man might appreciate a woman's cooking skills from time to time or a sympathetic ear when he feels low.

Let's look at the financial side of home sharing. Assume that the standard of living and lifestyle to which you would like to become accustomed requires at least $1,200 a month for rent and utilities. This amounts to $14,400 a year. That's quite a chunk of your budget, right? By sharing with two companions, your expenses drop to $400 a month, a savings of $9,600 a year—over a ten-year period, a savings of nearly $100,000. This is money you could spend on travel, a new automobile every once in a while, or any frivolous expense you might care to indulge in. If you manage to share an automobile between house-sharing companions, the savings are even more.

If you're a single home owner, you might find that a compatible companion or two sharing house payments and everyday expenditures makes perfectly good sense. While your expenses are cut drastically, you still accumulate equity in your house. Sharing household chores makes living easier and gives you more time to get out of the house and enjoy your retirement. With friends watching over the house and paying the expenses, you can travel without worrying. On the other hand, it could make equally good sense to sell the house, put the money into investments, and move in with someone else. (Of course, please consult your financial adviser and family members before making an important decision of that nature.)

How do you go about finding partners? A glance at any newspaper classified section often turns up individuals seeking home sharing. You might place your own ad (with a box number or telephone number so you don't receive unwelcome visitors). Screen the candidates carefully to make sure you like and trust them. It goes without saying that compatibility is the highest-ranking consideration in house sharing. It takes time and flexibility to find housemates who are compatible with your lifestyle and nature. Making a decision to live with someone requires far more "checking out" than merely a few conversations. References and credit checks are a must.

Retirement Communities

Not everyone can be comfortable pulling up stakes and relocating as a stranger in a strange neighborhood or living in someone else's home. A convenient, worry-free alternative for singles is the concept of a nonprepay retirement community, the kind where you simply rent by the month. In a living situation like this, you will find a large number of people of your age group from which to select your friends. Aside from medical insurance, clothing, and phone use, most of your basic expenses are covered.

The retirement communities we investigated in Oregon are typical of most sections of the country, offering quality living in secure apartments with fees starting as low as $1,200 a month. This charge includes two meals daily (served in a pleasant dining room), twenty-four-hour staffing, cable TV, social and recreational programs, off-street parking, and all utilities except telephone. These are generally large complexes, often with a social director who arranges bridge games, arts and crafts, evening entertainment, and other activities. A van will take you for shopping and doctor appointments. We've also looked at places that charge as much as $3,900 a month, but these places are so luxurious that it's like being on a permanent cruise. However, it isn't difficult to find similar accommodations for much less per month, but these will be smaller complexes, sometimes with only a dozen or so efficiency apartments. The amenities aren't as nice, and sometimes only dinner is served. With fewer residents, you could be stuck with people you don't care for, and you won't get much in the way of entertainment. But the homes are much more affordable; we saw one small apartment that rented for $900 a month, the same as a Social Security benefit for some folks.

There are several advantages to this type of living arrangement. Besides the fact that your monthly expenses are predictable, without having to make a serious commitment, you can explore the community to see whether it is desirable for your long-term retirement. One manager of a retirement facility pointed out that she encourages people to do a three-month trial before pulling up stakes in their hometowns or doing anything drastic.

"This is particularly important upon the death of a spouse," she said. "Too often the surviving spouse isn't capable of making rational decisions in the short run. She may feel utterly isolated, lonely, and trapped in an empty home. In a retirement community, she'll be surrounded by friendly people. Because she has no long-term obligation, this is a relatively painless way to try out a new lifestyle and to try on a new community for size."

One caution: Most residents of retirement homes naturally will be older—there are no multigenerational retirement homes. Look around and see if you'll find compatible companions, retirees of your own age and enthusiasm with whom you can relate. Just because you're retired doesn't mean you're old!

You'll find retirement establishments all over the country. To locate them, simply open up the yellow pages to "Retirement." To choose a retirement community in another city, visit your local library and ask for the out-of-town phone books. Then choose the city or town where you might want to retire, check the listings for something that sounds nice, and do some shopping for price and quality. Don't overlook the Internet—just "Google" the name of the community and "retirement." Charges vary widely, depending upon the community, the area's cost of living, and the quality of the facility.

Be careful about places where you must "buy in" to the facility or sign a long-term lease. There is nothing wrong with these concepts; it's just that if you are looking around for low-cost retirement alternatives, you probably aren't interested in putting up $50,000 in nonrefundable front money just to see whether you like your new retirement location. If you find you aren't happy, you would be far better off if all you were responsible for was a thirty-day notice before shoving off. Also, don't expect to find reasonable rents in a large city or in an expensive area. Like everything else in an expensive location, the cost of a retirement home is likely to be extravagant, too.

When you find something you can afford, check it out. The best time to visit is for lunch or dinner, when you can sample the quality and variety of the food. How is the place decorated? How does the staff interact with residents? Are they professional and caring? Is the place quiet or noisy? Do people seem friendly? Do they socialize well? Don't hesitate to speak with residents to see how they like living there. Many retirement communities have furnished guest apartments set up for trial visits. At the least, arrange to stay a weekend to get the feel of the place.

Traveling Singles

Many people view retirement as a time for foreign travel. After all those years of two-week vacations, mostly spent fixing things around the house, some travel seems to be in order. Unless your budget is so restricted that trips farther than the grocery store are out of the question, this is your chance.

Of course, it will have to be done as economically as possible. As a person who has specialized in budget travel, I can assure you that it can be done—and that it can be fun! In fact, a lot of the fun is just in seeing how inexpensively you can travel, particularly in foreign countries. Budget travelers often pass time comparing expenses. The person who found a great room for $20 is one up on the poor dunce who paid $25 and didn't even get breakfast.

If your budget won't even allow for a $20 room, sometimes you can travel to the great vacation hot spots and receive your room free as part of a work package. Our RVs and Retirement chapter tells about how to find part-time jobs in resorts during the height of the season and earn some money, as well.

Travel for singles can, however, be unfairly made expensive because of something called the "single supplement." That is, most hotels charge a single person the same price as two people in the same room. Some cruise ships are reluctant to book a single in the first place. It turns out that the real profit is the money the cruise ship takes in on drinks, gambling, and side excursions. They make twice as much when there are two people in a cabin. When taking a taxi, it costs just as much for one passenger as for two or more. And on and on.

The solution is to find a travel companion to share costs. Compatible friends enjoy their trips much more than singles, not just because of companionship, conversation, and sharing of experiences but also because they have more confidence to go more places and do more adventurous things than they would by themselves. And by sharing costs the travel budget goes much further.

If you have no adventurous acquaintances, how do you find a compatible partner? Sometimes it's difficult finding someone with the time, money, and desire to take a trip with a stranger. Senior-citizen newspapers often have classified ads from those looking for travel companions. If you Google "single travel" you'll come up with numerous offers for "single cruises." The convenient thing is they can find you a single companion so that you don't have to pay the single supplement penalty. The bad news is that you and your single companion will find yourselves on a cruise with 2,000 people but only a dozen or so are also single. The others are retired couples or newlywed honeymooners. Also, should the travel agency not get enough clients to fill their allotment, they can cancel the program.

Cruises for Singles

Singles should remember that when a "singles cruise" is promoted, it is usually just one small- or medium-size group of perhaps 10 to 100 singles on a ship where the rest of the 1,000 to 2,000-plus passengers are still mostly couples. Also, there are *always* many more single women than single men on any given cruise.

One other problem with booking a "singles trip or cruise" through a travel agency or a Web site is that some (or many) of those departures are later canceled because not enough singles signed up by the deadline. Ask lots of questions before making a nonrefundable deposit for any travel booking. Ask how many singles are firmly booked already. Because every cruise ship cabin and every hotel room is built for at least two people, the singles travel business is a most difficult one. Compatibility when sharing a small cabin or hotel room is also very important.

One way to find a traveling partner is through a singles travel club that helps singles in search of companions get in touch with each other. A good friend of ours, Jens Jurgen, was a pioneer in the field of travel partner–matching with his company Travel Companion Exchange. For twenty years Jens brought together travelers of similar interests through a newsletter and computer match-up service. Members listed their interests and the places they'd like to go and described the kind of travel companion they were seeking. The company is presently on hold due to family illness, but Jens kindly shared his experience with us about this kind of service for singles.

"This isn't intended to be a lonely hearts club or a dating service," says Jens Jurgen, the company president, "although it works well in that respect. We've had a lot of marriages. I remember one elderly lady who met and married a gentleman through the service. Then, a few years later I saw her name on the list again. Her husband died on a trip on the Orient Express, so she signed up to find another one!"

Jurgen says, "I realize that opposite-sex matches are not always platonic, but that doesn't trouble me. A good service caters to the needs of single people needing traveling companions." Romance isn't necessarily the objective. Jurgen points out that men often don't like to share with another male. "After the army, never again," seems to be the attitude. And women, although open to sharing with another female, often prefer a man. Some of the reasons given: "I like to have someone to dance with," and "I feel more secure with a male travel partner, and I like help with the luggage."

For inexperienced, elderly, or handicapped travelers, having a partner makes sense. Women traveling alone miss a lot by their reluctance to visit some very interesting places. It goes without saying that you must be very careful when using this kind of service. You need to make it quite clear what the traveling relationship will be and what it will not be. Jens suggests that you and your prospective companion meet and get to know one another before setting out on adventures. One woman complained that her lady traveling companion "smoked like a chimney and wouldn't drive under 80 miles an hour." A few meetings beforehand might have helped them avoid subsequent bad feelings. Though travel companions services are multigenerational in nature, there are plenty of retired members, with the majority of listings from people older than fifty—and some up to eighty-five years old.

Which singles' groups are recommended? Jens points out that Internet dating/personals or companion Web sites are a common source of scammers. So the key is to locate a reliable "travel companion" service rather than a "dating" service; you want to find a company devoted to matching single travelers who want the convenience and low cost of double occupancy. He says, "I can only mention a few that at least have now been around for a number of years: the Solo Travel Network (run by Diane Redfern) at http://cstn.org; and Travel Chums at http://Travelchums.com (though the number of 'members' listed seems to include even those no longer active). There is also a travel agency that sponsors a number of trips-cruises for singles: singlestravelintl.com, or phone 1–877–SOLO–TRIP."

RVs for Singles' Retirement

Single RV travelers have their own clubs. There are several of them, but the singles RV club we know best is called *Loners on Wheels* (LoW). The members we've interviewed are enthusiastic about the club and continually talk about what it has done for them. This is a singles-only club, although married couples are not discouraged from joining in the evening campfire get-togethers or dances. Members stress that this is not a lonely hearts club, although that's not to say romances do not bloom. Should a couple begin traveling together in the same rig, or if they get married, they are expelled from the club on the grounds that they have "committed matrimony." However, there's no ill feeling toward those errant members who have fallen by the wayside. In fact, there's a general celebration and a genuine invitation to keep in touch.

The club has its own home park in Deming, New Mexico. Members can stay there for $2.00 a day for boondocking (without water or electricity hookups) or $150 a month with utilities. You'll find LoW chapters in almost all states in the United States and all the Canadian provinces, with temporary regional headquarters in popular seasonal campgrounds where members congregate. Club rallies are held year-round, following the weather, in places like Florida, Texas, Mexico, California, Canada, and just about anywhere else RVers might want to visit. For full information, write to Loners on Wheels, P.O. Box 1060, Poplar Bluff, MO 63702; www.lonersonwheels.com.

As part of the research for this book, my wife and I decided to visit a LoW gathering to see firsthand what it was all about. So one balmy January evening, we drove our motor home off the pavement to make camp amid thousands of trailers, campers, and motor homes in the California desert setting of Slab City.

It was a pleasant, moonlit night, with a slight breeze blowing in from the nearby Salton Sea. We breathed sagebrush-perfumed air deeply as we walked across the sandy desert to where the Loners have their semipermanent headquarters. Several official trailers were set up around a large cement slab, which served as a dance floor at night and a shuffleboard court by day. A blazing campfire had drawn a dozen Loners, who were drinking coffee, cocktails, or hot cider. They were chatting and making plans for a square dance the next afternoon.

We explained that we were doing research for a book and were interested in talking to single retirees. We'd come to the right place; the campers were eager to talk to us. "Man or woman—life is a difficult experience to handle alone," remarked one single man who had just moved into retirement. "I've found the solution to my loneliness through RV travel and belonging to Loners on Wheels."

Majority of LoWs Are Women

As is the case at most Loners on Wheels campouts, at least 60 percent of the campers were women. I asked one lady, "How do you feel about safety out here in the desert?" She explained that before retirement, she had been a bank teller in a big city, adding, "During the two years before I retired, I was held up at gunpoint five times! Now ask me again how safe I feel here!"

Another woman, a widow, said, "If it weren't for this club and all of the wonderfully supportive friends in it, tonight I would be sitting alone watching television in a little two-room apartment in downtown Seattle." She smiled at her friends and said, "I've never felt safer in my life."

An eighty-five-year-old lady known as Duchess Grubb added, "This is a lifesaving group that has literally gotten people out of wheelchairs. We have campouts and rallies going on every month somewhere and caravans going in all directions." At that time, Duchess was living in her RV half of each year, commuting from her Pacific Northwest home—where she spent summers—to Death Valley and the Salton Sea for the winter. Duchess has since "retired" to a rest home in Seattle. Another seasoned LoW member is Lee Snow, age eighty-nine, who is the only surviving charter member of Loners on Wheels. She still drives the same rig she had when she joined, and she travels from Wisconsin to Florida for warm winters.

"Traveling with friends makes all the difference in the world," explained another LoW member. "I'd never have the courage to do it alone." With other club members in a caravan—always ready and willing to assist—RV traveling becomes relatively anxiety-free. Socializing over breakfast, cooking dinner together, or singing around the evening campfire, there is no time to be bored or to feel alone. Because most RV clubs have a philosophy of "Never let a stranger into camp without a hug," RV retirement becomes a heartwarming experience. For singles, it is the most economical retirement lifestyle we've seen. This gives "retirement on a budget" a special meaning.

For past editions of this book, we've interviewed LoW members, asking about their budgets. When we asked one single RVer if he could estimate his budget, he replied, "I don't have to estimate. I can tell you to the nickel. I spend $833 a month. That's what I get from Social Security, and I spend it all!" For this edition, we asked Jack Matlock for his take on budgets. (Jack writes a monthly column for the club's newsletter.) So one night, while seated around a campfire, Jack queried campers about their budgets.

He said, "One lady at the campfire lives on less than $600 per month. She's miserly with her air-conditioning but seems to eat and live well, and she certainly enjoys herself. Most have budgets of less than $1,500 and some as much as $3,000. The fact is, they all live within their budgets."

Jack pointed out some of the economic advantages of living in the Deming LoW park, saying, "Physical security is a must. We need to retire in a place where we can get medical help and where we can buy prescriptions at reduced rates. Living close to the Mexican border solves this need. Many of us here in Deming make the 30-mile trip to Mexico for dental and optical care and to take advantage of reduced drug prices."

Jack concluded by saying, "We need to break the apron strings attached to our families. Our kids love us but they simply don't have time to babysit us. They have lives of their own. That doesn't mean we have to break our relationships. It simply means we need to establish our own lifestyles. If our kids want to see us, they can come to visit. We don't have to live next door. We can retire with friends of our own and relieve our children of feelings of responsibility and guilt."

chapter nine

RVs and Retirement

Of all the lifestyles open to low-income retirees, few accommodate a limited budget as well as RV retirement. This presumes, of course, that your motor home, trailer, or camper is paid for, or at least that you aren't facing stiff monthly payments.

If you've ever owned an RV, chances are you've fantasized about how it might be to actually live in your rig instead of merely vacationing. You imagine yourself taking off and never landing, following the seasons, catering to your whims, happy as a seagull soaring in the breeze. It's an exciting, awesome idea. You can totally change your lifestyle, rent out the house, put things in storage, and set out with no particular destination in mind! Many people do just this. The best part is, for those searching for low-cost retirement, RV living can fill the bill. It depends on how you go about it, of course.

Times have changed, and RVs have changed with them. Today, uncounted thousands of retired folks spend months at a time in fifth-wheels, motor homes, and deluxe cab-overs. If you still believe RVs are for gypsies, a visit to your local RV sales lot will leave you slack-jawed in astonishment. Instead of the old portable toilet facilities of yesteryear, you'll find complete baths, including sunken tubs, showers, and designer vinyl. Microwaves and freezers are all but standard, as are three-way refrigerators that can operate on propane, the rig's 12-volt battery system, or 110-volt park current. Furnishings are plush and tastefully matched to the rest of the decor, and an ingenious use of space provides incredible storage room. It isn't surprising that many folks spend a lot of time in their RVs during retirement, when they finally have time to enjoy them to the fullest.

RV Parks Galore

RV destinations offer accommodations that vary in quality from super deluxe to extra grungy. Prices vary from costly to free. Later in this chapter you'll find out how you can even get paid to park! In addition to higher prices, higher quality parks have certain features in common: swimming pools, Jacuzzis, shuffleboard courts, restaurants, and sometimes even golf courses.

An all-important part of the better RV parks is a clubhouse. It's more than just a place to go for a cup of coffee and to meet other RV enthusiasts. The park clubhouse serves as the headquarters for the park's social activities. Dancing, bingo, arts and crafts, jazzercise, card parties, potlucks, and group tours are just a few of the organized pastimes available in the typical clubhouse. There's no excuse for ever being bored.

There are two kinds of RV parks. There are parks that cater to tourists in transit, places where people typically stay for a few days and then move on. These facilities can cost $30 to $50 a day, depending on what is offered. Full-time RV folks cannot afford these luxury places. They look for parks that cater to long-term residents, where space rents vary from as low as $100 a month to more than $500 depending on amenities. For example, one of the better RV parks in Tucson, Arizona, charges $375 a month (plus electricity) for the winter months but only $1,900 for year-round rent (that figures out to less than $160 a month). About half of the spaces are rented out for the year; the owners leave their rigs parked during the summer and return to their cooler hometowns. From October through May, the park hires a full-time social director, who arranges a complete calendar with tennis tournaments, swimming, hobbies, and just about anything else one might wish to do. "Our people don't just sit around twiddling their thumbs," says the park manager. "We don't give them the chance to be bored."

Rents for RV parks vary depending on quality and location. Many perfectly adequate RV parks charge as little as $190 a month.

Not long ago I read an ad in *Trailer Life* for an RV park in Mesa, Arizona. It advertised affordable rates and an astonishing range of attractions. I'll list them here so you can see what you get for your money: clubhouse, ballroom, lounge, library, pool/billiards, card parlor, Olympic-size pool/Jacuzzi, kitchen/snack bar, four tennis courts, putting green, golf driving cage, shuffleboard, horseshoes, exercise gym, lapidary shop, silversmith studio, woodworking shop, ceramics studio, arts and crafts facilities, table tennis, laundry/ironing rooms, and a sewing room. Apparently, the only hobbies missing are bungee jumping, goldfish swallowing, and underwater basket weaving!

Those addicted to slot machines will find many of Nevada's casinos very accommodating for RV travelers. For example, the last time we looked, Sam's Town RV park in Las Vegas charged $22 per night, which included (besides hookups) a fifty-six-lane bowling alley, 2,000 slot machines, two floors of casino with keno, and a race-and-sports book. And if that wasn't enough, they offered free dance lessons. Most casinos don't bother charging for parking; they simply request that RVs park in a designated area, but they provide no hookups. Naturally, they're eager for you to stay so you can spend your money in the casino. By the way, some of Nevada's gambling casinos, starting with Harold's Club in Reno, have made it a policy to hire senior citizens as part-time or full-time workers. How would you feel about dealing a few hands of blackjack next winter?

The variety of RV parks almost defies description. Those with their own golf courses present a country-club atmosphere, complete with nineteenth-hole cocktail lounges and gourmet dining rooms. Others sit right on the beach for easy access to surf-casting and splashing around in your bathing suits. There are even parks for nudists, where people splash around in their birthday suits! Ordinarily, you must be a member of the American Sunbathing Association to enter, but most parks allow trial visits by respectable-looking couples. And because park residents do laundry less frequently, they also save on laundry detergent.

What Will the Kids Think?

A big problem for many retirees who want to start "full-timing" in their RVs is the shock, disbelief, and disapproval of their children. They cannot believe their parents could do such a thing! The whole idea seems irresponsible to them. "Why do they want to worry us like this? Why do they have to do weird things? Why can't they stay home and be like everyone else?" They forget how we were appalled at the weird clothes and hairdos our kids used to wear or by their CDs of so-called music with lyrics we didn't want to hear!

As one lady put it, "My only real problem getting started into full-timing was convincing my children, relatives, and friends that I had not lost my senses. To them, 'grandmother' means dressing in a long skirt, apron, bonnet, and high-top shoes. She's a person who sits by the fire, knitting sweaters while cookies bake in the oven. 'Grandmother' certainly doesn't mean flitting around the country alone in an old motor home, dressed in a sweatshirt, jeans, and sneakers!"

If you want to humor the kids a bit, you can put a CB radio and cellular phone into your rig and get vehicle insurance with a good emergency road service provision. But in the final analysis, it's your retirement, and now it's your turn to worry them a little.

One caution all experienced full-timers will offer to newcomers: *Don't burn your bridges.* You may want to recross them should you decide that full-timing is not as romantic as you thought. If you own a home, you might consider leasing it out for a while, "just to make sure." Some make arrangements with their tenants to reserve the garage, a room, or part of the basement for storing their things. Renters can also forward mail and telephone messages.

RV Clubs and Retirement

Many RV travelers feel that part of the fun of owning a rig comes from belonging to a club. Rallies, campouts, and tours are just a few of the organized activities available through RV clubs. Newsletters keep members well informed about upcoming events. Depending upon the season and weather, club members meet at designated campgrounds, set up an enclave, and start socializing. There are clubs for rockhounds and prospectors, for jewelry making, quilting, handicapped travelers, computer buffs, and just about any other kind of hobby you can imagine (for which you aren't likely to be arrested). Anything you want to know about RV lifestyles you will learn by belonging to one or more clubs.

For the full-time RV traveler, however, club membership is more than just an entertaining pastime; membership is essential. Folks who scrape by on very limited budgets and who must squeeze the maximum value from every dollar do not hesitate to spend money for club dues. They consider club membership every bit as important as gasoline when living full time in their rigs.

Club publications present news of rallies and new campgrounds, and they keep you posted on other members' whereabouts. Some list free parking places provided by members for the overnight use of fellow members. The sticker on your RV announcing that you are a member acts like an invitation for other club members to introduce themselves. You are able to enjoy the inexpensive benefits of RV ownership without feelings of uneasiness about being a stranger among strangers.

Good Sam

The largest RV club of all, Good Sam, started years ago when a Utah trailerist sent a letter to *Trail-R-News* magazine (now *Trailer Life*). The letter suggested that the magazine offer subscribers a decal for their rigs, something that would indicate their willingness to stop and help fellow RVers in distress. The idea caught on and mushroomed into the Good Sam Club.

Because few insurance companies were interested in covering RVs, it seemed only natural that the club should provide policies tailored to members' needs. Before long it became the major insurer of travel trailers and motor homes.

Today the Good Sam Club boasts more than 750,000 members, with 2,200 chapters around the country. In addition to insurance with emergency road service, policyholders receive discounts at hundreds of campgrounds in the Good Sam Park program, a campground directory, a subscription to *Trailer Life* magazine, trip routing, and even RV financing.

(The insurance isn't mandatory for club membership.) Free services include mail forwarding, credit card loss protection, lost key service, lost pet service, commission-free traveler's checks, and a monthly news magazine, the *Hi-Way Herald*.

Trailer Life, by the way, is a valuable publication for RV travelers, whether full-timers or weekenders. It is full of important news, features on how to repair your rig and interesting places to visit, and analysis of general trends in the RV industry. Information on Good Sam Club can be obtained from P.O. Box 11097, Des Moines, IA 50381; (800) 234–3450; www.GoodSamClub.com.

Escapees

Several clubs specialize in serving the needs of those who live full time in their RVs. The best known and largest is the Escapees (SKP), with 12,000 members. Founded by Joe and Kay Peterson several years ago, the club has grown by leaps and bounds as more and more people discover the joys of full-time RVing. They maintain several RV parks scattered around the country, where members can stay at reduced rates, even boondock for just a few dollars a day.

The club publishes a monthly news magazine covering important news about rallies and get-togethers, new places to park, tips on equipment maintenance, and hints for making life easier on the road. Members report where they are and what they've been doing so friends can keep in touch. SKP members often remark, "We feel like we're part of a large, close-knit family."

Another important facility of the club is a mail forwarding and message service. An 800 number both accepts phone messages and allows you to retrieve them. Mail is forwarded automatically. This system solves the problem of keeping in touch with the world while gypsying. The Escapees' national headquarters is at 100 Rainbow Drive, Livingston, TX 77351; (888) 757–2582; www.escapees.com.

Free Lodging in State and National Parks

Perhaps the main reason you wanted an RV in the first place was to visit scenic national parks, recreational wonderlands, and picturesque parts of the country. Making camp alongside a lake or beside a sparkling trout stream—that's what it's all about, right? Most folks, restricted to a two-week vacation, have to squeeze into any campsite where they can make reservations. When park campsites are full, it's off to a $26-a-night commercial park with coveys of screaming children underfoot.

Every vacation season, however, county, state, and national parks are in need of volunteer workers. If you're retired and have your own transportable housing, you may make application as a campground volunteer host. If you're accepted, the park will reserve a prime campsite for you at no cost whatsoever! You can stay the season for free. Even better, a few parks will even pay you to park for the entire season! While the pay may be minimal, the work is also minimal, yet interesting and rewarding.

The host's duties consist of registering visitors, helping campers locate their campsites, and answering questions. For serious emergencies, a two-way radio or cell phone keeps volunteer hosts in touch with park rangers. Usually, the requirement is four hours of work a day in exchange for a free site hookup and perhaps a few benefits. One volunteer said, "We seldom keep to the minimum. It's too much fun."

Private resorts, campgrounds, and tourist attractions also need seasonal help, but they are expected to pay a salary or hourly wages. Sometimes regular housing units, such as cabins or rooms, are provided for workers without RVs. But living accommodations can be spared for only a few people—the rest of the rooms or cabins must be rented to make a profit. When you bring your own housing with you, however, it's a different story. These places love their RV staff members! And they know that when the season is over, you're out of their hair until next year.

Because many volunteer and paid jobs are in rustic locations, managers and employers are delighted to find seasonal workers who need nothing more than water and electricity hookups. When the season is over, the workers pack up and move on to better weather, leaving behind nothing but good memories. Often, before they leave, arrangements are made for the coming season.

Job opportunities are available as campground managers, bookkeepers, off-season caretakers, maintenance workers, and gatekeepers. The most common volunteer jobs offer free parking and hookups (but no salary) to campground "hosts," whose duties consist of answering the questions of new campers and making them feel at home. Other jobs require more responsibility and offer a salary.

We interviewed a couple who spent the summer at a county park on a scenic white-water river, a favorite place for river rafting and trout fishing. This was their first time doing this. "We sent out ten applications," Brenda said, "and within the week we received two positive replies. We took this one because it paid a monthly stipend as well as the free hookups." Her husband said, "They even installed a telephone in our trailer so we could be in contact with park headquarters."

When asked how much their summer on the river cost them, they did some mental calculations, and Joe said, "We were spending about $75 a week at the market. We know, because we only drove into town twice a week. Our only other expenses were laundry, telephone calls to our kids, and dinner out once a week." Brenda added, "Videocassettes, too. We rented four or five a week. No television here." After doing some work with a hand calculator, they came up with an average figure of $385 a month. They didn't mention their pay, but it surely covered a portion of their expenses.

Seasonal Retirement

Every winter, trailers, campers, and motor homes by the hundreds of thousands flock toward retirement destinations in Texas, Florida, California, and Arizona. This is an ideal compromise for those who refuse to give up their paid-for homes or who cannot stand the thought of leaving their grandchildren permanently. For winter's duration, they golf, bicycle, stroll the beaches—whatever suits their fancy—instead of huddling inside next to the fireplace. If they feel like fishing, they needn't chop a hole in the ice first. Money saved on heating bills back home pays for a large part of the trip.

By nature, RV travelers are friendly folks. They have to enjoy parking shoulder-to-shoulder with their neighbors. You'll find few strangers in RV parks. Winter travelers generally have two sets of friends: those who live in their hometown and those who live in the RV winter neighborhood. As winter parks begin receiving visitors, old friends meet and celebrate a joyous renewal of last year's companionship. "We've been coming here for the last six years," one lady told us, "and we have more friends in this park than we've ever made back home!"

Not all part-timers travel seasonally; some use their rigs to visit friends and relatives scattered around the country. Because weather isn't the most important consideration, they travel during the uncrowded and inexpensive times of the year. One couple we interviewed has two sons living on the West Coast, a son in New Jersey, and a daughter in Miami. "We make it a point to spend a month a year visiting each one," explained June, a petite brunette who helps drive the 30-foot motor home. "We never wear out our welcome, and we have our own home. We don't have to interfere with our children's privacy by staying in their homes."

Working and RV Travel

As we mentioned earlier, many RV travelers follow the seasons, visiting the nicest parts of the country in the best seasons and working at temporary jobs. They often earn enough to cover their expenses and don't have to touch their Social Security or other "mail-box income." The good news is that plenty of temporary jobs are available at most popular seasonal resorts. Employers love to have workers who bring their own housing with them—and who don't mind leaving when business drops off at the end of the tourist season. RV owners often receive preferred consideration over those who need conventional housing.

This is a great way to follow the weather and stay within a shoestring budget. Like a loose-knit club, thousands of RV full-timers travel the country, working their way from one vacation hot spot to another. They have their own "bible," a publication called *Workamper News*, which is chock-full of information on temporary job opportunities. Subscribers write enthusiastic letters to the editor telling of jobs like guiding visitors at the Wild Bill Hickok Museum in Deadwood, South Dakota; working in casinos in Lake Tahoe; selling Christmas trees in Wisconsin; doing office work in an RV campground in Florida; and managing a gift shop in Bar Harbor, Maine.

Desert Boondocking

The deserts of the Southwest draw hundreds of thousands of RVs, the vast majority driven by retired people, as they visit the cities and desert outback for winter stays. Snowbirds have become a major economic boon for host communities. Yuma, Arizona, for example, doubles its population of 50,000 every winter. Phoenix hosts around 200,000 seasonal residents, bringing almost $200 million to the economy. An enormous number of these winter visitors bring RVs with them.

The Southwest offers plenty of conventional RV resorts with the usual recreation facilities. But for many, the desert Southwest presents unique opportunities for "boondocking," an ingenious technique of camping without paying overnight fees. "Freebies" is another term for the same thing.

Most RV owners boondock occasionally; that's one of a rig's advantages. Roadside rest areas are perfect for getting sleepy RV drivers off the interstates. A supermarket parking lot can be a lifesaver when it's too late to find an RV park. A friend or relative's driveway is much better for a weekend visit than a motel or trailer park a dozen miles away.

But southwestern desert boondockers have raised the concept of boondocking to a fine art. A boondocker's badge of pride is the ability to spend the entire winter boondocking—enjoying sunshine, companionship, and recreation—without spending a nickel for rent. Needless to say, free housing and no utilities help enormously toward the notion of shoestring retirement, with the elimination of the two most expensive items in basic budgets: rent and utilities.

Desert boondocking started informally many years ago, when a few campers began pulling off the road onto government land to spend a few days or weeks just loafing. They'd simply set up camp wherever they pleased and make themselves at home in the sagebrush and cactus. The vast majority of southwestern desert lands in states such as Arizona and

California are public property—so nobody complained. Before long, the word got out that free camping in the desert was the perfect way to spend an economical and pleasant winter. Every fall, small cities of campers began blossoming all over the desert, staying until the following spring.

Rather than attempt to evict thousands of RVs, the U.S. Bureau of Land Management (BLM) began selling camping permits for the entire season and encouraging the boondockers to congregate in certain locations. The fee is a mere $25 a year, which goes toward providing drinking water, dumping stations, and cleanup. (This fee is due for an increase and may be higher by the time of publication.) Recently, the BLM started offering free campsites (presumably with utilities) for volunteers who will do a small amount of work, monitoring the permit-holding campers and checking sanitary conditions.

Don't get the wrong impression and equate boondocking with poverty. You'll see some rigs boondocked in the desert that cost more than many fancy homes. Their owners can afford to spend the winter anywhere they care to, yet here they are, happy campers in the cactus. They come from all walks of life, all trades, professions, and occupations. It's a lifestyle that isn't necessarily connected with a need for economical living.

Almost all desert boondockers are retired and have one thing in common: a love for outdoor winter retirement. To be sure, some really can't afford a winter vacation any other way. In fact, some have to live this way because their incomes are so low. So you will find shabby old trailers and campers on rusted pickups parked next to shiny new motor homes valued at $150,000. RV camping is truly a social leveler. This is democracy at the grassroots level (or is it cactus-roots level?).

In addition to the low rent of just $25 for the season, boondockers enjoy the lowest utility bills possible—they pay nothing. There are no 110-current plugs in the desert, no water hookups, no natural gas, and no garbage/sewer charges. Bottled gas cooks meals and sometimes provides light. Radios, televisions, and indoor lights are powered by 12-volt batteries, which are charged by solar panels. Conserving drinking water and battery power becomes second nature after a while. This is living at its simplest—and at its cheapest!

Those who prefer solitude simply wheel off the road wherever they choose—within the permit area, of course—and drive until all traces of civilization are out of sight. They set up camp and sometimes stay for weeks before having to make a run into the nearest town for supplies. They are disturbed by no sounds other than the distant yapping of coyotes or feisty little birds chattering away in the sagebrush. The BLM maintains several campgrounds in Arizona and eastern California near the Colorado River. Some have improvements, such as water and dumping stations, and one, near Holtsville, California, is even said to have a hot tub!

Arizona Choices

Now you might imagine that desert RV camping would be the very epitome of isolation. Oddly enough, desert camping can be perfect for the gregarious, the talkative, and those who love to make friends as well as for hermits. Those who enjoy company park their rigs near each other, with a campfire as the central focus. Those who like to be alone simply move farther into the sagebrush and tend their own campfires.

Every winter, the biggest RV boondocking area of all—Quartzite, Arizona—changes from empty desert into a virtual city. Although rigs don't park cheek by jowl, as they must in commercial RV parks, the campers have to get close together to make room for the others. Because so many friendly neighbors are camped nearby, folks who normally wouldn't dream of boondocking feel absolutely secure here.

Throughout late spring, summer, and early fall, Quartzite lives the life of a typical desert crossroads community, almost deserted. But when winter rolls around, things change quickly. During the winter, as many as 150,000 RVs converge upon Quartzite. When you drive toward Quartzite's center, RVs fill the desert as far as the eye can see. No one knows for sure how many people are there at any one time because rigs are continually arriving and departing or moving from one boondocking site to another. It's been estimated that there are a million visitors in the winter. This sounds exaggerated to me, but I have to admit there are plenty of people there.

Entrepreneurs of all descriptions set up shop, selling wares and services to the flood of RV owners who begin arriving in mid-fall. Hobbies become businesses, and pre-retirement skills once again become valuable. Signs on motor homes, campers, and trailers announce, ALTERATIONS AND TAILORING, AIR CONDITIONERS SERVICED, CERAMICS, AUTO REPAIR, and RENTAL LIBRARY. One motor home advertised a copy machine and word processing (presumably the rig had its own generator). People set up stands in front of their rigs to sell knickknacks, clothing, arts and crafts, trinkets, and essentials. Automobile mechanics carry tools in their pickups and essentially bring the garage to your vehicle while they make repairs. One man who deals in flea-market kinds of merchandise said, "Whenever my wife and I spend the winter here, we always take home more money than we left with."

During the winter Quartzite puts on a carnival mood. Making friends and going to potlucks, dances, and club meetings keep the social types busy; trading paperbacks, campfire conversations, and card games are for the quieter types. An outdoor ballroom called the *Stardusty* hosts twice-a-week dances. Then, when the late spring sun begins beating down on aluminum roofs, when air-conditioning begins to sound nice, the rigs abandon their makeshift city to the baking heat of the desert summer.

Many snowbirds boondock or stay in RV parks in the Yuma area. Near Yuma, just off Interstate 8, is Sidewinder RV Park. Sleepy Hollow is a few miles farther, just across the border from the Mexican town of Los Algodones. Last I heard, monthly rates were reasonable, in the neighborhood of $100. Sleepy Hollow features a band that plays for dances every weekend. The musicians are regulars who come here every winter.

Los Algodones is Mexico's answer to high-cost U.S. medical bills. Thousands of U.S. and Canadian citizens journey here every year to take advantage of bargain eye care, dentistry, low-cost prescription drugs, and general medical care.

Another encampment is located north of Yuma near Imperial Lake and Dam. Campgrounds bear names like Hurricane Ridge and Beehive. Government-constructed restrooms, holding-tank dumps, and fresh water make winter-long camping comfortable and inexpensive.

California's Unique Slab City

During World War II, General Patton searched for a desert training ground to prepare his armored division for war. He wanted terrain that simulated North Africa's desert, a place to get his tank crews in shape for the planned invasion. He found it near the small town of Niland, not far from southern California's Salton Sea. A large camp went up, and the troops readied for battle. After the war, the camp was dismantled and its buildings razed to the ground, but the cement slabs upon which the buildings rested are still there—thus the name The Slabs, or Slab City.

These cement platforms made wonderful RV pads, so it wasn't long before a few campers began spending winters in the sunshine of the southern California desert. The elevation is low, nearly sea level, making for winters that are as balmy and pleasant as the summers are hot and insufferable. The news quickly made the rounds of RV boondockers. Slab City became a rival to Quartzite. And instead of the nominal $25 a year, Slab City is free!

Between 5,000 and 10,000 people congregate here every winter; by June, all but a handful are gone. RVs of all descriptions and prices pull off the paved road, head into the desert, and park haphazardly, sometimes next to friends, other times seeking solitude. Compatible RVers cluster together, forming regular neighborhoods, each with a central campfire area surrounded by lawn chairs and chaise longues.

Some campers started a church complete with regular services. The church, in a large mobile home, doubles as an information center when services aren't under way. This must be how it was back in the covered wagon days, for amid all of this chaos there is an admirable sense of community and order. There is a heartwarming, natural sense of respect for neighbors' rights.

With no formal rules or regulations, the residents seem to know instinctively just what to do as individuals to make things work. Even though there are no law enforcement officers, there are few or no lawbreakers. When an occasional troublemaker drifts into Slab City, he or she receives a silent treatment that is followed by determined group action should the offender not catch the hint.

An unspoken notion of the Golden Rule inspires folks to care for their neighbors. Should a camper not appear outside by 10:00 in the morning, neighbors check to see if everything is okay. Most RV units have CB radios that serve as a telephone system. Some CBs are always monitoring channel nine, ready to call Niland, about 2 miles away, in the event of a medical or other emergency. At any given time, a retired nurse or two will be staying here, so medical assistance is always close by.

Although the vast majority of the Slabs' residents are retired, a few younger families join the community every year. A county school bus makes a daily stop to pick up the handful of children who live there.

Once a month, a government agency out of San Diego arrives with surplus commodities, and the Salvation Army drops in two or three times a month to distribute vegetables, canned goods, and other foods. Some campers need this help; most don't, even though they welcome the freebies. As one lady said, "When you're living on Social Security, you feel that anything the government hands out is something your taxes have already paid for!"

With no rent or utilities, there is little to spend money on at the Slabs. Several retirees tell us that they not only get by on their Social Security checks but they also save some of it every month! The Niland post office receives many retirement checks for Slab City residents. The extra money spent in the town doesn't go unnoticed by the town residents, who deeply appreciate their winter neighbors. The campers annually pump $4 million into the economy of Imperial County.

Not everyone will be happy at Slab City, though. My wife and I agree that it's fun for a while and that we thoroughly enjoy the extremely interesting mixture of campers. Yet a long-term visit here would grow tiresome for us. It's a long journey to the nearest library, bookstore, or shopping center. Before long, we catch up on our reading, get tired of playing bridge with neighbors, and weary of our own cooking. We begin dreaming of Chinese food and pizza with sausage and anchovies. For a while, we enjoy not worrying about deadlines or telephones, but the truth is, after a while, we miss them.

Texas's Rio Grande Valley

Another important destination for RV retirees is in the great state of Texas. RV parks throughout Texas draw travelers from all over the United States and Canada. Although Texas undoubtedly has boondocking locations, the emphasis here is on traditional RV parks. The main attraction is that part of Texas that borders Mexico: the Rio Grande Valley, a country famous for truck farms, grapefruit groves, and nowadays groves of RV parks.

Each winter, trailers, campers, and motor homes of all descriptions converge on the Rio Grande Valley and become seasonal abodes for several hundred thousand temporary retirees. "Winter Texans," they're called. They are welcomed by the local businesspeople and residents, who acknowledge the tremendous boost retirees give the economy. Orange groves, palm trees, and 80-degree afternoons make for pleasant living while winter winds paralyze the countryside back home.

Winter retirement in southern Texas isn't an especially new idea. It started back in the 1930s, when Midwestern farmers, their work shut down by cold weather, would make their way to the warmth and sunshine of the Rio Grande Valley. Pulling old-style house trailers or driving homemade campers, these cold-weather refugees began arriving in such numbers that the Rio Grande Valley area gained the nickname "the poor man's Florida." When RVs came into their own and shed the connotation of poverty, the Rio Grande Valley came into its own as a winter retirement Eden.

The number of winter visitors keeps growing. Ten years ago, about 50,000 snowbirds wintered in the Brownsville-Harlingen-McAllen area; today they number more than 200,000! There has been a boom in RV park construction to accommodate the crush. There are well over 500 parks around here, some with several hundred spaces each. One popular RV retirement destination is the town of Mission, near McAllen. More than 10,000 RVs arrive here every winter, with more than 100 RV parks making room for them. RVers almost double the year-round population of Mission, which bills itself as "the Mecca for Winter Texans."

An interesting contrast exists between the lifestyles of the desert boondockers and winter Texans. While the desert folks pride themselves on living frugally, organizing unique social groups and creating their own entertainment, the Texas crowd prefers having things done for them. RV parks are big business here, and they compete for winter residents by offering complete programs of entertainment and activities. Social directors plan pancake breakfasts, ice cream socials, square dances, and other events to get people mingling and having a good time. Swimming pools, hobby rooms, classes, indoor shuffleboard, tennis, dance halls, libraries, pool rooms, sewing rooms, and special halls for recreation and socializing are other common features. Even bare-bones parks usually have a lively recreation hall to go with the laundry facilities. Park rents here are more than $300 a month for the truly ritzy places to about $200 for the more ordinary ones—certainly within the range of a shoestring budget.

With such a tremendous influx of people every season, pressure is put on stores, restaurants, and service enterprises to keep up with the additional demand for goods and services. This naturally creates a demand for seasonal workers. Many retirees state that they have no problem finding work if they so desire. Many RV parks hire their extra help exclusively from their seasonal residents. Some RVers have "steady" jobs—they work for the same employer every year.

McAllen is the largest town in this network of retirement cities; Mission, Harlingen, and Brownsville fill out the list. Near the mouth of the Rio Grande is South Padre Island, a long, narrow spit of land that also draws RVs. The southernmost tip is covered by the town of South Padre, but just a few miles north civilization gives way to sand dunes, good fishing, and RV boondocking.

We've discussed only a small portion of RV seasonal retirement here. Excellent winter RV parking can be found throughout the southern United States from Florida to the West Coast. For summer travel the selection is even wider in the northern states and into Canada.

Wintering in Mexico

Because Texas and the desert Southwest wintering places are so close to the Mexican border, it would be surprising if adventuresome RV owners didn't venture farther south for sun and tourism. Of course they do, and they've discovered some delightful and economical places to spend the winter. RV caravans are very popular, with ten to thirty rigs traveling together as their owners have fun exploring Mexico. Hundreds of RV parks accommodate visitors. Some visitors prefer to boondock for free in Baja California.

My wife and I had become enamored with RV travel south of the border while in the process of writing a book called *RV Travel in Mexico.* Unfortunately, the book is out of print, but you might find a copy in your library.

When we began work on *RV Travel in Mexico,* we stocked our 24-foot motor home with fresh water, fishing gear, a couple of lawn chairs suitable for sunning, and plenty of reading material. The next few months were spent on a delightful odyssey through various parts of Mexico. In all, we did more than 3,000 miles of traveling, boondocking on lovely beaches, visiting colonial towns, sometimes overnighting by hooking up to electricity behind large gas stations, occasionally staying at luxury resorts where coats and ties were preferred in the restaurants, and making some enduring friendships. It's easy to understand how this carefree lifestyle can become addictive.

On Mexico's western side, the most popular RV winter retirement areas are found in the Baja California peninsula and in the mainland state of Sonora. Many beautiful and isolated beaches have no hotels or tourist accommodations, mostly because of a lack of water. Empty and pristine beaches abound along the beautiful Sea of Cortez and on the Pacific Coast. Without an RV, no matter how rich you might be, you can only glimpse these sights as you drive past. With your own rolling home, you can enjoy beaches and scenery that those poor millionaires must forgo. Boondocking in Baja is in!

Not unexpectedly, as more and more "winter Mexicans" crowd the Baja beaches, local residents see commercial possibilities. Along the Baja California coasts, many beaches belong to *ejidos* (Indian communal lands) under tribal control. Although all Mexican beaches are open to the public, *ejidos* can charge for overnight parking. That's why some of the more popular beaches are no longer free—although they might as well be because camping charges are so low. Typically, a caretaker makes the rounds every evening and asks for a couple of dollars or so for overnight parking—depending on the beach. In return, the caretakers make sure things are tidy and keep an eye out for suspicious characters.

The beach where we've spent the most time is Santispac, just south of Mulegé, about halfway down the peninsula. Hundreds of RVs arrive here every winter, beginning in October and staying until the weather begins heating up in April. With their rigs lined up along the beach, campfire pits in front, and sometimes a palm-thatch palapa built for shade, these temporary expatriates enjoy a bountiful season of companionship, fishing, swimming, and just plain loafing. Beach caretakers also keep their eyes on trailers and palapas left through the summer when Baja sunshine makes Death Valley seem cool. From the reports we get, theft is rarely a problem.

"The same folks tend to come to our special beach every season," explains one lady. "It's like a big homecoming every time another rig pulls in. With campfires every evening, it's like a winterlong beach party." Her husband adds, "With rent almost free, it costs us less than $300 a month to spend the winter in Mexico. It could be less, but we like to eat breakfast at the beach restaurant, and we often eat dinner in town."

For those who hesitate to boondock (although with a hundred rigs in a row, it hardly seems like boondocking), more than a hundred RV parks are scattered around Baja. You'll find one just about anywhere you'd care to visit, as well as a few in places you wouldn't visit on a bet. Facilities range from super-luxurious star resorts complete with gourmet restaurants to rustic fishing camps with no amenities other than hospitality, cold beer, and friendly faces.

By the way, 99 percent of your RV neighbors will be from the United States or Canada; very few Mexicans own RVs. Affluent Mexicans prefer to stay in first-class hotels when traveling. They don't quite understand why we think traveling in a small tin box is fun. (I don't understand it, either, but it is fun.)

Space rents for RV parks range from a couple dollars a day to as much as $35 a day at one luxury place we visited. One of our favorite commercial parks is at Bahía de Los Angeles. A few years ago, a cement patio and an electrical hookup cost about $10 a day. It's probably not much more today. A water truck passes through with drinking water and will fill your tanks for a small fee. The sea provides a bountiful harvest of clams and scallops, not to mention fish for those willing to toss a line in the water. Kids knock on the door every evening to see if you want to buy their freshly caught fish or live pin scallops still in the shell. A nearby restaurant serves excellent meals of fish, lobster, and tough but tasty Mexican steaks.

Several markets in the village supply basic foods, such as chickens, coffee, and sterilized milk. Folks on tight budgets depend on the sea for much of their food, with clam chowder, sautéed scallops, or rockfish fillets "Veracruzano" providing wonderful gourmet dinners. "We load up our cabinets with canned goods and such before we leave San Diego," said one lady visitor we spoke with in Bahía de Los Angeles. "We seldom have to buy groceries here other than eggs, tortillas, and fresh veggies. We feel as if we are eating for free."

"We made a deal for two months' space rent at $190, so I don't see how we could possibly spend more than $500 out of pocket for two months," said her husband.

When driving in Baja during our last trip, I counted the number of vehicles on the road and noted that more than half were RVs with U.S. or Canadian license plates. Sometimes it looked as if we *norteamericanos* had taken over the peninsula for our own campgrounds. My personal experience has been very positive in Mexico. The questionnaires we hand out to RV travelers in Mexico include a question about safety. Unanimously, people tell us they feel very secure driving in Mexico. Well, that shouldn't be too surprising: If they didn't feel safe, they wouldn't be there.

North for a Cool Summer

Seasonal travel is not the snowbirds' exclusive kingdom. Summer heat and humidity send thousands on the reverse trek. Retirees who select Phoenix or Tucson for retirement because of the lovely winter weather can be bored silly by the searing heat of July and August. That's why you'll see Arizona license plates in Montana, Michigan, and Maine during the summer. Spring and fall are beautiful in Missouri and Indiana, but summers are suffocating and might be spent better elsewhere.

We interviewed one Phoenix couple who visit the Oregon coast every summer. Their favorite town, Brookings, seldom sees summer highs above 70°F. The Phoenix couple said they always sleep under an electric blanket. "We've never used the motor home's air conditioner in Brookings," the husband said, adding, "We've never seen the temperature reach 80!" Other RV travelers visit here in the winter, as well, because fishing is good all year and it never freezes. Be prepared for drizzling winter rain, however.

Folks who choose to retire on the Gulf Coast of Florida because of mild winters dearly love to escape the hot summers there. The hills of West Virginia, North Carolina, Kentucky, and Tennessee offer welcome deliverance from Florida's steamy summers. The Atlantic Coast, particularly up around Maine, offers some delightfully cool places to park and relax. This might be the time to visit those Canadian RV friends you see every year in your winter neighborhood.

RV Budgets

The question of how much it costs to live full-time in an RV is a complicated one. All of us have different incomes and budgets. Those with huge mortgages on a deluxe motor home will naturally spend much of their income on payments. Some spend a lot of time driving from place to place, consuming gasoline or diesel fuel and staying in fancy resorts every night. Getting from one place to another isn't cheap—RV fuel consumption is much higher than that of a typical sedan. But the average RV full-timer moves only to change locations for the season, and ideally the rig will be paid for. Renting park space by the month rather than by the night reduces costs drastically. The truly economical lifestyles include a considerable amount of boondocking and freebies.

One lady who makes her home in a 24-foot RV told us, "Last winter, when I left my Michigan home base to go to the California desert, I found I could easily get by on $350 a month. Not including gasoline, of course, but I stayed on one spot except for going to the holding tank dump station." She went on to add that during the winter, before she started full-timing, her heating, gas, and electric bills at home totaled close to $300 a month, so getting by on $350 was easy.

Not everybody can manage full-timing on $350 a month, of course. We all know folks who spend more than that on cigarettes and booze. So how did our friend do it? She stayed at California's Slab City for zero rent. The gentle desert climate all but eliminated the need for heat or air-conditioning (Slab City has no utility hookups anyway). She used three 5-gallon tanks of propane for cooking and an occasional touch of warmth when the temperature dropped below 60°F outdoors. A solar panel supplemented her 12-volt system for lights, radio, and cassette player (TV reception is lousy in Slab City). Her total utility costs (bottled gas) came to less than $25.00 for the full three-month sojourn—an average of $8.00 per month.

"Since I'm single, my food costs are low," she said. "Neighbors at Slab City always share rides for shopping in Niland, so I drove the 2 miles to town just every other week or so. I needed to dump my holding tanks anyway. My gasoline bill was almost nothing."

In addition, she shared expenses with three other single ladies for a day trip to Mexico (about an hour's drive), plus one overnight expedition to challenge the slot machines and blackjack tables in Nevada (about four and a half hours away). "We shared a large room—at the senior-citizen rate of $33 with two double beds—and we took advantage of the 99-cent breakfast specials and the enormous buffets in the casino restaurants. That was the only month that I spent $350, and then only because I couldn't make the slot machines pay off!"

chapter ten

Mobile Home Alternative

As they near retirement, some people begin thinking of "drawing in their horns" by buying a mobile home. Many consider this an ideal way to live in comfort and convenience, in their own home, on a minimum amount of investment. By selling your conventional home and banking the equity, you can stay in your hometown without having to reinvest all the profit, and thus keep a sizeable bankroll as backup. Yet you maintain the security of being a homeowner without the high investment and real estate taxes that go with conventional property. As one couple puts it: "It costs us only $295 a month to live in our own home. That includes water, garbage, and sewer. We don't pay property taxes. Instead, we buy a sticker for our license plate every year." (Of course, this will depend on the local tax structure—some states tax mobile homes as if they were conventional homes.)

Not all mobile home parks are inexpensive; some charge as much for park rents as apartment rentals in the same neighborhood. Generally, space rents depend upon the facilities and scarcity of mobile home spaces in the locality. The least expensive mobile home we happened to look at was in the California desert near the Salton Sea. It was an 8-foot-wide, 32-foot-long Vagabond (1959 vintage) for $800, with space rent a mere $100 a month. (You probably wouldn't want to live there.) The most expensive used mobile home housing we've seen was a deluxe unit situated on a Florida golf course, priced at $350,000, with a space rent of

$1,180 per month. You probably wouldn't want to live there, either—at least not on a budget.

Mobile homes often are perceived with a lingering memory of the early days, when mobile homes were called "house trailers" and considered housing for vagabonds and losers. Trailer parks were stereotyped as being populated by welfare families with herds of grimy-faced children roaming the premises. In some cases this picture is still fairly accurate, but these parks are not where you would want to live in the first place. Especially not with herds of noisy, destructive children around.

The category of mobile home living you'll choose will be totally different. These are places that cater to middle-class retirees and working couples. Facilities are tailored to couples or singles who want exceptional personal safety, friendly neighbors, and a clublike atmosphere. This lifestyle attracts a great number of retirees who could easily afford more expensive housing but who prefer to place their home-sale profits into income-producing investments. The nicer locations are usually restricted to those over age fifty. (Try to avoid parks that accept youngsters and teenagers. They can sometimes ruin a mobile home park atmosphere!)

Several benefits accrue to this lifestyle besides low-cost, maintenance-free living, not the least of which are friendly neighbors and park clubhouse social activities. The better parks will have recreation and social halls—usually next to the swimming pool and barbecue area—where dinners, club meetings, bingo, and dances are regular activities. Actually, for a time my wife and I lived in an upscale mobile home park in San José, California. After only a few weeks, we knew dozens of neighbors and had invitations to visit for dinner or cocktails.

Some luxury mobile home parks offer amenities such as Olympic-size swimming pools, hot tubs, Jacuzzis, tennis courts, and spacious clubhouses. You can find just about everything you expect in expensive apartment complexes and luxury condo developments. In Florida you'll have no trouble locating a mobile home park featuring an eighteen-hole golf course! You don't have to do landscaping or maintenance of anything but your own small plot of ground. Often you don't even have that chore, since landscaping is commonly taken care of by park employees.

Because mobile home communities are enclosed by fences and have limited outside access, they are exceptionally safe places to live. Some of the more expensive places have security guards posted at the entrances around the clock. In any case, because homes are close together and because residents know each other far better than in traditional neighborhoods, criminal activities are rather quickly noted.

The standard width of a mobile home today is 14 feet, with lengths up to 70 feet. Some older ones are 12 feet wide. When two of these units are joined together, forming a "double-wide," you end up with a fairly nice-size home. If you've ever visited one of the expensively furnished display models at your local mobile home sales lot, you've probably been dazzled at the luxury and spaciousness.

Purchasing a Mobile Home

What does it cost to live in a mobile home? That's like asking what it costs to live in a house—it all depends on the value of the house and the quality of the neighborhood. We've seen spaces in acceptable parks renting for as little as $150 a month, and others for much, much more. For example, we looked at a park near Sarasota, Florida, that featured a landscaped lakefront, a clubhouse, and tennis courts, plus the inevitable swimming pool—all for around $370 a month. Used two-bedroom mobile homes were priced at $19,000 to $35,000, with new units starting at $65,000. A social director arranged a full schedule of activities for the park residents.

We also visited a generic mobile home park in St. Petersburg, a nice place but without upscale items such as lakes, golf courses, and the like. The only facility besides a small clubhouse was a swimming pool. A couple had just recently purchased a unit with one bedroom and a small office for $12,500. "We could have bought for as low as $8,500," said the wife, "but that was a little too downscale for me." They had retired from northern Illinois, drawing down a small equity in their home. "Not enough to do much more than make a good down payment on a Florida condo," the husband said. "So when we found this place—with a mobile home costing no more than a used car—we bought immediately. Now we have our own place plus a nice bank account."

Another park just a few miles away was full of older units, mostly ten to twenty years old, more closely spaced. The major facility was the laundry room, which traditionally serves each park as a place to meet, socialize, and exchange gossip. According to residents, all of whom were retired, there was a satisfactory level of social activities, which were organized by residents on an informal basis rather than by the park management. It was quite pleasant and peaceful, with mature trees for shade. A few homes displayed FOR SALE signs, including a single-wide, one-bedroom place for about $6,000. Park rent was $195 a month. Space rent farther out in the country was even less expensive, as low as $165 a month according to some park managers. Yes, that's in Florida.

It's interesting to note that most parks—particularly the higher-quality ones—prohibit posting FOR SALE signs on homes. You might drive through a park and conclude that there is nothing for sale. When you don't see any signs, simply inquire at the park manager's office. The rule forbidding the posting of signs is supposedly just to keep things uncluttered, but I suspect that the real motivation is management's desire to filter out undesirable tenants they do not want buying into the park. In fact, many parks have a policy of having to approve a sale, or the mobile home has to leave.

Remember, selling prices often depend more on the scarcity of land and competition among parks, and don't necessarily have anything to do with the cash value of the mobile home itself. A mobile home owned by a private party, located in a city where spaces are scarce, could sell for $50,000. The identical make and year, located in an area where lot vacancies are plentiful, however, might be worth only $25,000. When land is valuable and in demand for conventional housing, few developers are willing to invest in mobile home parks. That's why in smaller towns, where land is cheaper, mobile home prices and park rents are lower.

Pitfalls for Mobile Home Buyers

It's true: A mobile home can be an excellent way of cutting back on living costs. On the other hand, if you're not careful, it could turn out to be a seriously costly and risky investment. If you're not careful, mobile home living becomes as expensive as owning a conventional home.

Examples of Mobile Homes for Sale

Below are some random prices of mobile homes in various locations around the country. The range of asking prices varies widely—since we haven't personally looked at these places, some mobile home parks could be located in unattractive areas, but for economical home ownership, mobile home living is hard to beat.

FLORIDA

Deerfield Beach: 12' x 48' (966 sqft), two bedrooms, one bath, plus enclosed porch. Partially furnished. Carport, laundry room, landscaped, sprinkler system. Park rent $300. Asking price $15,000.

Near Orlando: 12' x 56', two bedrooms, 1.75 bath, includes an insulated Florida room, carport, and utility room. Home is sold unfurnished. Lot rental fee $283 month. Price $7,500.

Near Cocoa: A block from the beach. Older 10' x 44' one-bedroom on large lot. Completely furnished. Lot rental fee $264 month. Utilities $85. Asking price $6,500.

Near Disneyland: Golf course, heated swimming pool. Two-bedroom, two-bath home, fully furnished, including hot tub. Lot rental fee $470 a month, includes all community facility charges. Last tax bill $180. Asking price $80,000.

Central Florida: 1,440 square feet, two bedrooms, two baths with furnished Florida room. Lot rental fee $410 per month includes grass cutting, fertilizing, free golf, and all amenities. Last tax bill $40 per year. Asking price $69,000.

COLORADO

Colorado Springs: 14' x 70' two bedrooms, two baths, with great views of Cheyenne Mountain and overlooking Colorado Springs. Clubhouse, pool, recreational facilities. Monthy rent $300. Asking price $12,500.

Colorado Springs: 64-ft. double-wide, three bedrooms, two baths, central air, fireplace, washer-dryer, carport. Park has pool, clubhouse, and recreation facilities. Rent $580. Asking price $18,500.

(continued)

ARIZONA

Mesa: 56' double-wide, two bedrooms, two baths, hobby room, sundeck. Situated in a first-class, 55-plus park. Rent $380. Taxes last year $184. Asking price $27,500.

Glendale: 12' x 60', two bedrooms, one bath, fenced area for pets. 55-plus community, new pool and clubhouse. Park rent $259, electric bill $58. Asking price $9,000.

MISSOURI

Springfield: 14' x 60', two bedrooms, one bath, central air, oversize deck, completely remodeled. Park has pool and rec. room. Rent $190, utilities $40. Price $10,900.

Some problems can be avoided if you can keep from being blinded by the beautiful furnishings or a dealer's glowing sales pitch. In fact, we advise *not* buying from a dealer, for two reasons. The first is that a brand-new mobile home has a devastating rate of depreciation—like a new automobile, only worse. You lose thousands of dollars the minute it's removed from the dealer's lot. You could get stuck with something you later might have to sell for a loss! Buy a used unit, from a private party, that's already set up in a park and ready to move in, depreciation already taken. Then, should you decide you don't like mobile home living, you should be able to sell for as much as you paid for the unit.

The second reason: Park space is often at a premium. Even though the homes are "mobile," they are almost never moved once they are set up. Therefore, when you buy a *new* mobile home, you'll have to find a park with a vacant space. This means your choice of where you live will be determined by wherever a vacant mobile home space might be available. Instead, shop for a nice mobile home park in the neighborhood of your choice, and *then* see what's available for purchase.

The first rule of buying a mobile home: Make sure not to go overboard and buy something you cannot afford! *If you can't pay cash, you can't afford it!* Why? Not only because of depreciation, but because high interest rates and park rent combined can cost more than renting a nice conventional home. You don't get thirty-year loans on mobile homes, so payments are higher. You would be better off with a long-term mortgage on a conventional home, a place that you might be able to sell someday for a profit instead of taking a loss on depreciation.

Another thing to consider: Although you own your mobile home, the land it's sitting on belongs to someone else. You are simply renting a patch of land from month to month. A problem arises when the park is in an area of rapid development. You could suddenly find that the owner of the property wants to kick everybody off and turn the land into a shopping mall or an industrial park. The property has become too valuable to be kept as a mobile home park. This happens all too frequently. When a developer offers big bucks, the park owner can easily succumb to the temptation to get rich quick instead of depending on your monthly rent. You'll have to find someplace to move.

Investigate: Scope out the mobile home park situation in the area thoroughly before making any decisions. Talk to park residents where you are thinking of buying. Go to the laundry room and start asking questions. This is easy to do because the laundry room is the nerve center of a mobile home park, a place where folks visit often and where they are unusually friendly and talkative. While waiting for their clothes to dry, they happily talk each other's ears off. Ask residents if they have worries about the park's future.

If you ask about the park's management or the owner, be prepared to hear all the good and bad things about living there. You don't need a situation where tenants are continually skirmishing with management. An aware and caring park ownership rarely hires this kind of employee. When they do, you can guess that the owners are not aware and caring.

The fifteen-year rule: Some mobile home parks try to maintain spiffy images by continually upgrading homes in their developments. Replacing older units with glitzy new models keeps the park looking new, thus justifying higher rents. Managers can't go around evicting older units, but when possible they invoke a "fifteen-year rule." That is, whenever a mobile home more than fifteen years old is sold, it must be removed from the park rather than being sold to a new owner. If spaces are at a premium in the area, the mobile home becomes practically unmarketable. Most buyers of used mobile homes want a place to live in, not a mobile home that they have to move.

It is therefore essential to know management's policy on older homes, particularly if you are thinking about saving money and purchasing one that is thirteen or fourteen years old. A few states, such as Florida, and some cities have laws prohibiting this age discrimination. Mobile homes can only be evicted for unsafe or unsightly conditions. Folks in the laundry room will tell you about this. When a mobile home is kept in good condition, one fifteen or twenty years old can be an excellent buy, provided it isn't in danger of eviction.

Family parks: A final caution is against moving into a "family" park—particularly one of those older, run-down places. Young, low-income families who live in these parks, often on welfare, will crowd into a small trailer with three or four youngsters. Keeping the kids outside, playing in your yard, is the only way the parents get any peace and quiet. Too often they exert no control and don't show any serious concern for their kids' behavior. When you have a gaggle of children trooping through a park in search of entertainment, you not only have noise but you are also bound to have vandalism. Youngsters cease to be cute when they start unplugging your electricity, drawing pictures on your automobile, or picking your flowers to take home to mommy. Adult parks are customarily quiet, and chances are much better that you and your neighbors will have something in common.

Rock-Bottom Mobile Home Living

Many of those older, 8-foot-wide units that were popular before the wider ones came into vogue are still around and still in livable condition. In their heyday, they were built for full-time living instead of just summer vacations. They are solidly built, sometimes of galvanized steel, and well insulated. Instead of small space heaters, they usually have oil or gas furnaces with forced-air heat. Because they have only a small interior space to heat in the winter or cool in the summer, utility bills are almost a joke. The units that survive make excellent, inexpensive living quarters, and if push comes to shove, they can be moved easily. A pickup or an old Cadillac with a good equalizer hitch can zip them away—no problem—with no special permits or wide-load warnings front and rear required.

Because these survivors are old-fashioned and clumsy-looking, with birch-finished interiors instead of today's plastic and simulated-wood panels, these older units often go for incredibly low prices. You won't find them in newer mobile home parks because they've long since been kicked out to "upgrade" the park. But they make comfortable living quarters and have surprisingly efficient interiors for storage and everyday living. Beds and living room furniture are usually built in, so you won't have to buy furnishings. They also make great temporary homes when building a conventional home on your lot. You do need to inspect these units carefully for water damage and dry rot, however, and you must make sure that the undercarriage is sturdy and not rusted through.

The next step up from the 8-footer is the 10-foot-wide mobile home. These are more spacious and often have 8-foot expansion rooms, which make the living rooms or bedrooms a spacious 18 feet wide. When both living room and bedroom are expanded, the home is called a "double expando." You don't feel as if you are in a trailer when you're in one of these. They sell for a bit more than the older units but far less than the newer 12-footers.

An Affordable Winter Home

Older, inexpensive mobiles are ideal for summer homes in the mountains or winter retreats in the desert for escaping freezing weather and outrageous utility bills. For example, we looked at one park in Yuma, Arizona, that caters exclusively to retired folks who live elsewhere but enjoy the warm Arizona sunshine for the winter. Almost all units are about twenty years old but in good condition and furnished.

The park's landscaping featured natural desert plants, so there was virtually no upkeep problem for the winter residents. (Cactus doesn't require mowing.) Space rent in this seniors-only park, with a pool and spa, was $275 a month including utilities. When residents go home for the season, they pay $60 a month for the space through the summer (when the mobile home park is virtually abandoned except for the managers). It's a good deal for the park owners because for half the year they don't have to bother with tenants, and it works out well for the winter residents because they don't have to tow an abode back and forth every season. They would have to pay $60 a month for RV storage back home anyway. When we last visited in the area, we saw a 12-by-52-foot two-bedroom for $8,900.

Winter visitors start arriving at this Arizona park around the middle of November. When they have a quorum at the clubhouse, they elect officers for the season, appoint committee members, and decide on a calendar of events. A recent calendar included trips to nearby Mexico, Las Vegas, and Disneyland. Dances, potlucks, and card games completed the social schedule.

"We can't afford to stay home," one lady said. "In our Wyoming home, we would be spending at least $400 a month to heat our place. And when the north wind blows, nothing will keep the house warm." She was wearing shorts and a halter as she rode a bicycle around the park. Her husband was out playing golf.

We asked what she figured for a budget during the winter months. She replied, "With $275 for rent, about $350 for food, $100 for entertainment, and $200 for miscellaneous, we manage everything on my husband's Social Security check."

Buying a Mobile Home and Land

You might want to buy your own mobile home space as a way to be absolutely sure that your mobile home park won't be bulldozed to make way for WalMart. Some developments sell lots rather than simply renting them. Therefore, when you buy a home in one of these developments, you'll pay the seller for the land as well as the mobile home itself. A new development usually offers a package deal; they sell you a mobile home, set up and ready to move in. One park we visited in Arizona was offering an attractive two-bedroom mobile home with a carport, utility room, and screen room. The development had a twenty-four-hour guarded gate, a swimming pool, and tennis courts.

When buying into a development, make sure you actually hold title to the land and not just a "revocable lease." A good salesman can make a lease sound exactly like an iron-clad deed. Also be aware that even though you own the lot, you will be liable for monthly maintenance and member-ship fees. These could be as high as rent in a similar-quality park.

For inexpensive, quick housing on your own land, you can't beat a mobile home. All it takes is someone to move it onto your lot, and you have plumbing, electricity, and a comfortable place to live. By the way, the best way to buy a mobile home for your property is to look for one of those distress sales mentioned earlier, one of the fifteen-year-rule disasters that must be moved at any price. When a mobile must be moved, you can cut the asking price drastically.

You will, of course, need to check local regulations very carefully before placing a mobile on your lot. Many localities absolutely prohibit them on private land. In addition, you need to investigate several other things, particularly if you plan on buying property out in the country. The following items must be considered:

- Are electricity and telephone services available? If you have to pay to install telephone and power poles several miles to your place, you might end up paying more for that than you did for the land and mobile home combined.

- A good water supply is essential; if city water isn't connected to the property, you'll need to know how much it will cost to bring it in. The alternative is a well, which could be expensive, depending upon the locality. Even if a well is possible, you need to be assured that the water is drinkable. I have a friend who spent several thousand dollars drilling a well through layers of hard rock, only to find that the water tastes like sulfur and smells like rotten eggs. Makes for unpleasant showers, to say the least.

- If a city sewer hookup isn't in the picture, you'll likely need a permit for a septic system. Sometimes this is impossible to obtain. Percolation tests may be required, and if your property can't qualify, you could end up using the bathroom at the nearest filling station. If your luck is really bad, it will be a pay toilet—keep a plentiful supply of coins on hand.

- If your land is truly out in the country, you must be sure that you have access easements across other people's property to reach your land. This is not only important for a road or driveway but also for stringing power and telephone lines. If your neighbors aren't friendly, the only way to reach your property could be by parachute.

- Check your deed for timber and mineral rights. Usually these aren't important, but if your land is in a mining or timber-harvesting area—as parts of the Ozarks are—you could find bulldozers strip-mining your front yard or chain saws rearranging the landscaping.

The total investment in a mobile home on private land can be minimal, but it does entail a bit of work to get set up. Sometimes the obstacles are much more formidable than meet the eye. Frankly, I believe it's better to let someone else do the work; I'd prefer to buy something already set up and ready for occupancy.

During our research travels, we found exceptional buys in mobile homes on their own lots in the wooded Ozarks area of Missouri, Arkansas, and Oklahoma. One lovely place was a five-minute drive from a boat ramp on Lake Tanycomo. The double-wide mobile home was set back among a growth of pine trees, almost hidden from the road and surrounded by more than ten acres of wooded solitude. Of all the landed mobile home setups we've seen, the Ozarks offer the best bargains.

It should go without saying that you need to be positive that country living is what you really want. If your spouse craves fishing, hunting, and communing with the outdoors, but you can't stand the sight of dead catfish or the thought of doing without HBO on cable TV, it may be time to discuss a compromise.

chapter eleven

Researching a New Hometown

If you've analyzed your situation and decide that moving to a less expensive location is the solution for your retirement on a shoestring, the next question is *where?* Bookstores are full of retirement guides and magazines suggesting where to relocate for retirement. Helpful as they are, in the final analysis, you have to do much of your own research. Feature articles in magazines and newspapers often tempt you with articles such as "The Twenty Best Towns in the U.S.A." Books might list "One Hundred Best Places to Retire." But when you go to make your choices between towns, you'll notice that each author or magazine writer has a personal opinion as to which are the "best" towns. Each list is different. If there actually were "twenty best towns" in the country, wouldn't at least some writers agree which ones are best?

There are several reasons for nonagreement about which are the best towns. First of all, you can't rate a town as you rate a baseball team. With a baseball team, we can check statistics and past performance—and the conclusions are obvious. Rating a place to live is much more complicated. In the final analysis, ratings are simply personal opinions on the part of the writer. Furthermore, the writer's next article had better rank a *different* set of "best towns" or the editor won't buy the article. I say this because I've written several of these articles myself—having to rank the "twenty best"—but I always stress that the twenty places are our *personal* favorites and leave plenty of room for disagreement.

> **Tip**
>
> An excellent way to scope out a town, to see if you will
> enjoy living there, is to find a short-term apartment rental.
> These can usually be found in a motel setting, small
> rooms, but livable for a month or so. This gives you a
> chance to see how shopping is and which part of town is
> best for permanent digs.

What Magazine Articles Don't Tell You

Most magazine articles and retirement guidebooks are written for an audience of fairly affluent people, or at least not those who are thinking about retirement on a budget. Retirement writers tend to assume their readers live in an ideal world of country clubs, fancy restaurants, and split-level ranch homes. Some do, others don't. The retirement researchers count the number of museums, operas, theaters, and symphony orchestras in a city and use them as criteria for a good place to retire. Of course, these amenities do add a touch of class to your retirement, but how many times a month will you be going to the opera, a symphony performance, or a museum? Some retirees would consider the number of municipal golf courses, bowling alleys, or public libraries far more important.

Retirement writers sometimes judge the quality of medical care by counting the number of doctors in the area, the amount of money invested in hospitals, and the number of CAT scanners available to physicians. Special praise goes to communities with a medical school. Frankly, I'd be more interested in whether doctors are accepting new patients. Do they accept Medicare? What's the cost of an office visit? How much will I pay for a hospital room? And what's this nonsense about a medical school? I'd rather have my vasectomy done by a journeyman doctor than a nervous student, thank you very much.

Favorable ratings are often awarded on the basis of conditions that don't affect retirees. For example, good schools, high employment, and a booming business climate lead writers to boost a town's popularity rating, while horrible weather and high taxes are often ignored. Quality elementary schools and good recreation programs for kids matter less to retirees than outdoor recreation for adults, quality senior citizen centers, and safe neighborhoods. The problem with full employment and thriving business conditions is that they usually result in high prices and expensive housing. Unless you are counting on finding a job, a booming economy is irrelevant.

The bottom line is this: By giving the same weight to concerts, museums, and medical schools as to climate, reasonable housing costs, and personal safety, many retirement guides paint a picture that's simply unrealistic for the nonaffluent.

Of course, the better retirement guides are excellent sources of data on towns and cities that would otherwise be difficult to find. Guides can present a world of information that can help you decide whether a place is a viable candidate for retirement. But in the final analysis, you have to go there and see for yourself. You have to see what the retirement guide cannot tell you—will you love it or will you hate it?

Analyzing a New Community

Following is a list of requirements my wife and I personally consider essential for a successful retirement relocation. Your needs may be different; feel free to add to or subtract from the list, and then use it to measure communities against your standards.

Safety. Can you walk through your neighborhood without glancing fearfully over your shoulder? Can you leave your home for a few weeks without dreading a break-in?

Climate. Will temperatures and weather patterns match your lifestyle? Will you be tempted to go outdoors and exercise year-round, or will harsh winters and suffocating summers confine you to an easy chair in front of the television set?

Housing. Is quality housing available at prices you're willing and able to pay? Is the area visually pleasing and free of pollution and traffic snarls? Will you feel proud to live in the neighborhood?

Nourishment for your interests. Does your retirement choice offer facilities for your favorite pastimes, cultural events, and hobbies? If you fish, are there accessible lakes and streams? If you're an art buff, are there art centers or museums?

Social compatibility. Will you find common interests with your neighbors? Will you fit in and make friends easily? Will there be folks who share your own cultural and social background?

Affordability. Are goods and services reasonable? Can you afford to hire help from time to time when you need to? Will your income be high enough to be significantly affected by state income taxes? Will taxes on your pension make a big difference?

Medical care. Are local physicians accepting new patients? Does the area have an adequate hospital? Do you have a medical problem that requires a particular kind of medical specialist nearby?

Distance from family and friends. Are you going to be too far away or in a location that nobody wants to visit? Would you rather they wouldn't visit?

Transportation. Does your new location enjoy intercity bus transportation? Many small towns have none, making you totally dependent on an automobile or taxis. How far is the nearest airport with airline connections? Can friends and family visit without driving?

Senior services. Senior centers should be more than merely places for free meals and gossip; there should be dynamic programs for travel, volunteer work, and education. What about continuing education programs at the local college?

Make Research a Game!

Finding your next hometown can be loads of fun. First, make a wish list describing your ideal location.

For example, your list might look like the following:

- No sidewalks to shovel in winter
- Small town not more than forty-five minutes from a city with job possibilities
- Near an interstate and an airport with commercial service
- Within two hours' drive from the ocean or a large lake
- Local college for adult education
- At least one public golf course
- Plenty of hiking and biking trails
- High-speed Internet connection
- Good health-care facilities

Then, get out the maps and go to work!

Use Your Vacations to Investigate

If you decide to move away for retirement, then ideally you'll start your retirement search long before your employer shakes your hand and says good-bye. Instead of going to the same old place for vacations, try to visit someplace different each time. Look at each location as a possible place to live.

Even if you are already retired, you need to do some traveling if you plan on moving somewhere else. Your travels needn't be expensive. Pick up some camping equipment at the next garage sale in your neighborhood— a tent, sleeping bags, and a cooking stove. Just about anywhere you want to visit will have either state parks with campgrounds or commercial camping places, like KOA, where you can pitch a tent. Many RV parks have special spots for tent camping. Your local library will have a camp-ground directory to help you locate a place in or near your target town.

Check out real estate prices. Look into apartment and house rentals. Does this town offer the kinds of cultural events you will enjoy? A cultural event could be anything from light opera to hoisting a glass of beer at the corner tavern; the question is, will you be happy you moved there? Just looking closely and imagining that you truly intend to move there will tell you a lot.

While you are there, be sure to drop in at the local senior-citizen center. Talk to the director and the members of the center to see just what services will be available should you decide to move there. A dynamic and full-service senior center could make a world of difference in your every-day life. Don't take it for granted that the senior center will have every-thing you need. Some are very dreary; others are exciting places to visit.

A very important consideration is public transportation. Over the years, a large number of smaller towns in the United States have been stripped of intercity bus service. The Greyhound Corporation was permit-ted to buy out its major competition, Trailways, and shut down the least profitable runs. If you choose to live in one of these towns, you ought to be aware that you will be totally dependent upon an automobile. If at some time in the future you are without a car—because you've become unable or cannot afford to drive—you'll be trapped. Your grandkids can't visit you by bus, and if the nearest airport is 100 miles away, you'll not be able to meet the incoming flight. They'll have no way to get from the air-port to your home. Yes, you could take a taxi, but places that don't have bus services may not have a fleet of taxis at your disposal, either. Besides, by the time you make a few 200-mile round-trips by cab, you could have purchased your own taxi. These conditions are something you probably wouldn't notice on a regular vacation. But you can pick up on them if you pay attention and ask the right questions.

When you're investigating a town, one of your first stops should be the local chamber of commerce. A world of information can be found there. The level of enthusiasm and retirement advice offered by the chamber staff clearly tells you something about the town's elected officials, the business community, and their attitudes toward retirees.

Most chamber offices love to see retirees move into their towns; they recognize the advantages of retirement money coming into the economy and the valuable contributions retirees can make to the community. These offices will do just about anything to help you get settled and to convince you that living in their town is next to paradise. However, don't be surprised if the person behind the counter isn't the least bit interested in your idea of retiring in the town. My experience has been that some chamber of commerce offices are staffed by minimum-wage employees who seem to resent folks coming in to ask questions and interfering with their reading. When this is the case, you can guess that the level of services and senior-citizen participation in local affairs could be inadequate. This is not always true, but the local chamber of commerce generally reflects the business community's interest in retirement attraction.

Newspaper Research

Between periods of travel, you can do your research at the local library or by mail. Almost all libraries have out-of-town newspapers. The larger the library, the wider the variety. If you live in a small town where your library can't provide the newspapers you want (particularly those from another state or smaller towns some distance away), one way to obtain them is to write to the chamber of commerce in the place you are interested in and explain that you need a copy or two to make decisions about retiring there. You can also write to the newspaper office (look in the phone directory section of your library for the local phone book and the name of the paper). Some real estate brokers will gladly mail you copies of the local newspaper because they know you will probably use their services when and if you decide to buy. We once had a real estate office send us a three-month subscription to the local paper to help us make up our minds.

A newspaper is a valuable research tool. The most important section in an out-of-town paper is always the classifieds. Here you can check the prices of homes, rentals, and help-wanted ads. Compare them with those in your hometown newspaper, and you begin to get a picture of relative costs. This gives you an indication of what kind of earnings you can expect should you seek part-time work, as well as what kind of competition you will have for jobs. Some classified pages have a special "managers wanted" section, where you'll find positions managing apartment buildings, motels, or trailer parks. Typically, these jobs offer free rent and perhaps a salary in return for a minimum amount of management work. Be careful, however, that you don't end up working full time just for rent!

If mobile home parks advertise spaces for rent, you know that the situation should be okay for buying a mobile home. Compare the prices of used items—furniture, appliances, automobiles—to prices listed in your local paper's classifieds. If prices are much higher, you can figure the cost of living is also higher.

Check the rest of the paper to get a flavor of what the town is like. See if supermarket prices compare to those at home, particularly if the same national chains operate in both places. Sometimes identical specials will be priced differently; this comparison also tells you something about the cost of living.

Look at the newspaper's editorial pages to observe the publisher's political stance. It's very interesting how this can influence the thinking of a community. Look over the news stories to see if they are heavily slanted politically or if they strive for a neutral position. Particularly revealing are campaigns for or against services and spending for senior citizens and low-income residents. If you are uncomfortable with the direction of the political slant, this may be something you can investigate when you arrive in the town. You can't be sure how local people think or vote by the way a newspaper presents its opinions, but often—when this paper is the only source of local news—these opinions are accepted locally as fact. If you have strong political views, you might feel uneasy in a community where you are in a tiny minority. Check to see how crime is reported; the way a newspaper reports crime news tells you much about a town's safety.

Newspapers should announce senior-citizen activities, cultural events like lectures and free concerts, and news of community college classes open to seniors. Look for this menu of activities. See which ones are free, which ones cost money, and which activities might interest you. A newspaper with a large section devoted to senior-citizen news indicates a high level of interest in the well-being of retirees. Look for retiree political action groups. Wherever senior citizens band together to vote, the level of senior services and benefits rises proportionally.

Out-of-town telephone books are valuable adjuncts to newspapers for information. You can check for retirement homes and apartment complexes that cater to seniors and get the address of the local housing authority office. If subsidized housing is available, the housing authority can tell you how to find it and how to apply. A telephone book's yellow pages can give you a picture of the business life in town. The number of banks, supermarkets, shopping centers, and other commercial entities tells you something about the vitality of business. This is where you check for bus service and taxi companies. Look at the listings under "airlines" or "airport" to see if there is a local airport and which airlines service it. A telephone book also gives an up-to-date listing for the chamber of commerce office and the government agencies such as Housing and Development and Social Services. A letter to each of them could yield valuable information about the locality. A nonreply also tells you something.

After you've researched a community thoroughly by library research, you still need to visit in person.

Internet Research

Just a few years ago, the Internet was unknown except for a few universities and government agencies who were sending inter-department messages by modem connections. If you wanted to send a document by modem, you dialed the recipient directly, announced that you were going to transmit, and waited until you were connected to send. About that time, my publisher and I tried sending a manuscript over a 1200-baud modem direct dial, home-phone to office-phone connection. That was considered a fast modem at the time (about a thousand times slower than the one I now use). We waited for two hours for the transfer to complete transmission, until we finally gave up. The long distance phone bill was almost $40.00 dollars—it cost $6.50 to mail it the next day! Today I can send a manuscript of a 300-page book by Internet in about ten seconds!

Why do I mention this? Even when the Internet became a practical reality a few years later, few readers knew what I was talking about when I would urge them to learn to research through the Internet. That audience was the tail end of the generation just preceding yours. Yours was the generation that *invented* microcomputers, high-speed modems, Internet, and other forms of cyber technology. I don't have to tell you how much information is available simply by punching a few keys and clicking buttons on a mouse. I would bet that 70 percent of those between the ages of forty-five and fifty-five know more about computers than I do.

However, for the benefit of those few holdouts who stubbornly refuse to learn to use computers, it's time for a sermon. There is *no excuse* for not being connected to the Internet! We're not talking about a large investment. Used computers today are so cheap that they are practically free. In fact, many people throw out perfectly good computers every day because they feel that they must have the latest and fastest machine available. At our local dump, we have to *pay* a $5.00 fee to the dump to accept a computer or a monitor screen for the landfill!

All you need is one of those old discarded computers, a telephone connection, and you're in business. For an Internet connection, several inexpensive connections are available, starting around $5.00 a month.

Some offer free service: Juno is the first that comes to mind—at www.juno.com. Among others offering free Internet are Kmart, Ace Hardware, and dozens more. They'll give you free disks for going online and toll-free numbers to get you started. There's hardly a reason to use a stamp anymore. Instead of collecting a monthly fee, these providers earn income by posting a few ads on your pages (just like a newspaper; you don't have to look at the ads). Can't afford a used computer? Check with your local library. Today most libraries have computers with free Internet connections. Chances are you will have an Internet café in the nearby shopping center where you can go online for a dollar an hour or so.

If you've never touched a computer before, don't worry. Learning the Internet is easy. It isn't as if you have to take classes or learn anything more than a few basic operations. The experts who've developed the Internet have deliberately made it simple to understand. You don't even need to know how to type. Hunt-and-peck is just fine. Ask a friend to show you how it's done, or maybe the neighbor's kids. If you have a grand-child, she'll be delighted to give you a lesson.

The core procedure for doing retirement research is to use a "search engine" (don't worry, your granddaughter will understand). My favorite search engine is called Google. You simply type *www.google.com* into the blank at the top of the screen, then enter the name of the town or city you want to investigate. Like magic, a long string of Web pages that refer to your query will appear. Virtually every town or city in the country that has retirement possibilities will have several Web pages to tell you every-thing about the community. More information than you would ever want to know! Instantaneously! Usually you'll have dozens of pages to look at. Type in the name of the community and add the word "retirement," and you'll find the list narrows down, with each page providing pertinent information for those thinking of relocating there. Or add the words "recreation," and you'll know how many golf courses a community has, walking and biking trails, and even fishing and hunting advice.

You can learn about the town's history, culture, cost of living, real estate market, rentals, climate, recreational opportunities . . . and on and on. When you encounter a particularly interesting page, you simply press the "print" button, and your granddaughter's printer churns out that page so you can put it in your file.

The amount of Internet information about most communities is truly staggering. Some of it is fluff, of course; every community wants to put its best foot forward. But the hard facts and details are there for you to absorb. Most pages will have e-mail addresses inviting you to ask questions. Real estate companies always list e-mail addresses that you can use to ask detailed questions.

Searching for information is only half of what you need to know about the Internet. The other great advantage of having a computer in your kitchen is sending and receiving e-mail messages. It's a wonderful way of communicating with friends and family without the cost of postage or long-distance telephone bills. You just enter the e-mail address of your friend or your granddaughter, hunt-and-peck your message and send it away. E-mail is totally free.

And, of course, you'll take your computer with you when you move. When you are miles away from your kids and grandkids—who are scattered all over the map anyway—you'll enjoy keeping in daily touch with them. The more you use the Internet, the more you'll communicate with the world and the less you'll spend on postage and phone calls. There's hardly a reason to use a stamp anymore.

Investigate Medical Care

Another significant-cost item that varies from one part of the country to another is medical care. Of course, doctors and hospitals are expensive everywhere, but in some areas—notably larger cities—medical costs are out of control. In many localities, even an inexpensive hospital charges $1,000 per day just for the room. Aspirins can cost several dollars each. And this is an economy hospital! The more expensive ones charge $2,000 per day. How many days can you afford at these rates? Therefore, local medical expenses are something to consider before you decide to relocate.

It's not only the expense of medical care you need to research but also the quality. Do not take the word of the local chamber of commerce as to the marvelous medical facilities they have and the new hospital that's just been remodeled. Too often this "hospital" is nothing more than a health clinic or an emergency facility with a dozen beds. Anything more serious than can be treated with antibiotics means an ambulance ride to the next town to the nearest real hospital.

Don't feel smug because you are old enough to be covered by Medicare. Many doctors today are refusing to participate in Medicare or belong to HMOs, which are under the Scrooge management of insurance companies. If you have some condition that requires a medical specialist, you would be wise to inquire whether you can be covered or if you will have to drive 90 miles to the next city to be treated. The government, along with private insurance companies, is trying to force doctors to work on a piecework basis, with an emphasis on saving money rather than quality health care. It's understandable why many doctors are refusing to participate. Not only that, but many general practitioners find Medicare patients a bother and limit the number of patients they will accept or refuse to deal with Medicare at all.

chapter twelve

Climate and Personal Safety

For many people, retirement means moving to a warmer climate. After experiencing a lifetime of freezing winters, they dream of living someplace where they won't have to shovel snow or change to special tires every November and carry snow chains in the trunk. They know they'll love warm winters because they've occasionally spent a two-week vacation in Miami or Phoenix and fondly remember how delightful the warm air was. Also, they remember what their neighbors back home were doing: shoveling snow and cleaning ice off their windshields.

When the time comes for you to leave your job—or when your job leaves you—you might remember how you felt in Miami or Phoenix. You also remember the vacation interlude was rather expensive, with a deluxe time-share or a high-priced motel. "We can't afford that," you might say, as you make plans for toughing out winters for the rest of your life. At this point, you may abandon your dream of Florida, Arizona, or California retirement.

However, if you consider the facts carefully, you might discover that suffering through cold winters isn't necessary after all. Just because the more popular areas of Florida, Arizona, or California are expensive doesn't mean *all* places are expensive. The trick is to find an area where housing prices haven't gone wild. The interesting thing is, depending on how you do it, retirement in a benign climate can cost less than staying at home in a cold climate. There's no reason you can't enjoy retirement on a budget *and* mild winters. You just have to find an affordable location.

Shoestring retirement is often possible in milder climates for several reasons. As mentioned previously, heating expenses can be one of the biggest budget-busters. Automobiles are even more costly. It stands to reason that your automobile will last longer without winter road salt eating away the underside of your car, and changing antifreeze is no longer an issue. Walking to the supermarket and shopping isn't a hardship in mild winters, so you have a chance to save $3.00 a gallon on gasoline. With other prices more or less similar, inexpensive housing is the crucial factor.

Granted, pleasant weather draws affluent people who look on $400,000 homes as beneath consideration. Yet ordinary working people have to live there as well. Cities like Palm Beach, Scottsdale, and Palm Springs aren't exactly places where you might expect to live on a budget. But you'll always encounter communities, not too far from the luxury neighborhoods, where prices are reasonable and where living without snow shovels is possible on a restricted budget. Stores and businesses that cater to the wealthy residents need clerks, janitors, and other workers. The residents employ maids and gardeners. These people have to live somewhere, and those nearby communities are where you'll find affordable housing. If you are looking for work, your chances of finding something satisfactory may be just as good as or better than in your hometown.

The Perfect Climate

Everyone seems to have a different definition of a "perfect climate," but the truth is that there's no such thing. It's all in the eye of the beholder. Folks in Maine dearly love their summers but complain that winters are cold and dreary. Their neighbors who retire in Florida adore Miami winters but complain because summers are too muggy. Hawaii has near-perfect weather, but you'd better take a shopping bag full of money if you expect to stay very long. Having said that, I remember being surprised to find many relatively affordable neighborhoods in Hawaii. Not on the beach, of course, but usually fifteen minutes or half an hour away from the spiffy expensive layouts, you'll find ordinary homes at well below average prices.

Personally, I consider parts of California, inland Oregon, and Washington to have the best overall climate in the nation—sunny summers with low humidity and relatively free of bugs. Winter days often require nothing more than a sweater or windbreaker. Some places, particularly near the ocean, see little frost or snow—sometimes none all season. In the winter of 1990, we were living in Grants Pass, Oregon, when an unusual cold snap burst water pipes throughout the area. The temperature dropped into the 20s and stayed there for about three days. Residents there aren't used to protecting pipes from freezing weather. Extreme cold spells are so unusual that folks don't think about freezing pipes. But when we lived in Michigan, we not only wrapped exposed pipes with insulation but we also used electric warmers—or else. Winter weather wasn't considered unusual unless the temperature dropped to 20 *below* zero!

Cold Weather Robbery

Readers will have little trouble detecting a definite bias in my writing—a bias against winter ice, dirty snow, and slush. I fully realize that not everybody is trying to escape snow shovels. Many folks sincerely enjoy winters, with ice fishing, skiing, and lovely Christmas-card scenery. Therefore, I'll try to be careful not to sound like a chamber of commerce advertisement for Florida. But the fact is that cold weather can be very detrimental to your pocketbook—partly because of heating bills and partly because of the extra wardrobe required for cold weather, with down jackets, padded boots, and long underwear adding to the seasonal expenses.

One unrecognized cost of cold weather is the subtle destruction of your automobile. Batteries deteriorate quickly in cold weather. Cold-weather starts wear out engine cylinders by dragging moving parts against each other without the benefit of free-flowing oil for lubrication. Antifreeze and snow tires also batter away at the budget. Unlike winter clothing, auto repair and maintenance are ongoing expenses that cannot be put off until next year. When you move to a salt-free environment, your car's life expectancy depends on the number of miles you drive, not on the number of winter months you drive. When you need to buy another automobile every three or four years, your restricted budget gets stretched to the breaking point.

Climate, Exercise, and Health

Another way cold weather can be costly is in terms of doctor bills and shortening your life expectancy. Medical and health experts agree that one of the biggest dangers to retired folks' health is inactivity. Many medical researchers, cardiologists, and scientists are coming to the conclusion that exercise is the key factor in health and long life. Exercise, many believe, may be much more important than diet or preventive medicines.

Unquestionably, people living in warm climates tend to spend more time outdoors. They get out and exercise, doing healthful activities instead of huddling next to the fireplace with eyes glued to the television set. Bicycling, swimming, tennis, and daily walks for your health and recreation can add years to your life. In mild winter climates these are year-round activities. In cold-weather climates folks exercise only occasionally during the winter, if they exercise at all.

Some of you will say, "Yes, it would be nice to escape winter, but have you ever tried taking a brisk walk or playing tennis in Atlanta during August?" They have a point, although it is clearly possible to get the exercise out of the way early in the morning or to wait until after sundown. Those who cannot stand the muggy humidity of the southern states can always opt for low-humidity western states.

For some folks, the solution to the climate problem is to become "snowbirds" and enjoy the best of all worlds. Snowbirds are those free spirits who choose to escape winter's anger by flying south for the season. When summer's heat threatens to become oppressive, it's back to a kinder, gentler climate. Snowbirds luxuriate in balmy Phoenix winters and enjoy springlike summers in Montana. Those who choose RV retirement epitomize the snowbird lifestyle.

Some escape winters by going south of the border, choosing an inexpensive, part-time retirement in Mexico, Guatemala, Costa Rica, or other countries. Personally, my wife and I choose to do our snowbirding in Costa Rica at our home on the Pacific Ocean. We've also fled to Mexico,

Guatemala, and South America to avoid winter. All of those locations feature a cost of living about half that in the United States.

Snowbirding is possible through creative housing schemes. Some people rent their homes or apartments for a nominal income while they are on "vacation" in the sunshine. Some retirees make regular arrangements to work at a resort motel, a state park, or a lake marina—with free rent as part of the arrangement—thus enjoying summer resort weather while their neighbors shiver through the season back home. Others take similar positions in popular winter resorts in Arizona, Texas, or other warm-winter retreats. These jobs are easier to find that you might think.

Many top high-tech companies are located in mild-weather places like San José, Portland, Seattle, and Austin. Although many choice jobs have been outsourced to other countries, some skills are still needed. Casual and part-time positions can often be secured. Casino jobs in Las Vegas and other casinos throughout Arizona and California are often reserved for older workers. Casinos like to hire those willing to work flexible schedules, sometimes just four hours a day.

Finding a Low-Crime Area

Locating a crime-free area is an important objective for anyone searching for a new retirement home. Unfortunately, as you might guess, there is no such thing as a totally "crime-free" community. There are, however, many "low-crime" areas around the country, and they are relatively easy to locate—easier if you're rich.

Why rich? Because it turns out that the lowest crime rates in North America are found in the most affluent neighborhoods! I discovered this fact while studying the FBI's crime statistics for cities in the United States with populations higher than 10,000. Until then, I had always assumed that most burglaries and robberies would naturally take place in the wealthiest neighborhoods. Not so; the richest neighborhoods generally have exceptionally low rates of burglary, larceny, and robbery. This is true for several reasons. First of all, law enforcement in wealthy neighborhoods tends to be more efficient than in poor neighborhoods. Also, these locations tend to have fewer teenagers in residence—the presence of young people is a basic factor in the number of burglaries. And finally, strangers with criminal intentions tend to "stand out" in wealthy neighborhoods and can be reported to police before they get a chance to commit a crime.

None of the foregoing will be of comfort to those who are looking for economical yet safe retirement neighborhoods. However, many low-cost places to retire are just as safe as such expensive spreads as Palos Verdes and Palm Beach. Read on, and we'll explain how to find them.

Although crime rates in the United States are decreasing dramatically throughout the nation, some areas are still plagued by crime and violence. If you are old enough to remember, you'll recall that when you were a child, your neighbors never bothered to lock their doors at night, and children played outside until long after dark. Crime rates were much lower than today. Part of this was due to a much lower rate of drug use, which is directly responsible for much of today's problems. Stealing is a lot easier and more profitable than working, especially for those who are supporting a drug habit and who must turn to crime.

What's the answer? Some say we need to get tougher on criminals. But how do we do that? We already have a higher percentage of our population locked up than any other civilized nation in the world. Recently, the United States passed the two-million mark for prison inmates. That means one out of every 147 Americans is in prison! We can't build prisons fast enough; prisoners are being kicked out of jail before their terms are up in order to make room for more criminals! The truth is that you and I can't do much about crime except to look for a safer place to live.

Why Some Places Are Safer

The number of police officers does *not* determine low-crime areas. Some large, crime-ridden cities have so many cops patrolling the streets that they get in each other's way. There were more police on the streets of New York City than soldiers on the ground in Afghanistan in 2006. Nevertheless, the crime rates remain high. On the other hand, in some communities with only a handful of part-time police officers, burglars are as scarce as honest lawyers. A large police force is usually a *response* to crime, not an indication of a town's safety.

Obviously, the larger the city, the higher the crime rate. But even in large cities you'll find areas of tranquility, often not too far from the problem areas. When checking out a neighborhood for possible retirement, look for mature, low-turnover neighborhoods where residents know each other and the average resident is at or near retirement age.

The age of neighborhood residents is important. When a working-class neighborhood is overrun with young people—particularly males between the ages of fifteen and twenty-two, most of them underemployed—you are looking at a troubled neighborhood. When seeking a rental or a home to buy, cruise the neighborhood and look for teenagers hanging out on the street corners. Try to find a neighborhood with older, mature residents; your chances for peace are better there. Walk the streets, stop to talk with people working in their yards or walking their dogs. You'll quickly get a feeling for personal safety. (Of course if the person working in the yard offers to lend you a gun for protection or if the dog bites you on the leg, you probably don't want to consider that area.)

One way to identify high-crime areas is by studying the local newspapers and seeing how crimes are reported. You can tell how safe a town is by the importance accorded various crimes. When murders, robberies, and burglaries in an area are reported routinely or not at all, you can be sure that the place has a high crime rate. But when a bicycle theft makes headlines, you've found a safe community.

You can't blame the newspaper. Murders are so common in some cities that if all of them were reported on the front page there wouldn't be room for other news. Unless victims are newsworthy enough to have their names published, their murders are reported as casually as a stock market report.

The lesson is this: When murders and rapes are reported on page 23, if at all, you can assume that violent crime is epidemic. On the other hand, if a burglary makes front-page headlines, then burglaries can't be all that common. If a newspaper publishes a detailed police log, read it over carefully. In towns where police are involved in important cases such as rescuing a cat from Mrs. Smith's tree or recovering a bicycle stolen from Jimmy Jones's front yard, it's likely that crime isn't exactly out of control.

Safety Tips

Your local office on aging and the police department can help you make your home or apartment more secure. In most communities these organizations sponsor crime prevention projects and work together to publish educational materials about crime prevention.

Often your police department will be happy to make a free "burglary audit" of your home. They'll send a police officer to your home to check on your home security and make suggestions for your safety. Some of the more common security recommendations include:

- Always lock your garage, even if you are at home or are just stepping out briefly.
- When you are out of the house, lock your windows as well as your doors.
- Cut back bushes near doors and windows.
- Install dead-bolt locks and night chains.
- Install and use a peephole in your door.
- Keep outside areas well illuminated.
- Keep valuable personal property in a safe-deposit box rather than at home.
- Do not keep large amounts of cash in the house.
- Do not hide an extra set of keys to your home in an obvious place, such as under the doormat, on the ledge above your door, in a planter box, or in the mailbox.
- If you go away on a trip, use timers to keep lights on inside and outside the house in the evening.
- Stop mail and newspaper deliveries and ask a neighbor to pick up circulars and packages from your driveway.
- Hide your empty garbage cans.
- Arrange for someone to maintain your yard.
- Turn your telephone bell down.

FBI Statistics

Over the years I've used the FBI's Uniform Crime Report to analyze various cities as to the crime rate, but there were several things that puzzled me. Towns that I knew to be exceptionally peaceful often showed up on the charts as terribly crime ridden. Other places where I wouldn't park our car on the street overnight looked exceptionally safe! Part of the explanation is the method individual police departments use to report crime. Some departments don't even bother reporting crimes such as rape and arson because they aren't considered to be extra-serious crimes. Not wanting to make their departments look bad, sometimes police change the results to make crime rates lower than those in neighboring communities. On the other hand, some conscientious departments routinely report the theft of a tricycle or a fist fight between town drunks as crimes.

The FBI warns about this inconsistency in the report, so none of the above is a surprise. But what seems curious is that some places, especially towns with large tourist populations in the season, would appear to be exceptionally dangerous, with murder, assault, rape, and robbery at high levels. It turns out that when you lump 50,000 tourists with a community's year-round population of 20,000, you end up with an exceptionally high level of incidents. The FBI takes the crime statistics of 70,000 people and divides it into the 20,000 regular inhabitants.

Another flaw in the FBI's statistics is that they do not show the nature of crimes reported. When a town shows several murders and many assault cases a year, the report doesn't indicate whether these incidents were the result of holdups, burglaries, or other crimes against ordinary citizens, or whether they involved youth gangs fighting over turf and their share of the shrinking drug market. Very few senior citizens will be involved in drive-by shootings because of a bad drug deal. What might be dangerous for a gang member can be perfectly safe for a senior citizen.

Example: According to FBI statistics, our California hometown is one of the safest in the country because of the low number of crimes reported. And we feel very safe. Yet not 20 miles away is a small city with a very high murder rate. Why? Drive-by shootings and wars over drug turf. Do the retired people who live in that city feel safe? Yes, they do. The problems do not happen in their neighborhoods, nor do they occur in the city's downtown area—only in neighborhoods where retired people wouldn't live on a bet. In fact, this city was called one of the country's "top retirement destinations" by a leading retirement magazine not too long ago. The lesson here: Do not rely on statistics as to whether a community is safe. Do your own analysis as I pointed out above, then ask the folks living in your target neighborhood how they feel about crime. The Uniform Crime Report can be accessed on the Internet at www.fbi.gov/ucr/ucr.htm. But remember the background when looking at the figures.

chapter thirteen

College Town Retirement

Twenty years ago, when my wife and I began doing research for our first book on retirement, we began the first of many trips across the country. We looked at hundreds of small cities and towns over the years—evaluating them as possible places we could recommend as retirement destinations. After a while, we discovered something curious. It turned out that most of our favorite towns and smaller cities seemed to have one feature in common: Most had a college or university with a large number of students and faculty in residence. At first we thought this a coincidence. After all, how could a school affect a community for anyone but those connected with the college or those retirees who are interested in higher education? How could the mere presence of a college make a town a better place to live?

After much puzzling over why our favorite towns were different from the others, we finally stumbled upon the key. College towns are dinosaurs—suspended in a time warp. Prove it to yourself: Walk into the downtown section of a typical college town, and you'll feel like you are stepping back in time. You're looking at the way our hometowns were when we were youngsters! Remember how it was then? The center of town was alive. It was the place to shop, have lunch with friends, browse the bookstore, or take in a movie. Something was always happening downtown. You couldn't stroll through the town center without seeing a half-dozen friends and acquaintances. Drivers would honk at friends as they passed by. Downtown was the social focus of the entire community. That's the way it used to be. That may be what retirees today are unconsciously looking for.

Starting about forty years ago, Small Town U.S.A. began undergoing profound changes. Large shopping centers began opening up out on the Highway 161 bypass, cutting prices until the small stores and businesses in the town itself couldn't compete. They either joined the movement to the strip mall or they closed their doors. Today many of these towns are hollow shells. The downtowns are deserted. You'll see little more than abandoned buildings, deserted storefronts, empty sidewalks. Stroll through the town center, and the only people you see are those patronizing the secondhand stores—the only businesses left. The one positive thing you can say is, there are plenty of parking spaces.

But this didn't happen in most college towns. Why? Because students and faculty simply are not going to hang out at a strip mall. They want a lively, user-friendly downtown within walking distance of their dorms and offices. Yes, when they shop for groceries or a refrigerator, they have to go to the strip mall. But when they want to buy a sweater, have lunch with friends, or listen to a jazz combo in a pub, they think "downtown." With several thousand students, faculty, and school employees as customers, this means plenty of traffic in the town center. As long as there are people downtown, there will be stores, shops, and businesses downtown. And as long as there are stores, shops, and businesses, the other residents of town go there as well. You'll even find the old-fashioned single-screen movie theater—showing foreign or classic movies perhaps—and it's still named the Bijou or Rialto! It's like going back in time forty years.

A university not only influences the intellectual atmosphere but also indirectly affects the business, entertainment, and dining traditions of the area. A university lures intellectuals from all over the country, creating an air of sophistication unknown in most towns of moderate size. Yet when you stroll along a downtown street, strangers are likely to nod and say hello as they pass. After all, this is not just a small town, it's a college town. Most people are connected with the university. We're all neighbors.

Although some university towns boast expensive and exclusive neighborhoods, they also provide neighborhoods with reasonably priced to inexpensive real estate. There is always a demand for affordable housing to meet the low-budget needs of students, employees, and beginning faculty members. Living costs are usually no higher than those in other similar-size towns in the area. After all, as many as half the community's residents are students who don't hold steady jobs, so there aren't a lot of extra wages bidding up rental and real estate costs.

Any time you combine a large number of university students with lots of retired folks, local businesses naturally respond with reasonably priced services, nicer shopping facilities, and good but affordable restaurants. Neither students nor retirees are overburdened with money, but they do appreciate quality at affordable prices.

For retirees operating on a restricted budget, one of these towns could be the doorway to an exciting new lifestyle as you make new friends who share your interests.

Even if you have no intention of going back to school, you'll discover many benefits of retirement in a university setting. Most institutions provide the community at large with a wide selection of social and cultural activities. You don't have to be a registered student to attend lectures and speeches (often free) given by famous scientists, politicians, visiting artists, and other well-known personalities. Concerts ranging from Beethoven to boogie-woogie are presented by guest artists as well as the university's music department. Stage plays, from Broadway musicals to Shakespeare, are produced by the drama department, with season tickets often costing less than a single performance at a New York theater. And of course there's football, basketball, baseball, and other sports with low-cost or even free entrance. Some schools make special provisions to allow seniors to use their recreational facilities. Art exhibits, panel discussions, and a well-stocked library are usually available to the public.

College towns generally have at least one large bookstore where you'll enjoy one or two free events each week. Sometimes you'll have the opportunity to meet a best-selling author and listen to her discuss her latest work. In some bookstores you can sip a coffee and listen to a string quartet while you browse.

Because of the high level of sophistication, most college towns support bars and restaurants that feature entertainment, often well-known talent. Ordinary towns nearby seldom have this attraction. Throughout the southern states, where some of the more delightful college towns are located, "local option" has "dried up" surrounding counties, but most college towns have managed to reject the notion of prohibition. After all, what is a college experience without beer? What is a good meal at an upscale restaurant without wine with dinner?

There is one economic downside to retirement in a college town: vigorous competition with students for part-time work. Unless you have a special skill or can do some teaching, you may have plenty of spare time to enjoy retirement by taking free classes and doing volunteer work. That's not so bad. On the other hand, students have a tendency to drift in and out of jobs, often quitting during summer vacation. Some employers prefer steady year-round employees, even if on a part-time basis.

When choosing a college town for retirement, there are several items to look for. Of course, in any town you'll need to check out health care, transportation, and personal safety. College towns usually rank high in health care; many have a university hospital as well as a medical school. Because so many people travel to and from college towns, the communities usually have intercity bus service such as Greyhound, with a commuter airport nearby. Because many students don't own automobiles, there's always local bus service. And as in most small towns, crime rates are usually low.

Something to think about: Just because a community has a college, it's not necessarily what we would consider a "college town." When a school is basically a technical trade school or religious institution, for example, it often doesn't interact with the community. The important thing is when the school reaches out to the community, inviting residents to events such as plays, concerts, lectures, and sporting events. A good school will offer free or reduced tuition for seniors and will have non-credit classes tailored for mature students.

Choose Your Neighborhood Well!

Inexpensive neighborhoods are popular with college students as well as those looking for bargain housing. Should you buy or rent a home next door to a frat house or other student housing, you could find yourself bombarded twenty-four hours a day by full-tilt music blasting from monster speakers at a decibel level that routinely peels paint from automobiles as they drive past.

Taking College Classes

Scientific research shows that we don't necessarily lose our capacity to learn as we age. Furthermore, the common belief that memory always fades with each passing year is simply not true. Numerous psychological experiments prove that those who regularly exercise their minds hold up quite well.

You don't have to go back to school, but as long as you're retiring in a college town, why not give continuing education a try? More and more, dynamic seniors with active lifestyles are enjoying the pleasant, invigorating mental exercise of part-time classes. And this time around, they sign up for subjects they *want* to study, rather than what's required to get a degree!

More than two-thirds of all colleges and universities offer reduced rates or even free tuition to mature citizens. Many communities have special centers, schools, and programs tailored to older adults' needs. You won't feel like the proverbial sore thumb when you're in a setting where many students are your age or older.

Nervous about going back to school? Never been in a college classroom? Don't worry. For a mature adult, it's a snap. Professors are usually much closer to your age than to the age of other students. They'll tend to treat you as an equal but might talk down to younger students. Most schools allow you to audit courses, which means you take the class but don't have to worry about tests, finals, or term papers. You get the benefits and fun from the course without the tension. Below are some courses selected at random from a schedule offered by Valdosta State University in Georgia:

- Home Fruit Growing
- Instant Piano for Hopelessly Busy People
- Basic Watercolors
- Early Twentieth-Century Artists
- Starting a Home Business
- Creative Ideas for Filling Your Memory Book

If a university classroom seems a bit much for your ambitions, then try adult education classes. They're usually offered in the evenings, often in the local high school or community college buildings. You'll find a broad assortment of offerings—everything from philosophy to auto repair. The bonus is that in many college towns you'll find that the adult ed instructor is also a university professor, moonlighting for extra money or simply because he enjoys sharing his special expertise.

Don't overlook your local two-year community college. Most towns either have a school or have one within driving distance. Although some are specifically for trade and entry-level professional training, others have wonderful offerings of low-tuition or tuition-free classes especially oriented toward mature students. Many community college classes are non-credit, mostly for personal improvement or hobbies, with subjects such as flower arranging, fly-fishing, cooking, book discussions, or woodworking. But you'll also find practical courses that could be useful in starting a home business, such as income tax preparation, dog grooming, and childcare certification. University level or adult ed, it doesn't matter—you'll find yourself among a group of lively, interesting people. Just the kind of folks you would like for friends.

University Retirement Sampler

Following are some places we particularly like, towns where folks retire primarily because of the university setting. Of course, many other college towns throughout the nation offer everything that my favorites do. Doing your own investigation could turn up a setting that better suits your taste in climate, recreation, and location. You can take advantage of continuing education just about anywhere you choose to retire. As mentioned, most small cities without a university will usually have a two-year community college. It's just that in some towns, the university is the centerpiece of local attention, the focus of social and cultural activities. This creates a situation in which everyone can participate in the excitement generated by the university. The following places are my personal favorites:

Oxford, Mississippi

Stately antebellum mansions, enormous magnolia trees, live oaks and flowers in profusion, an ancient courthouse with a statue of a Confederate soldier—all of these combine to make Oxford a model of a gracious university town in the Old South. This is my all-time favorite college town. A city of 20,000—half of them students—Oxford is large enough to provide quality services but small enough that you'll meet friends just about every time you go to the supermarket or walk to the library.

Although upscale homes have soared in value in the past few years, there are plenty of affordable neighborhoods with inexpensive prices and rents. A nice mixture of Yankees and Deep South natives adds spice to the flavor of retiring here. If you're not from the South, you won't be a stranger because the 140-year-old university lures intellectuals from all over the United States and from all over the world, creating an air of sophistication unknown in most isolated southern towns. Retirees find

TYPICAL WEATHER—OXFORD, MISSISSIPPI						
Temp. (F°)	Jan.	April	July	Oct.	Rain	Snow
Daily Highs	51	75	93	76	56"	5"
Daily Lows	31	50	69	49		

Oxford a wonderful place for education; everyone older than fifty-five can take three hours of classes tuition-free per semester and can audit as many classes as they care to.

Columbia, Missouri

This is more than a "college town"; it's more properly called a "university city." Much larger than Oxford, Columbia blends the sophistication of a small city with an exciting academic environment. Instead of just one university, three well-known institutions of higher learning make education a major industry here. Some programs offer free tuition in return for volunteer work after graduation. Kansas City and St. Louis are two-hour interstate drives in either direction for those who can't live without occasional major league sports or other amenities of big-city life.

Making the decision to retire in Columbia is made easier by a unique chamber of commerce program. Retiree volunteers greet visitors and take them on a "windshield tour" of the city. They drive you through neighborhoods ranging from economical to deluxe, past the town's colleges, golf courses, and hospitals.

TYPICAL WEATHER—COLUMBIA, MISSOURI						
Temp. (F°)	Jan.	April	July	Oct.	Rain	Snow
Daily Highs	36	65	89	68	36"	23"
Daily Lows	19	44	67	46		

Ashland, Oregon

Couples with mixed interests, who want more than intellectual stimulation, might check out Ashland. Set in southern Oregon's gently rolling hills, Ashland is an excellent retirement choice for outdoorsy, sports-oriented people. Great hunting, fishing, and skiing are available in the nearby Cascade Range, with crystal-clear rivers teeming with world-class salmon and steelhead trout. White-water rafting on the wild and scenic Rogue River draws adventurers from all over the country. One of the best climates in the nation makes outdoor sports enjoyable year-round; Ashland's 20 inches of yearly rain is a third to half that of most popular midwestern and southern cities. It's wonderfully sunny here most of the year.

Ashland offers all the usual cultural amenities of a small college town (it is home to Southern Oregon University) and more. Its renowned Shakespeare festival draws thousands every summer, and year-round community involvement in the college's activities keeps retirement interesting. A charming downtown offers excellent restaurants and shopping. As a final incentive, real estate costs are typical Oregon, ranging from cheap to affordable, although—as with Oregon real estate in general—prices have risen somewhat in the last few years.

TYPICAL WEATHER—ASHLAND, OREGON

Temp. (F°)	Jan.	April	July	Oct.	Rain	Snow
Daily Highs	48	65	95	70	22"	4"
Daily Lows	32	38	60	42		

Corvallis, Oregon

Corvallis sits midway between Eugene and the state capitol of Salem (45 miles either direction), two hours from snow skiing, and an hour from the Pacific Ocean beaches. Outdoor recreation is plentiful in this mild four-seasons climate, with everything from mountain biking and hiking on a network of trails to river rafting and golf. There is a wealth of performing arts and festivals as well as galleries, antiques shopping, and wineries. In and near the city you'll find more than fifty parks and wildlife preserves.

Oregon State University is known as the largest and oldest institution of higher learning in Oregon, employing more than 7,000 faculty and a student body of 19,000. The town's population is about 50,000, with just the right balance between residents and students. Several advanced technology businesses have found a home in Corvallis, including Hewlett-Packard, located on a 174-acre campus with about 4,000 employees. Other high-technology firms have offices here, and others are operated as satellite entities, providing possible job opportunities as well as ambience of a university town.

Weather in the Williamette Valley is mild throughout the year. Despite Oregon's reputation for rain, Corvallis receives an annual rainfall of about 40 inches—less than New York, Chicago, and even Miami! There's about 6 inches of snow and enough rainfall to keep things green most of the year. Summer days are pleasantly warm, with an average maximum temperature of 80 degrees from July through August.

TYPICAL WEATHER—CORVALLIS, OREGON

Temp. (F°)	Jan.	April	July	Oct.	Rain	Snow
Daily Highs	46	61	83	65	46"	6"
Daily Lows	34	39	51	42		

Gainesville, Florida

Home of the University of Florida, Gainesville is a culturally stimulating city of 96,000 inhabitants in a state famous for its culturally unstimulating cities. It doesn't look like Florida, either. Were it not for an occasional palm tree, Gainesville could easily be mistaken for a college town anywhere in the Midwest. Old-fashioned residential areas with tree-shaded streets justify Gainesville's official nickname, "the Tree City."

You needn't be a student to participate in the many activities connected with the university. A cultural complex with museums of art and natural history and a performing arts center serve the public at large. There is also an excellent two-year college that accepts most students older than sixty tuition-free. The extensive curriculum covers classes such as dog training, computers, and antiques collecting.

If a town of 96,000 is too large for you, the nearby communities of High Springs and Archer are a fifteen-minute drive away. Housing costs less here, and small farms are affordable.

For outdoors types, there's plenty to do. A dozen nearby lakes invite anglers. Golf and tennis facilities abound, and beach fun at either the gulf or the Atlantic is a short drive away. The closest saltwater fishing is in Cedar Key, a 49-mile drive.

TYPICAL WEATHER—GAINESVILLE, FLORIDA						
Temp. (F°)	Jan.	April	July	Oct.	Rain	Snow
Daily Highs	67	81	91	81	52"	—
Daily Lows	42	55	71	59		

Boulder, Colorado

Without hesitation, we recommend Boulder as one of our favorite university towns. The city is surrounded by snow-covered peaks looming in the background, and Rocky Mountain National Park is just minutes away. Skiing and other winter sports are famous throughout the region, and summers are typically Colorado-perfect. Yet it's not exactly isolated—Denver is only 27 miles away. The University of Colorado, of course, is the centerpiece of this small city of 95,000.

The university's student influence is most obvious in the city center as you stroll along the downtown pedestrian mall known as Pearl Street. A picturesque historic preservation district becomes the focal point of the city. In an atmosphere reminiscent of San Francisco or Paris, you'll encounter mimes, jugglers, and musicians mingling with the passersby, adding a touch of magic to the scene. All generations mix here to meet for coffee, shop the boutiques, or perhaps browse a bookstore.

The University of Colorado encourages retirees to enroll in classes for credit or as auditors. But for those who don't feel up to total immersion in the university's curriculum, an extraordinary senior center operated by

TYPICAL WEATHER—BOULDER, COLORADO						
Temp. (F°)	Jan.	April	July	Oct.	Rain	Snow
Daily Highs	41	60	85	65	15"	43"
Daily Lows	16	33	57	37		

Boulder Housing and Human Services gives classes in everything from papermaking to computers. They even offer sailboat instruction on Boulder Reservoir and day trips to archaeological sites and theaters in Denver. Coupled with an active volunteer program, this is one of the better senior programs we've seen.

Chico, California

Only a twenty-minute drive from tree-covered mountains and excellent fishing and hunting, and just a little farther to winter skiing, Chico is the site of a California state university. This is a typical Sacramento Valley town with about 75,000 residents, complete with an historical district, quiet residential neighborhoods, and live oaks and huge ash trees on topography as flat as a pool table. The thing that lifts Chico above most small, agriculturally centered valley towns is its university and vibrant academic timbre. Like all California state universities, Chico State encourages senior-citizen participation with free and reduced tuition rates. Cultural events, such as concerts, plays, lectures, and foreign films, are plentiful and usually free.

Chico weather, as in all Sacramento Valley towns, is both a blessing and a drawback, depending on your opinion of how hot summer should be. You can find days on end with temperatures in the 100-degree range. Balance that against the warm, seldom-frosty winter days with practically no snow, and Chico's weather comes out a winner. After all, when the summer gets going, that's the time for you to head for the nearby mountains for a picnic beside a cool stream or a day's prospecting and panning for gold in the Feather River. A twenty-minute drive takes you to the Feather River Canyon mountain country, where homes are hidden by huge pine trees.

TYPICAL WEATHER—CHICO, CALIFORNIA						
Temp. (F°)	Jan.	April	July	Oct.	Rain	Snow
Daily Highs	54	71	98	79	21"	2"
Daily Lows	37	47	66	52		

Danville, Kentucky

One of the prettiest towns in Kentucky, Danville is home to Centre College, an outstanding school that consistently receives high academic ratings. Located in a historic part of the state, Danville is just a few miles from Harrodsburg—the birthplace of Abraham Lincoln—and several Civil War battlefields. Incidentally, both Abe Lincoln and his Confederate counterpart, Jefferson Davis, were born in Kentucky, less than 100 miles apart.

Danville was named one of "Six Great Low-Cost Towns for Retirement" in *Where to Retire* magazine (winter 1999 edition). The magazine took into consideration culture, entertainment, beauty, safety, climate, medical care, and cost of living.

Danville has a population of 17,000, but it is only 35 miles from Lexington, a city of 350,000. The town is located in the famous bluegrass country, known for rolling farmlands, horse farms, and pleasant rural scenery. Danville is a place where people are friendly, the streets are safe, and citizens are committed to keeping it that way.

Senior citizens are a vital part of the Danville area community. A well-equipped senior center provides activities that include lunches, speakers, shopping excursions, day-long outings, dancing, and fitness sessions. The center also provides periodic health screenings and transportation for elderly persons.

Temp. (F°)	Jan.	April	July	Oct.	Rain	Snow
TYPICAL WEATHER—DANVILLE, KENTUCKY						
Daily Highs	40	66	86	68	46"	16"
Daily Lows	23	44	66	46		

Fayetteville, Arkansas

Up in the northwest corner of Arkansas, the college town of Fayetteville consistently receives favorable publicity as a great place for retirement. Its low cost of living, nearby outdoor recreational opportunities, and a community-friendly college are all part of the attraction. Not exactly a small town, Fayetteville has a population of 50,000, plus almost 15,000 students at the University of Arkansas.

This part of Arkansas has some of the most beautiful Ozarks scenery in the entire region, starting just a few miles from downtown Fayetteville. In the foothills is Beaver Lake, with 28,000 acres of fishing and boating.

The University of Arkansas is Fayetteville's heart and soul. The school, its students, and the faculty add excitement and vigor to the city. To savor fully the magnetism of the community, you must visit Dickson Street, near the campus. This colorful, entertaining street is filled with bistros, restaurants, and art galleries.

The university is ranked as one of the top schools in the country in the number of chief executives produced for major U.S. companies. (Bill Clinton taught law at the university before he entered politics.) The nearby town of Rogers is the home of Northwest Arkansas Community College, with 2,600 students to add to the educational scene.

TYPICAL WEATHER—FAYETTEVILLE, ARKANSAS

Temp. (F°)	Jan.	April	July	Oct.	Rain	Snow
Daily Highs	48	74	94	76	40"	7"
Daily Lows	27	49	71	49		

Athens, Georgia

Here is a prime example of how a university can shape a town's architecture, business structure, and social ambience. Downtown Athens looks exactly as a university town should look. Its main street is arched over by large trees and lined with old-fashioned cast-iron lampposts with glass globes. Sidewalk tables and chairs in front of cafes invite residents to linger over a cup of coffee. Students, residents, and tourists stroll the streets, browse stores and shop, or simply sit on wrought-iron benches, observing the passing world with an unhurried casualness only students and retirees can afford.

It's obvious that the downtown isn't just for the university's 26,000 students. Residents as well as visitors from nearby communities come to browse bookstores and specialty stops for articles not normally found in small Georgia cities. They love to dine in downtown Athens's exotic restaurants serving not only traditional southern-style cooking but also wood-fired pizza, Mexican enchiladas, Indian tandoori, and Japanese cuisine. This is one of our favorite college towns.

TYPICAL WEATHER—ATHENS, GEORGIA

Temp. (F°)	Jan.	April	July	Oct.	Rain	Snow
Daily Highs	52	74	89	74	50"	3"
Daily Lows	33	50	69	51		

chapter fourteen

Foreign Retirement

At one time, American retirees in Europe, with a few dollars in their jeans, felt like millionaires, sipping fine wine in Paris cafes, savoring beef Wellington in London restaurants, or playing roulette in Monaco. A seventeenth-century stone cottage with a view of the Mediterranean rented for $700 a month, and a sumptuous meal—including wine—cost $15. Retired North Americans routinely traveled abroad to spend several months a year in Provence or on the Costa del Sol because it was cheaper than staying home.

No longer. Today you'll feel indigent in most of Europe. That Mediterranean cottage will now cost $5,000 a month, and that sumptuous meal has a sumptuous price. Even European economy prices would be expensive here at home. But if you have a dream of an exotic foreign retirement, don't despair. There are still a few countries where a limited income budget can sustain a dignified, comfortable, and stimulating lifestyle. Instead of retirement in Europe, look closer to home—to Mexico and Central America. Long stays or permanent retirement are practical on a budget backed only by Social Security. Most important, these countries welcome retirees.

Before we go any further, I'll make an important point: Moving to a foreign country just because it is cheap can be a huge mistake. Yes, you can easily live on a shoestring budget in some countries, but if you *have* to live on such a budget, my recommendation is don't try it in a foreign country! Unexpected expenses can and will arise. Without a safety net, you may well find yourself in a pickle. Many people discover they aren't cut out for the inconveniences of living in a foreign setting, and they feel the need to return home. If you can't afford the money to return, you are trapped.

Back home, those with low income and few resources have city, county, and state agencies to make sure they are somehow taken care of. But Mexico and Central American countries do not provide welfare assistance even for their own citizens—and they certainly won't help you. Welfare in the Third World is the responsibility of family and friends—not the government. If you run out of money, you'll either be on your own or else dependent upon the charity of fellow North Americans. Furthermore, if you are truly indigent, the host government can take a very dim view of your being there. You are rarely permitted to work in foreign countries unless you are a legal resident, and you could get into trouble if you try.

Also, becoming a legal resident of a foreign country can be difficult for low-income retirees because a minimum monthly retirement income is required to qualify for a resident visa. If you fall below this minimum, you are limited to six months' stay at a time; then you must leave the country. Actually, the income needed isn't very much. Usually an average Social Security check will qualify you for residency. Of course, many expatriates are satisfied with six-month stays, choosing to spend cold winters in their foreign retirement home, then back to their northern residence for the best part of the year at home.

A final consideration is that neither Medicare nor Medicaid is recognized outside the United States. You will be on your own as far as medical and hospital bills go. The bright side of this picture is that doctors and hospitals charge a fraction of what they do back home, and inexpensive medical plans are usually available for joining the country's health programs. Many retirees simply use the inexpensive local medical system and return home for Medicare treatment for problems that are complicated or expensive.

Therefore, if you do have backup funds for emergencies, you might enjoy the excitement of living in another culture. There's no question that you can do it in style on a budget. In Mexico, Costa Rica, and Panama, your generic Social Security check of $900 to $1,500 a month can cover all expenses. The higher amount provides a quality lifestyle that would be totally unthinkable in the United States or Canada on the same money. Many retirees cover all basic expenses, dine out frequently, do some traveling, and even hire part-time servants.

While it's true that living costs are dramatically lower in some countries, you must remember that there are limits to your lifestyle; nothing is free. If your liquor bills are $800 a month, you'll be hard-pressed to survive on your Social Security checks of $1,000 monthly. If you decide to rent an elegant house with a swimming pool for $1,000 a month, you'll need to make some drastic adjustments to your food budget!

The big plus of foreign living is that you'll find it extremely easy to make friends with your new neighbors—native people as well as North Americans. A special camaraderie arises among expatriates in a foreign setting. They come together as if by magnetism. You'll find close friends among people you would never have even spoken to back home. There are no strangers in an expatriate community.

You'll also have adventures exploring scenic coasts, spectacular mountains and forests, and picturesque villages. My wife and I enjoy living abroad so much that we spend up to half of each year at our second home in Costa Rica. We've previously lived in Mexico and have traveled extensively in South America, where some truly inexpensive countries welcome retirees.

By the way, in the following descriptions of retirement in Mexico and Central America, I may use the word *gringo*. Understand that this is not a pejorative term in Latin America. It generally means any person who is light-skinned and who speaks English as a first language. Latin Americans sometimes call Germans and Swedes *gringos* simply because they are often blond and light-skinned. The practice is similar to our using Aussie for an Australian or Brit for anyone from the British Isles.

Let's start our discussion of foreign retirement with Mexico. It's the most accessible foreign country suitable for budget retirement.

Retirement in Mexico

Twenty-two years ago, Don Merwin and I coauthored a book called *Choose Mexico for Retirement*, describing how to retire in that country on a monthly expenditure of $400. This fantastically low budget even allowed for servants and travel about the country! In those days Mexico was truly an economic paradise for North Americans retiring on a shoestring.

Our book sold 50,000 copies the first year. (It's still in print, by the way, with a new edition due in 2007.) Thousands of retirees from the United States and Canada used the guidebook to discover the joys and benefits of retirement in a friendly country that welcomes foreign neighbors. The newcomers found fascinating lifestyles in colonial cities, picturesque villages, and tropical beach settings. Living graciously on a minimal budget was only part of the equation. The vast majority didn't make the move to Mexico because of finances. The attraction was an opportunity for gracious living among other expatriates, a choice of perfect climates, and immersion in a different culture. The fact that the equivalent of a Social Security income provided a standard of living far better than they could hope for at home for the same money was merely icing on the cake.

As you might expect, the cost of living has risen steadily over the years. Although today it would probably require three times as many dollars to maintain the $400-a-month lifestyle of twenty-two years ago, we must realize that costs have risen in North America over those intervening years as well. A minimum budget today would be in the neighborhood of $900 to $1,200 a month.

What can you do with $900 in Mexico today? That's about $225 a week—about four times what most skilled laborers earn. On a budget of $900, it's possible to rent a modest home or apartment, eat well (including dining out at least once a week at a nice restaurant), and take care of all your basic needs. Maybe even hire a part-time maid to clean the house one morning a week. On incomes of $1,200 to $1,500 a month, a couple can do some traveling and afford to hire a maid and a gardener. This budget even covers medical insurance. One thing that makes this lifestyle possible is that you won't need to spend money on heating and air-conditioning.

Don Merwin and I take turns occasionally spending a month or so in Mexico in order to update *Choose Mexico*. During a recent visit, my wife and I traveled to a popular retirement area, rented an inexpensive apartment for a month, and kept scrupulous records of our expenditures. We found that a basic monthly budget would come under $800, so rest assured that it is still possible.

A semiretired couple who live in Mazatlán had this to say: "Labor, food, and locally manufactured goods are much less expensive than their counterparts in the United States. We go to the movies here every week—a ticket costs $2.00, and popcorn is 80 cents. Our maid, who comes in six days a week, eight hours each day, is paid approximately $50 per week, and she is very well paid by Mexican standards. On the other hand, if you want to buy imported electronics or appliances, be prepared to pay plenty for them."

In one respect, year-round retirement here isn't as easy as it used to be. The Mexican government has increased the minimum income requirement to qualify for full-time residency. At one time a couple needed just $550 a month in retirement income; today it's around $1,000 for a single person and $1,500 for married couples. However, this income requirement is cut in half if you own your own home in Mexico, which brings the amount needed for residency to only $750, well within the range of most Social Security checks.

If you cannot qualify financially, you aren't completely out of the picture. Tourist visas are good for six months' stay at a time. A large number of retirees don't care to live in Mexico full time anyway. They prefer to spend November through March enjoying the sunny weather here, and they then return to enjoy the best part of the year at home.

Where North Americans Live

Mexico is a large country with an amazing variety of climates, landscapes, and panoramas. From tropical Pacific beaches to high, snow-clad mountains, you can find almost any kind of environment imaginable. The climate on the central plateau is often described as "perpetual spring," and the Pacific and Gulf Coasts enjoy "perpetual summer." You make your choice from a menu of climates.

Many locations in Mexico make wonderful places to retire, too many to be described here in a few paragraphs. From Baja California to the Yucatán Peninsula, retirement locations are described in the book *Choose Mexico*. Many bookstores and most libraries have copies, so before you make any decisions, check it out.

Previously, we discussed RV travel-retirement in Mexico during the winter months. This can certainly be done on a budget. But spending a summer in Baja California would be only slightly less uncomfortable than spending a summer in a pizza oven. The Mexican mainland is where most North Americans choose conventional retirement living.

Some folks dream of finding an out-of-the-way place where the residents are all natives, a place where retirees can live an idyllic existence. However, unless you are fluent in Spanish, you'll probably want to try your retirement in a place where plenty of other North Americans can keep you company. That isn't because Mexicans aren't friendly; it's simply because you'd soon become bored and suicidal with no one to communicate with.

One area with lots of expatriates and a perfect spring climate is Guadalajara and environs. More than 30,000 North Americans call this region home. Between the city and the many small communities around Lake Chapala, you'll find many clusters of English-speakers among whom you will immediately be accepted as friends. Helping newcomers get their start in Mexico is part of the tradition here. Rents can be expensive in some Guadalajara neighborhoods and lakeside communities, but you'll have no problem finding accommodations to match your budget just a short distance from the high-priced places. We have a friend who recently found a small house near the lake for less than $200 a month.

Others prefer the tropics, settling in romantic places like Acapulco, Puerto Vallarta, or Mazatlán. Although these places have a deserved reputation as expensive jet-set resorts, you'll discover that there are always low-cost homes for rent, although they may be away from the beaches. The more popular the resort, the more low-cost housing is needed for the many Mexican employees who work for tourist businesses. This is where you'll find housing bargains in working-class neighborhoods.

Driving in Mexico

Most Mexican highways are adequately paved but not designed for high-speed driving. Mexican drivers tend to drive slowly on the highway; many feel that the slower they drive, the longer their vehicles will last. It's best to adopt this local practice; it's a lot safer that way. The worst thing about most Mexican highways is that they often lack shoulders and have neither centerlines nor markings on the side of the pavement. This is all right when driving during the daytime, but it's not safe at night. A slight miscalculation or oversteering when oncoming headlights blind you could send you over an embankment. An encounter with a Brahma bull sleeping on the pavement can be deadly for the animal and for you. Repeat after me, "I will never drive at night in Mexico!"

An even more important piece of driving advice: Never drive in Mexico without Mexican automobile insurance. Non-Mexican insurance is not valid. Fortunately, insurance is inexpensive if you buy from the right source. Don't believe guidebooks that tell you that all Mexican insurance costs the same. Details on insurance and other essentials can be found in *Choose Mexico* or any good travel guide for Mexico.

Is Mexico safe? This frequently asked question is frustrating for anyone who has traveled in Mexico. The misinformation and distorted views of Mexico held by many North Americans are difficult to dispel—until they actually travel there. The truth is that the Mexican people are gentle, polite, and law-abiding. The law is very strict and tough on habitual criminals. Upon the third conviction, a convict automatically receives a twenty-year sentence. As you can imagine, this policy discourages professional criminals. People who have retired in Mexico will often tell you that they have no fear of walking the streets of an average Mexican town at any time, day or night. That's not to say Mexico doesn't have its share of crime, particularly in the bigger cities; in Mexico, as anywhere in the world, the larger the city, the more crime.

I've heard many horror stories over the years about someone's brother-in-law's friend who had difficulties with the police after being involved in a minor accident. Well, I suspect that the rest of the story is that the brother-in-law's friend didn't have insurance. In my years of driving in

Mexico—nearly 100,000 miles to date—I've never been unfairly hassled by the police. I've been stopped many times for speeding, but each time I knew full well that I was breaking the law. I just hadn't expected to get caught. (An apology and a ten-dollar bill solves the problem.) I've interviewed many Americans who have been involved in accidents in Mexico; they've had nothing but praise for their insurance companies and the local authorities.

In an issue of *Loners on Wheels Newsletter,* a retired single lady driving her motor home toward Cancun, Mexico, described an accident this way: "Two days into Mexico, like a turkey I stopped for a feathered turkey sitting in the road. A big green truck loaded with oranges didn't stop. The trucker's insurance paid for my damages. It's strictly against the law in Mexico to hit anyone stopped on the road! The police and my insurance adjuster couldn't have been nicer. Two days later, the garage had miraculously patched up my RV, so my trip continued."

I'm sure bad things happen in Mexico just as they can occur anywhere. I'm convinced, however, that the incidents are few and far between.

Retirement in Central America

To a person who hates winter and who loves foreign living, the Central American countries of Costa Rica and Panama are extremely attractive. From the age of eighteen, when my parents retired in Mexico, I spent every winter I could enjoying that country's sunny warmth and charming tropical beaches. Then, in 1973, my wife and I discovered Central America during a three-month vacation through Guatemala, Honduras, El Salvador, Nicaragua, and finally Costa Rica. That trip began my ongoing love affair with Central America.

Although we enjoy visiting Guatemala, Honduras, and El Salvador, these are not countries that attract many North American retirees. This isn't because they aren't beautiful and interesting; it's because these countries are somewhat dangerous. Not for tourists, but for foreign residents who undergo risk of kidnappings. Honduras and El Salvador are undergoing a plague of youth gangs patterning themselves after our Los Angeles barrio gangs.

Therefore, the countries of Costa Rica, Panama, and Nicaragua are the places where the vast majorities of expatriates are relocating, either for retirement or for going into business. It's difficult to know for certain how many U.S. and Canadian citizens have relocated to these three countries. My guess is around 50,000. The majority live in Costa Rica, although a considerable number prefer Panama, and a growing number are choosing Nicaragua.

Costa Rica

Costa Rica has always avoided the civil and military strife that often mired its sister republics in quicksands of turmoil and tragedy. Costa Rica's devotion to democracy and peaceful cooperation with its neighbors helps the country to retain its enviable position as a showcase for prosperity, respect for law, and personal freedom. It's also been a preferred place for retirement and a new beginning for North Americans.

Costa Rica's traditions prompt people to call it "the Switzerland of the Americas." Of all foreign countries, the highest percentage of foreign retirees are found here. Among a population of some four million people, nearly 40,000 are North Americans who live here as retirees or business-people.

One of Costa Rica's major attractions is its wide range of climates. You can choose between a year-round spring climate in the central plateau or a lush, tropical beach with year-round summer climate. About half of the population lives in the temperate highlands in the center of the country. That's year-round, not seasonal! From the center of the country, around the capital of San José, it's only a two-hour drive west to the Pacific Ocean or two hours east to the Caribbean. Take your pick.

Nature lovers journey here from all over the world to enjoy rain forests, cloud forests, and abundant wildlife, as well as gorgeous beaches with world-class surfing and ocean fishing. The little nation is celebrated for its peaceful ambience. In fact, Costa Rica doesn't even have a military! It abolished its army more than fifty years ago, thereby avoiding the political sickness that often infects Latin American countries: military dictatorships. Money that in other countries is squandered on corruption or funneled into the Swiss bank accounts of high-ranking officers is instead spent on schools, hospitals, and roads. The lack of an army and the existence of a large middle class are key factors in Costa Rica's exceptionally high standard of living.

Inflation has climbed slowly here over the past few years, with the ratio of the dollar to Costa Rican currency following suit. At this writing, the country's monetary unit, the colón, trades at about 520 to the dollar. The colón floats in a free market and is not controlled and manipulated by the government as currency is in some countries. Therefore, as prices rise, the number of cólones we receive for the dollar goes up as well. This system keeps prices steady for foreigners with dollar bank accounts. For example, over the past five years, prices in cólones have doubled as the currency's value dropped. But a dollar is now worth twice as many cólones, so relative costs remain constant. The result is a low cost of living, not quite as low as in Panama but much lower than in the United States or Canada.

The average U.S. Social Security check is more than twice the average middle-class Costa Rican income. The income requirement for a couple to become *pensionados* in Costa Rica is at least $600 a month in Social Security income. And it's entirely possible to get by on this amount. It would require a lot of economizing, but it is done all the time by North Americans. A $600 paycheck is considered an excellent income for most Costa Rican families. That's about what a college professor earns, or about double what a skilled construction worker earns. However, again I caution against living in a foreign country without adequate funds. It would be unwise to try living here if you had no backup resources and if $600 was all you could count on.

To give you an idea of prices in Costa Rica, our basic phone bill is less than $7.00 a month, with local calls almost free. Where we live, our electric bill rarely tops $20.00 a month because our home has neither a furnace nor air-conditioning—we don't need them. It never gets so warm that our ceiling fans don't do the job. Groceries generally cost less than they do back home; local produce is downright cheap, although imported goods can be expensive. Medical expenses are affordable. The most expensive hospital room in San José—in a modern, well-equipped facility—will set you back not much more than $100.00 a day. That's for a private room with bath, telephone, TV, and an extra bed for family members if they wish to stay overnight. For about $50.00 a month, retired residents can buy into the Costa Rican medical system; that's everything fully covered.

Most North Americans will say that one of the best parts about living in Costa Rica is its friendly citizens. This is an egalitarian country without strong class distinctions. The people are outgoing, happy, and full of humor. They sincerely like North Americans, perhaps because we are so much like them. The educational system here is one of the best in Latin America, with literacy levels approaching that of the United States.

Tourist visas are restricted to ninety days, with an additional ninety-day extension possible. That's plenty long enough to get the flavor of living here and to decide if it's an appropriate place for retirement. Many people use Costa Rica as a place for an inexpensive winter escape from ice and snow up north, so a tourist visa is all they need. In San José, where most retirees live, or at least start out living, you might rent one of the many apartments that are available by the week or month to experience the essence of living within the culture. I recommend that you use the excellent bus system to travel around the country to look for your ideal location, although if you can afford it, an auto is quite convenient.

North Americans in Costa Rica, unlike those in other foreign countries, don't feel the need to cluster together in expensive compounds or gated communities. We tend to feel comfortable in just about any neighborhood. Therefore, suitable rentals usually can be found in middle-class neighborhoods for $350 to $500 a month, or even less if you look around.

Becoming a retiree in Costa Rica requires a lot of navigating through red tape and various government ministries, filling out forms in triplicate while the bureaucrats use their rubber stamps to mark everything in sight. It's best to hire a specialist to take care of things for you. You'll need proof that your income is at least $600 a month, a police report from your hometown, and other items. If you aren't retired, you have to prove an income of $1,000 to qualify for residence. For complete details, consult my book, *Choose Costa Rica for Retirement.*

However, it really isn't necessary to go for *pensionado* status unless you plan on living in Costa Rica full time. Many foreigners prefer not to apply for residency. They renew their three-month tourist visas every three months by traveling across the border into Nicaragua or Panama for a seventy-two-hour visit in an inexpensive hotel. Then they are eligible for another three-month stay in Costa Rica. Technically, they are only supposed to do this once in a six-month period; however, the government is very lenient with this situation. There's always the chance that they might become strict and insist on residency for full-time residents. You can keep in touch with latest developments on Costa Rica by checking my Costa Rica Web site at www.discoverypress.com/update and/or checking my Choose Costa Rica Bulletin Board at www.discoverypress.com/CostaRica.

Costa Rica's expatriate community is an interesting mixture of those who came here to retire and those who want to be in business. Expatriates are generally younger than those in traditional communities in foreign nations. The younger people like it because there are almost no restrictions about owning a business or buying and selling properties. Even with a tourist visa, one can own property and operate a business. Without a resident visa, you aren't supposed to actually perform work in your business, but you can manage it.

My friends claim that I tend to be uncritical about places I like, stressing the upbeat and minimizing the downbeat. So be aware that Costa Rica, like the other foreign countries mentioned in this chapter, is a Third-World nation. Bureaucracy is maddening, roads are not up to our standards, and servants tend to have a mañana attitude. And there is crime. (Is there anywhere in the world that's crime-free?) But the quality of crime is different from that back home. Outright robberies and violent crimes are so rare that they make headlines in Costa Rica. Petty theft is the common problem, with things being taken from unlocked cars and pickpockets on crowded streets. Most retirees in Costa Rica will tell you that overall personal safety is as high as, or higher than, in their hometowns up north.

Getting to Costa Rica can be quick and expensive by airplane, or slow and inexpensive by bus or automobile. My wife and I have traveled all three ways. When we have the time, we enjoy the drive, and the bus trip is fun, too. Our last drive took a month as we visited friends in Mexico and Guatemala along the way. We did lots of sightseeing, taking in Mayan ruins and wonderful beach resorts; it was a monthlong vacation. Buses are exceptionally inexpensive, with deluxe buses zipping through Mexico, complete with movies and "flight attendants" serving drinks and meals.

Panama

Panama is attracting a great deal of interest from those looking for a foreign country for a new beginning. A long and narrow country, Panama is located between Costa Rica and the South American country of Colombia. It's shaped like a long, lazy S that is only 50 miles wide at its narrowest point. It's possible to swim in the Pacific and the Caribbean in the same day and be home in time for dinner. Panama's population is around three million, with two-thirds of *mestizo* descent, in addition to a swelling population of American retirees and those doing business here.

Panama's government is a constitutional democracy, and like Costa Rica Panama has abolished its military. Panama City is the country's commercial and economic center, ultramodern and well-kept, bustling with commerce and elegant residential neighborhoods.

Why Panama? Like Costa Rica, a choice of tropical or temperate climates, affordable real estate, and a government and people who welcome foreign expatriates. Americans are not new to Panama; some expat families date back almost a hundred years, to the era of the construction of the Panama Canal. The country's infrastructure shows the investments the United States made over the years in the form of wonderful highways and electrical networks. Like Costa Rica, Panama's government has a reputation for being friendly and welcoming. Panama's North American expatriate community is always ready to welcome newcomers.

Basically, the country is divided into three general zones. A highland area of cool mountain communities, where many people have fireplaces for evening comfort, contrasts with warm tropical regions where air-conditioning is a must. Another zone is tropical beaches, mostly on the Pacific, where palm trees and surf are the attraction. The third zone is known as Bocas del Torro, which is a collection of islands on the Caribbean side of the country.

Another attraction that Panamanian expatriates like to point out: The cost of living is lower than in Costa Rica. Real estate prices have been on the increase, but as yet haven't matched some of Costa Rica's more expensive areas. Full-time servants are the norm here. A housekeeper and a gardener are considered essential household budget items for most middle-income lifestyles. A maid earns about $150 a month, a gardener about the same.

To become a legal Panamanian resident, the government requires evidence of $600 monthly income for a couple to qualify for a visa. But a longtime North American resident of Panama argues, "You certainly cannot live *well* on that amount. You would have to learn to like rice and beans. Most folks are more comfortable with a budget of $1,500 to $2,000 per month." You can also go into business in Panama, but it requires a little more red tape than in Costa Rica. For example, you need to have a special business visa, you may be required to employ a certain number of workers, and there may be some other red-tape requirements.

At this writing, retirees moving to Panama haven't spawned a frenzied immigration rush, but the trend is gaining momentum. In 2005 the government granted nearly twice as many retiree visas as in the previous year. A large number of retirees live in Panama seasonally, preferring to spend the best seasons of the year in the United States or Canada, then escape harsh weather by returning to their second homes in Panama. This can be done on a tourist visa. Even as tourists, foreigners can own property in Panama with the same ownership rights as Panamanian citizens.

As is the case in most of Central America—because of Panama's nearness to the equator—year-round temperatures remain constant. Two seasons are recognized: winter and summer, each characterized by the amount of rainfall, not by the thermometer. People think in reverse of our seasons: *Summer* is the dry season, which is from the middle of December to the beginning of April. *Winter* is the rainy season, all of the other months. This doesn't mean constant rain, just showers interspersed with sunshine. Newcomers often complain about strong winds that can blow during the dry sunshine months. This is common to most of Central America, and residents become accustomed to it. One of the benefits of living in Panama and Costa Rica is that both countries are out of the hurricane corridor that ravages countries from Nicaragua north to the Carolinas and even to Boston.

The cool Chiriqui highlands on the Pacific slope of the Continental Divide would probably be our choice were we to move to Panama. Volcán Baru, Panama's highest peak (11,412 feet), towers over all and is visible from the Costa Rican border. Boquete is the largest town in the region (pop. 18,000). With an almost European look, Boquete is about a forty-minute drive from David, the nearest city. Because of the 4,300-foot altitude, there's a cool year-round climate where temperatures rarely get above 79 degrees. Yes, this is in the tropics! Some folks sleep under blankets year-round!

Bocas del Toro is situated among a picturesque archipelago on the northwest coast of Panama. After the Panama Canal, this is probably the country's most popular tourist destination. Many, but not all, of the islands are inhabited, with miles of sandy beaches lined with coconut trees, and coral reefs for snorkeling and diving. The islands' rain forest hosts troops of monkeys as well as endangered red frogs.

Nicaragua

This is the third Central American country that we consider to be a viable candidate for North American retirement living. There aren't nearly the number of North Americans living here, but the interest is picking up. One drawback to expatriate living in Nicaragua is the overwhelming poverty here. The country suffered through several years of civil war between the left-wing Sandinistas and the right-wing remnants of the Somoza government that was overthrown by the Sandinistas. This, combined with corrupt politicians who drain the public treasury of funds, keeps the country one of the poorest in the hemisphere. Despite the

United States's role in supporting the rebels and keeping the war going for years, the Nicaraguan people don't appear to harbor any resentment. They are very welcoming to newcomers.

However, one result of the economic system is that real estate, wages, and cost of living are truly low. At this point, tourism is just beginning to take off, so it might be the time to invest in beach property or in one of the few inland towns where tourist facilities are becoming successful. House-hold servants are employed by just about all North American expats.

We can recommend two Nicaraguan places. One is the small city of Granada. A historic site located on the shore of a large lake, Granada used to be the place where oceangoing ships from eastern U.S. ports docked during the 1849 gold rush days. Passengers would disembark here and travel another 10 miles to the Pacific, where they would take another ship headed for California. In addition to being picturesque, Granada has the largest North American expatriate community. Compared with Costa Rica and Panama, Granada's expat population isn't very large, but it's growing.

The other place where there are expats in residence is San Juan Sur, a growing beach community. The beachfront is dotted with restaurants, small hotels, cabinas, and beach houses for foreign residents. At present, the tourism is not very high, but again, this increases every year.

Join the Peace Corps!

For foreign living on a budget, here's the best option of all: Join the Peace Corps! It isn't as crazy as it might seem at first glance. The Peace Corps actively seeks out mature citizens, even retirees who have much to con-tribute. You're never too old to serve in the Peace Corps. Volunteers must be at least eighteen years old, but there is no upper age limit. The oldest Peace Corps volunteer ever was eighty-six when he completed his service.

For the first time in their lives, many newly retired find themselves without commitments to a career or family, so they find fulfillment and excitement in helping others. In addition, they're getting paid for it! They're having the time of their lives and at the same time are participat-ing in programs that affect literacy, health, and hunger and help promote world peace and friendship. Retired singles and couples have put their expertise to work in Africa, Asia, South America, Central America, and the Pacific Islands.

About ten years ago our friend, John Dwyer—who was a publishers' representative—surprised all of us by joining the Peace Corps when he was approaching retirement age. I happened to be working in Guatemala while he was taking his training in a little mountain village above the town of Antigua. I envied his new life and wished I could do the same. I was honored to attend his graduation ceremony. John was the only gray-haired graduate among a class of twenty-something volunteers. The following is his story, in his own words.

"Joining the Peace Corps in 1991 at fifty-six years of age changed my life in a very positive way. I always had an interest in international affairs and cultures. My army service in Japan was my first immersion in a foreign culture. I found it enchanting and wanted to travel more. Life interfered. Time passed, I got married, raised a family, and thought my dreams of international travel would go unfulfilled. A chance conversation with a friend of my son changed those thoughts. The friend had just returned from Peace Corps service in Jamaica and was relating his experiences to me. I was curious. He told me that he had served with volunteers of my age and encouraged me to apply. My international ambitions returned. I contacted the Peace Corps, applied, and a year and a half later was on my way to Guatemala to train as a Small Enterprise Development volunteer. After training I was posted to a bustling agricultural center in the arid 'Oriente' of the country.

"Life was exciting. I made wonderful friends of both the hospitable Guatemalans and my fellow volunteers—most recent college graduates. These friendships have endured to this day. I must say that not all of my personal experience was exciting. Peace Corps is a government agency, and there is a certain amount of bureaucracy. However, the understanding one gains from immersion in another culture is priceless. The impact of my Peace Corps service has led to journeys that only dreams are made of.

"In 1996 the Peace Corps—working with the United Nations—was recruiting volunteers to work in the first post-war election in Bosnia-

Herzegovina. I hesitantly volunteered. Since that first, reluctantly taken international election assignment, I have worked, in different capacities and for different organizations, on ten international election missions. My election work has taken me to Bosnia, Republika Srpska, Serbia-Montenegro, Croatia, Macedonia, Albania, Russia, and Ukraine. I participated in the implementation of two post-war elections in Kosovo. My work in the Balkans led me to Afghanistan. There I managed camps of internally displaced persons (IDPs) in Herat and did development work in Kandahar. All of it interesting, rewarding, and exciting work.

"When I entered the Peace Corps, I had traveled to four countries; I have now traveled to thirty-five and am currently awaiting further assignments. All of these fulfilling experiences have occurred since my fifty-eighth birthday—and all of them occurred as a result of my Peace Corps experience."

Most Peace Corps assignments require a four-year college degree; however, if you don't have a college education, you can still qualify by having three to five years of work experience in a needed specialty such as a skilled trade or business management. When evaluating your application, the Peace Corps considers the "whole person," looking at your life experiences, community involvement, volunteer work, motivations, and even your hobbies. It's possible for married couples to qualify as volunteers, both working and living in the same community. In fact, about 10 percent of Peace Corps volunteers are married. Peace Corps recruiters can help you evaluate the skills and experiences needed to qualify for a foreign assignment.

Do you need to speak another language to get into the Peace Corps? Not at all. During your training period, you'll receive intensive language instruction to prepare you for living and working in your foreign community. Some countries prefer volunteers who have mastered the native language, such as French or Spanish, but it is not often a requirement. The Peace Corps is prepared to teach more than 180 languages and dialects.

Peace Corps volunteers receive living expenses and a monthly stipend to cover incidental needs, so there is no need for them to spend savings or other income. At the conclusion of your volunteer service, you will receive a "readjustment allowance" of $225 for each month of service. Therefore, if you complete your full term of service, you will receive $6,075 tax free. This severance pay comes in handy for making a transition back into life at home. The compensation you receive from the Peace Corps doesn't affect your Social Security earnings. Because all expenses are paid, many older Peace Corps volunteers bank their entire Social Security, pension, and interest income during their two-year tour of duty.

The Peace Corps provides two vacation days for every month of service. That's twenty-four days a year that you can use to travel home for a visit or entertain family and friends who come to see you. Most volunteers use their vacation time to visit other countries in the region and learn about other countries' people, cultures, and traditions. The cost of your vacation travel is your responsibility, but once you are there, you can travel inexpensively, traveling like a native rather than a tourist.

At the end of your tour of duty, you qualify for career, education, and other advice and assistance through the Peace Corps' Office of Returned Volunteer Services (RVS) and its Career Center in Washington, D.C. RVS publishes a bimonthly job bulletin and career manuals, provides self-assessment tools to help returned volunteers explore career options, and facilitates career-planning activities.

Here is a terrific opportunity to make a contribution to world peace, utilize your life's experience helping others, and have the time of your life. Be aware that there are always more applications than openings, so getting a position in the Peace Corps isn't a slam dunk. But you just might have the skills and experience that are needed.

Your regional recruiting office is the best place to get more information about your suitability for Peace Corps volunteer positions. Also, many recruiters were volunteers themselves, so they can explain firsthand what it's like to be in the Peace Corps. For information or an application, write to Peace Corps, Room P-301, Washington, DC 20526; or call (800) 424–8580. By going online to www.peacecorps.gov, you can get complete information about the Peace Corps, download an application, apply for a passport, and everything you need to join.

chapter fifteen

Choosing Your Hometown

Eventually you'll have to start narrowing your choices of possible places for relocation. The affordability of the type of housing you'll need and the cost of living in your new hometown will be important. Another important consideration to keep in mind when sizing up an inexpensive community: a possible lack of community services for retirees. Towns where population and tax money are dwindling sometimes have few funds left over for retirement centers and other amenities for retirees. If you're going to have to work—at least part time—your decisions will be different than if you are going to be fully retired. After all, that small town by a wonderful bass lake might be an ideal place for relocation, yet the chances of finding a job utilizing your special skills might be slim to none. Unless, of course, you specialize in mowing lawns or pumping gasoline.

Golf Course Communities

Don't assume that those "golf course" communities are exclusively for golfers. Statistics show that in some localities, far less than 50 percent of the residents actually play golf. Many choose to live there because of the plush surroundings and the secure feeling of a gated community. The clubhouse is the community social center, with dinners, dances, and other regularly scheduled events.

Job Training

Often a town will have a community college that offers classes in retraining, learning various trades, or entry-level professional training. This gives you a chance to brush up on job skills or even learn a new trade. Many schools offer practical courses you can use when starting a home business. For example, you can learn dog grooming, income tax preparation, and receive child-care certification. You might want to attend school in your current hometown before relocation.

If you will need a job, even part time, you might try to find one before you start making decisions on where to relocate. You know better than anyone where job opportunities in your line of work might be found and how to apply for them. If you can use an employment agency or "head-hunter," or if you can send out a résumé, so much the better. But sometimes the only way is to apply in person, particularly because many companies don't bother to advertise new or vacant positions; they depend on employees to take over a new position or else to recommend friends. That would mean traveling to various prospective job locations.

Traveling to several towns to interview for job possibilities gives you the opportunity to scope out the place as a potential hometown. By the way, some or possibly all of your job search expenses can be tax-deductible. Legitimate expenses are such items as meals, transportation, mileage (at 36.5 cents per mile), parking expense, tolls, hotels, and so forth. Keep detailed records of all expenditures, and check it out with a tax preparer.

Finding Reasonable Housing

It's no secret that housing prices in some parts of the country have risen to the height where they've become impossible to consider for economical retirement or relocation. This may be one of the reasons you've decided to leave your hometown. I have to admit that I just cannot adjust my mind to the selling prices of homes in some U.S. markets. Remember when a million bucks was a fortune? In many communities today, a millionaire is someone who owns a slightly above-average home. In the California town where my wife and I live—on the central California coast—home prices have risen so steeply we are shocked. Seems like every year, it's another 14 percent increase in prices. If we hadn't bought thirty years ago, there is no way we could pay, or *would* pay, today's prices.

To solve the housing crisis, our local government has contracted to build "affordable housing units" to accommodate low-income families. The price of an ordinary, "affordable" home will begin at $400,000. (No, that isn't $400,000 per city block. That's per low-cost house!) Well, compared with a median sales price of about $800,000 in an ordinary neighborhood, I suppose that is affordable.

The point is, real estate prices haven't exploded *everywhere*. Many parts of the country, even in California, have seen modest changes in the economy other than inflation connected with the price of gasoline and utilities. Housing has gone up everywhere, of course, but not to the extreme it has in other regions. The following chart illustrates differences between towns in the same state.

The first pair: college towns in California. Notice the average cost of homes and rentals. Remember that these are average prices, which means as many as half of the homes are selling for much-below-average prices. In Chico, for example, I found several homes listed between $85,000 and $99,000. The rents are figured on calculations by HUD in determining fair market rents when subsidizing housing.

CALIFORNIA COLLEGE TOWNS

Chico, California	City	County	California Avg.
Average Home Price	$180,559	$160,263	$304,168
Median Rental Price	$493	$426	$563
San José, California	City	County	California Avg.
Average Home Price	$490,490	$551,084	$304,168
Median Rental Price	$996	$1,064	$563

Next is a comparison of selling prices and rental costs between two Phoenix, Arizona, suburbs. Scottsdale, of course, is one of the more upscale communities in the region. Again, these are *average* prices, which include some of the million-dollar places as well as the budget-priced homes. You'll have no problem finding homes priced well below average.

ARIZONA, PHOENIX AREA

Glendale, Arizona	City	County	Arizona Avg.
Average Home Price	$150,384	$171,061	$167,791
Median Rental Price	$601	$548	$425
Scottsdale, Arizona	City	County	Arizona Avg.
Average Home Price	$306,378	$181,031	$167,791
Median Rental Price	$691	$548	$425

(Statistics from HomeGain, 2005; Web site: www.homegain.com)

Florida is the most popular state for retirement in the nation. Yet even the average price of homes are way under national average. As you can see, even upscale Boca Raton isn't as super-expensive as one might imagine, at least in comparison with states such as California.

SMALL FLORIDA CITIES

Ocala, Florida	City	County	Florida Avg.
Average Home Price	$110,341	$108,064	$156,148
Median Rental Price	$434	$372	$462
Boca Raton, Florida	City	County	Florida Avg.
Average Home Price	$285,213	$205,673	$156,148
Median Rental Price	$802	$686	$462

Towns with Below-Average Living Costs

Below are some of the more inexpensive places in the country. As you can see, the below-average price of housing has a lot to do with low living costs. Utilities and health care are also important. Note the below-average cost of medical care in these towns. A caveat is that small towns are not always famous for high-tech hospital care. Often the local hospital is best described as an emergency clinic.

These towns are listed as random examples only. Although we've visited most of these towns and have written about some of them, we cannot vouch for all of them. Some are excellent places for a new beginning, others are okay, and some can be politely described as "provincial." Some might be ideal for witness protection programs.

TOWNS WITH BELOW-AVERAGE LIVING COSTS*

Town	Cost of Living	Housing	Health Care
McAlester, OK	81.0%	73.4%	89.7%
Cookeville, TN	84.9	74.9	106.4
McAllen, TX	85.3	74.8	100.0
Clarksville, TN	86.2	74.9	91.8
Fort Smith, AR	86.4	73.5	97.8
Lubbock, TX	86.7	77.0	99.8
Hot Springs, AR	87.1	76.7	86.3
Murray, KY	87.1	74.9	81.1
Tupelo, MS	87.1	71.4	85.8
Harlingen, TX	87.3	78.3	96.5
Kingsport, TN	87.9	77.5	98.4
Knoxville, TN	88.4	77.4	90.0
Springfield, MO	88.7	76.9	91.5
Corpus Christi, TX	89.0	81.9	90.1
Bowling Green, KY	89.7	79.0	83.0
Muskogee, OK	89.8	79.8	95.5
Dothan, AL	90.0	76.9	81.4

(continued)

TOWNS WITH BELOW-AVERAGE LIVING COSTS*			(continued)
Town	Cost of Living	Housing	Health Care
Cedar City, UT	90.2	73.3	85.3
Ashland, OH	90.6	73.5	93.3
Pocatello, ID	90.7	77.5	95.8
Pueblo, CO	90.7	81.9	95.3
Winston-Salem, NC	91.0	82.1	100.3

* Percentages based on the national average cost of living.

Towns with Above-Average Living Costs

Listed below are some more expensive places. With higher-priced real estate and medical care, it should be obvious that the higher priced places on this list would be out of the question for most people thinking of budget retirement. But folks who live there, who already have housing they bought years ago before the market went crazy, find a comfortable living situation. Many food and miscellaneous items such as clothing and gasoline aren't priced too much above other places. If you can find an affordable place to rent or buy (yes, bargains can usually be found anywhere), your budget won't necessarily be pushed out of shape.

TOWNS WITH ABOVE-AVERAGE COST OF LIVING*			
Town	Cost of Living	Housing	Health Care
Asheville, NC	101.7%	113.8%	97.1%
Cape Coral, FL	102.1	106.0	106.9
Albuquerque, NM	103.2	107.8	96.7
Lake Havasu City, AZ	105.4	109.7	102.9
Bakersfield, CA	106.2	98.9	99.0
Eugene, OR	109.5	120.2	111.9
Las Vegas, NV	110.2	124.4	110.0
West Palm Beach, FL	110.4	120.4	102.8
Chapel Hill, NC	113.9	128.7	95.5

Town	Cost of Living	Housing	Health Care
Santa Fe, NM	114.2	138.8	100.5
Burlington, VT	115.6	129.7	106.5
Glenwood Springs, CO	119.2	136.9	111.5
Hartford, CT	120.9	141.5	117.9
Prince William, VA	122.9	160.4	106.0
Providence, RI	127.8	168.2	107.6
Boston, MA	136.8	179.6	129.2
Washington, DC-VA	138.3	205.8	120.6
Bergen-Passaic, NJ	139.6	200.4	109.5
Framingham, MA	141.1	200.3	117.3
Stamford, CT	152.4	240.6	119.1
Los Angeles, CA	153.0	245.2	114.0

* Percentages based on the national average cost of living.

chapter sixteen

Retirement Recommendations

When our editor first suggested that we list our favorite economical retirement locations, it sounded like an easy task. After all, my wife and I have visited and inspected many, many parts of the country in the course of our research travels. However, when we sat down to compile our list, we discovered that we had to choose from a list of almost 300 places we had visited over the past fifteen years of retirement explorations.

We find it next to impossible to choose just a few favorites. We would miss too many desirable retirement havens by restricting our list to specific towns or cities. Furthermore, space in this book doesn't allow detailed analysis of our recommended communities. In my book

Northern and Southern Summers

A common misconception is that the Southern summers are horribly hot and steamy. The following chart compares Southern summers with Northern summers. Notice there isn't a whole lot of difference in temperatures or humidity, except that Southen states have shorter and less frigid winters. Compare the number of days over 90°F with the number of days below freezing in this table. The truth is, the South is horribly hot and steamy in the summer, just as the North is horribly hot and steamy. Okay?

Where to Retire (Globe Pequot, 2006), you'll find further details on each community mentioned here as well as many others.

You will notice that the states and communities listed in this book generally enjoy milder winters and that we tend to emphasize locations in the South or Southwest for economical retirement. Some of the Southern communities mentioned are among the most economical in the nation for real estate, rentals, heating costs, and general cost of living.

CLIMATE OF SELECTED NORTHERN AND SOUTHERN CITIES

City, State	Average Humidity	Days over 90°F	Days under 32°F	July Avg. High (°F)	July Avg. Low (°F)
Atlanta, GA	70	19	59	86°	69°
Birmingham, AL	72	39	60	88°	70°
Clarksville, TN	71	37	75	90°	69°
Memphis, TN	69	64	59	88°	72°
Raleigh, NC	71	25	82	88°	67°
Kansas City, MO	69	40	106	83°	69°
Wichita, KS	66	62	114	87°	70°
St. Louis, MO	70	37	107	85°	69°
Chicago, IL	67	21	119	79°	63°
Philadelphia, PA	67	19	101	86°	67°

Southern States

We fully realize that Southern states suffer unfavorable press over the years, leaving a negative impression on those who are not familiar with the South. People from other parts of the country might wonder whether they would be welcomed as neighbors. It's true that most Southern communities are politically and socially conservative, but "Southern hospitality" is still the tradition in all but the most backward and remote communities. Having said that, I need to add that I hesitate recommending Southern retirement in rural farm communities, especially to folks with non-Southern big-city backgrounds.

When you have little in common with your neighbors, it's easy to feel left out and lonely. When most neighbors are in some way involved in agriculture, ordinary conversations tend to dwell on the price of soybeans or the best way to deworm hogs. When your agricultural experience is limited to watering houseplants, you find you have few words of wisdom others care to hear. When your accent sounds funny to your neighbors and when your tastes in movies, politics, and food are different (or when you don't even own a pickup), you could feel like an alien.

However, if there is already a population of outsiders, or "Yankee," in place, you'll probably fit in just fine. Most of the places we liked in the South and that we recommend are places where out-of-state people have retired and love it. After doing considerable research on small cities and towns in the Southern and Mid-Southern states, we quickly changed our opinions about living in the South. Politics aside, we found some of the most desirable and welcoming communities in Southern states.

We personally feel that the communities presented here would satisfy *our* retirement needs, but that doesn't necessarily mean they would be suitable for *you*. I can't stress too much the need to investigate for yourself not only the cost of living in your new hometown but also the friendliness and sincerity of your new neighbors. Just because a place has a low cost of living doesn't mean you'll be happy living there. It probably would seem obvious, but except for an occasional large Southern city such as Atlanta, you probably won't want to be looking for jobs. Pay is notoriously low in the South.

Alabama

One of the states most active in retiree recruitment, Alabama has dozens of small cities and towns with active Retirement Advantage committees to recruit retirees. For detailed information about these communities, call (800) 235–4757 or check out wwww.alabamaadvantage.com. You'll receive the state's retirement magazine as well as information about the towns that are awaiting your visit. One of the advantages to relocating here is extremely low property tax rates. In the towns we researched, taxes on a home worth $90,000 were typically less than $500 a year. And $90,000 will buy you a lot of house in Alabama.

The countryside varies from the Appalachian Mountains in the northeast to rolling farmlands in the center and wire grass flatlands in the southern part of the state. The weather is typically southern, with mild winters and hot summers. Ozark and Enterprise, located in the southeastern part of the state, are exceptionally friendly and welcoming to retirees. Quality real estate is affordable, with plenty of rentals available in Enterprise, and high-quality homes in Ozark listed at almost giveaway prices. Florida's beaches are only a ninety-minute drive away. There's a cosmopolitan makeup to the local citizenry; folks come from all over the country, not just the Deep South. A large percentage of new retirees are ex-military.

TYPICAL ALABAMA WEATHER—MONTGOMERY

Temp. (F°)	Jan.	April	July	Oct.	Rain	Snow
Daily Highs	57	77	92	78	49"	0"
Daily Lows	36	53	72	53		

Right on the beach, the communities of Gulf Shores and Orange Beach offer great saltwater recreation in Alabama's only beachfront communities. Be aware that this area took it on the chin during the last two hurricane seasons, and devastation was severe. They are currently rebuilding, and by the time this book is off the press, it may be livable again. Among the dozens of places in Alabama trying hard to convince you to join the community are Jasper, Mentone, Anniston, Gadsen, and Scottsboro. These all feature very low cost of living and real estate at 1990s prices. But understand these areas are not for job hunters—well-paying jobs, or jobs of any description, would not be part of the package.

Florida

Florida has always been the darling of East Coast retirees. Although it is losing some of its magic because of hurricanes, the state still draws more retirees than any other state in the Union. Around a thousand people a day move here. Those who think Florida is expensive may have a surprise coming. We feel that the state offers some of the best retirement bargains, dollar for dollar and feature for feature, in the country, as well as some of the most expensive real estate going. Yet not far from the high-price spreads, you'll almost always find working-class neighborhoods where real estate and rents are reasonable.

The state's climate ranges from exceptionally mild to semitropical. While midday temperatures in the summer, heavy with humidity, can be oppressive, outdoor activity in early mornings and evenings is the preferred mode of exercise. Some of the interior regions of Florida are very reminiscent of the Midwest in looks and price.

TYPICAL FLORIDA WEATHER—DAYTONA BEACH

Temp. (F°)	Jan.	April	July	Oct.	Rain	Snow
Daily Highs	68	80	90	81	48"	—
Daily Lows	47	59	73	65		

Daytona Beach is on the peninsula's Atlantic side, and although not exactly inexpensive, you'll find less-costly communities just a short drive away. Daytona's 23-mile-long white sand beach is perhaps its most famous feature, and it's one of the few places in Florida where autos are permitted to drive along the shore. Besides good beaches and pleasant winters, excellent senior-citizen services add to the value of retirement here.

On the northern Gulf beaches, you'll find affordable communities like Panama City and Fort Walton Beach, but tourism runs up the cost of living. Around Pensacola you'll find a selection of towns ranging from ordinary to almost luxurious. The state's western beaches have a string of towns that are rather expensive, yet with pockets of affordable housing tucked away here and there. Some of these communities were hit by hurricanes in the 2005 season, but they came back quickly.

Inland Florida quickly becomes rural once you get away from the metropolitan districts. Places like Ocala, Destin, Leesville, and other small cities have homes, farms, and acreage priced less than you might expect. This is our favorite area. A short drive east or west takes you to either the Atlantic or the Gulf. Also, just east of the Tampa–St. Petersburg area is a semirural area where very affordable real estate and inexpensive mobile-home living make for true shoestring retirement. Mobile-home living here is the least expensive mode of Florida retirement.

Georgia

Georgia can be divided into three regions for retirement: the Atlantic Coast, often called the Colonial Coast; the northeastern part of the state, in the foothills of the Appalachians; and the central area around Atlanta. Atlanta, of course, is where the job market is for those who plan on working at least part time. The state is full of small towns suitable for retirement, but whether many out-of-state retirees move there is another question. So far, the state of Georgia hasn't become deeply involved in retirement recruitment, although there is some activity at the local chamber of commerce level.

Long a favorite with retirees looking for inexpensive places to live, Georgia's northeast corner has suffered from too much popularity; the cost of housing has increased quite a bit in the last ten years. Rabun County is the perennial favorite, a collection of tiny villages, Clayton being the largest. Nearby Habersham County is the second most popular place for retirement, with Clarkesville and Dahlonga the largest communities. A good number of out-of-state immigrants have bought homes here. Again, this would not be a place to find part-time work.

TYPICAL GEORGIA WEATHER—ATHENS						
Temp. (F°)	Jan.	April	July	Oct.	Rain	Snow
Daily Highs	52	74	89	74	50"	3"
Daily Lows	33	50	69	51		

The Colonial Coast is a collection of exceptionally expensive places as well as some rather moderately priced communities. Jekel Island, Skidmore Island, and parts of Savannah are far out of reach for a restricted budget. But the mainland city of Brunswick is just a short drive from the spiffy island places and abounds in affordable places for rent or sale. Other communities offer similar real estate bargains.

Kentucky

Kentucky has any number of low-cost places to retire. Finding the most appropriate small towns may take some investigating, however. As in many small Southern towns, you could feel a bit out of place if you are the only "outsiders" in the community. Exceptions will be found wherever there are retirement committees, but there are few such programs in the state. You'll need to look carefully if you are "furriner."

For retirement anywhere, it's hard to beat a college town. Bowling Green, Murray, and Danville are three Kentucky university locations we've investigated. You're always sure to find kindred spirits who've moved from other states because of the school and attendant benefits. Of the three towns, only Bowling Green is "wet," where you can order wine with a meal. Somerset, toward the lower section of Kentucky, is another place becoming popular with retirees.

TYPICAL KENTUCKY WEATHER—LEXINGTON

Temp. (F°)	Jan.	April	July	Oct.	Rain	Snow
Daily Highs	40	66	86	68	46"	16"
Daily Lows	23	44	66	46		

Louisiana

A fascinating mélange of historical and cultural ingredients, Louisiana is becoming interested in attracting retirees. Not long ago we discovered the historic town of Natchitoches, one of the oldest towns west of the Mississippi and famous for its stately homes dating from the 1700s. This is also a university town that attracts retirees from all parts of the country. Natchitoches has a low cost of living and friendly residents. The movie *Steel Magnolias* was made here using local residents, scenery, and homes. Nearby is the Toledo Bend Lake area and towns such as Leesville and DeRidder, which have very active retirement committees.

TYPICAL LOUISIANA WEATHER—BATON ROUGE

Temp. (F°)	Jan.	April	July	Oct.	Rain	Snow
Daily Highs	61	79	91	80	56"	—
Daily Lows	41	58	73	56		

West and south of Baton Rouge is "Cajun Country," the most famous part of Louisiana. At one time, Cajuns were noted for their closed society. They jealously maintained their French language and their private ways of living. Times have changed, however, thanks to television, modern transportation, and open communication. Retirees are welcome, and living is easy in this charming region. This area is for folks who like "country," who fit into a down-home atmosphere, and who relish crawfish gumbo. Popular towns are Houma, New Iberia, and Lafayette. New Orleans has never been on our "recommend list" and will not make the list for some time to come. (By the way, I was born in New Orleans.)

Mississippi

Mississippi's "Hometown" retirement program is the most vigorous and enthusiastic of all the retiree-attraction programs in the country. With twenty cities "certified" as excellent places to retire, there's a chance you'll find a place you like. As an added incentive for retirees, Mississippi recently passed legislation exempting all pensions from state income taxes. For a list of Mississippi's twenty certified retirement cities, write to Hometown Mississippi Retirement, P.O. Box 849, Jackson, MS 39205 or call (601) 359–5978; www.visitmississippi.org/retire.

One of our favorite towns in the state, Oxford is described in the chapter on College Town Retirement. Other towns worth investigating are Columbus, an old-style southern city, and Hattiesburg, a city of

49,000 people just ninety minutes from the gulf. The gulf area's Biloxi and Gulfport were always on the top of our list of Gulf of Mexico towns, but since the hurricanes of 2005, it may be awhile before they regain their place as desirable retirement locations. The other place in Mississippi that we consider appropriate for out-of-state retirement is Natchez. The entire town seems to be a museum of pre-Civil War mansions. Property was surprisingly reasonable at the time of our last visit. However, for those who are planning on working part time, Mississippi probably won't be on your potential list. Most other Mississippi towns that we've looked at seem to be rather "countrified."

TYPICAL MISSISSIPPI WEATHER—MERIDIAN

Temp. (F°)	Jan.	April	July	Oct.	Rain	Snow
Daily Highs	57	78	93	78	53"	5"
Daily Lows	34	51	70	50		

North Carolina

We're convinced that some of the most beautiful and scenic places in the world are found in the Blue Ridge and the Great Smoky Mountains. October, when leaves are turning, is a marvelous time for a visit. Hardwood trees display a full explosion of color, with brilliant reds, yellows, purples, lavenders, and all colors in between, while evergreens provide a conservative background of green. We've also made the rounds in the spring, when the dogwoods, azaleas, and mountain laurel trees are in full bloom.

This mountain region has been prime retirement country for more than a century. Places like Blowing Rock, Boone, Newland, and other gorgeous settings in the Great Smoky Mountains draw many retirees in search of milder summers and picturesque winters. Living costs here range from very low to very high, so shopping around is strongly recommended. Asheville was once on the list of affordable places to live, but popularity has taken its toll—with higher real estate prices.

Two things make North Carolina popular with people from the Northeastern part of the country: the fact that this is the least "Southern" of the states, and the presence of much high-tech industry and job potential. In the Raleigh-Durham area, the huge Research Triangle Park employs thousands of scientific and high-tech specialists.

TYPICAL NORTH CAROLINA WEATHER—ASHEVILLE

Temp. (F°)	Jan.	April	July	Oct.	Rain	Snow
Daily Highs	48	69	84	69	48"	17"
Daily Lows	26	43	62	43		

The Piedmont and coastal regions of North Carolina also have many reasonable places for retirement, but you'll have to look around. Because so many people are moving in from the North and Northeast, prices have skyrocketed in some towns.

South Carolina

Like North Carolina, South Carolina has a mountain region, a piedmont, and a coastal region. Charleston is South Carolina's jewel, but there are few inexpensive neighborhoods. But just west is Summerland, an old-fashioned hometown not far from glamorous Charleston. Farther north is the waterfront city of Georgetown, where antebellum homes are as common as bungalows. While not exactly priced for the restricted budget, they are relatively affordable.

TYPICAL SOUTH CAROLINA WEATHER—COLUMBIA

Temp. (F°)	Jan.	April	July	Oct.	Rain	Snow
Daily Highs	56	77	92	77	48"	2"
Daily Lows	33	51	70	50		

In the Piedmont region, Aiken is a lovely Deep South city where a mixture of Northern and Southern newcomers take full advantage of retirement opportunities. Aiken's robust business district makes it look larger than it actually is. It's the shopping and employment center for a large area. With a university shaping its ambience, the community ranks high in our view.

Tennessee

Tennessee is a popular state for retirement for those who don't want to go too far from their hometowns in the North or Northeast. Retirees can easily return for a visit whenever they please, and the grandkids can visit often. Resort developers are taking advantage of this market by building golf-course housing complexes.

TYPICAL TENNESSEE WEATHER—CLARKSVILLE

Temp. (F°)	Jan.	April	July	Oct.	Rain	Snow
Daily Highs	46	71	90	72	48"	11"
Daily Lows	28	48	69	48		

Because of the large military base nearby, Clarksville has become a popular retirement place for servicemen from all parts of the country. An exceptionally friendly population and reasonable costs are the pluses. Clarksville sits conveniently on an interstate highway that whisks you to the big city of Nashville in less than forty-five minutes. The nearby town of Dover is typical of a small Tennessee town, with very low living costs. Dover is becoming popular because of its proximity to the Land between the Lakes and its outdoor recreational opportunities.

Crossville sits in a rolling wooded and agricultural countryside, typical of many midsize towns in Tennessee and Kentucky. Nearby Fairfield Glen attracts retirees from Michigan, Ohio, and Indiana, but the prices are higher than in Crossville itself. Two golf-course communities nearby offer properties at relatively moderate prices.

Virginia–West Virginia

Earlier in the book we discussed special conditions whereby retirees find that an economic slowdown, such as a factory closing, an industry change, or a military base closing, pulls the floor from under the real estate market and causes the cost of living to drop dramatically. All too often, this occurs in places where you wouldn't care to visit much less live. Empty factory buildings, rotting fishing piers, mining dumps, or denuded forestlands don't exactly create an ideal retirement atmosphere, even though living is cheap. There has to be more.

Some areas of the Appalachian region of Virginia and West Virginia didn't suffer from the above ailments because they started out with a prosperous infrastructure in the first place. Before the economic decline, residents were highly paid union members, who had the wherewithal to build upscale homes. Now, because of an economic downturn, it is one of the most affordable regions you can find. This area, self-styled as "Four Seasons Country," has a number of delightful small towns that are great for retirement. The bonus is that an active retirement welcoming committee is eager for you to take up residence there.

TYPICAL VIRGINIA WEATHER—CHARLOTTESVILLE

Temp. (F°)	Jan.	April	July	Oct.	Rain	Snow
Daily Highs	47	71	88	71	44"	15"
Daily Lows	27	45	67	47		

Our favorite places here are the towns of Tazewell and Richlands in Virginia and the small city of Bluefield, which straddles the state line. Incidentally, Bluefield State College reaches out to the community with its Creative Retirement Center. On the West Virginia side are Princeton and Beckley, two lovely towns with plenty of low-cost housing. Two remarkably charming towns in West Virginia are Fayetteville, in a wooded valley to the north, and Lewisburg, a colonial town toward the eastern portion of the state. Homes built in the 1700s are not uncommon here, and quality homes on large parcels of land are absolutely affordable. For information about this region, contact the Creative Retirement Center, P.O. Box 4088, Bluefield, WV 24701; (800) 221–3206; info@mccvb.com; www.retirewv.org.

Arkansas, Missouri, Oklahoma, Texas

The states of Arkansas, Oklahoma, and Texas have some interesting and economical places for retirement. The Ozark Mountains are the centerpiece of recreational and scenic values in western Arkansas and eastern Oklahoma. Texas has few mountains except in the western part, but it has lots of Gulf of Mexico beaches for recreation.

Wages and prices in general are low, especially in smaller towns, so the cost of living is favorable. Most locations enjoy a true four-season climate, with occasional light snows in the winter and delightful fall and spring seasons. Summers, of course, are similar to those in the Southern states. Texas has a more varied climate, with milder winters near the Gulf and a drier climate the farther west you travel.

Arkansas

Because it's not far from large population centers such as St. Louis, Kansas City, and Chicago, Arkansas has been drawing many retirees from those locations. The four-season climate features fairly mild winters, combined with Ozark Mountain scenery in the northwestern third of the state. Most Arkansas towns are "dry," except in some of the more populous areas.

TYPICAL ARKANSAS WEATHER—LITTLE ROCK

Temp. (F°)	Jan.	April	July	Oct.	Rain	Snow
Daily Highs	50	74	93	76	49"	5"
Daily Lows	30	51	71	50		

We recently discovered the town of Mena in the Ouachita Mountains, an offshoot of the Ozarks. The local retirement committee has several enthusiastic volunteers who've moved here from far northern locales. Housing is very reasonable, and personal safety is exceptionally high. Not far away is the college town of Fayetteville.

Bull Shoals, Mountain Home, and Lakeview are lakeside communities offering real estate bargains and reasonable living costs. Added attractions are friendly neighbors, good fishing, and lovely scenery. Traditional retirement areas like California and Florida are losing retirees, who move here to take advantage of an exceptionally low crime rate and gorgeous scenery. About 60 miles north of Little Rock, Heber Springs and Greers

Ferry draw many retirees who love fishing. The towns overlook a 40,000-acre lake with 300 miles of wooded shoreline and waters overrun with bass, stripers, walleye, catfish, and lunker-size trout. The Hot Springs area is another popular retirement locale.

Missouri

Those wonderful amenities found in popular retirement places such as California or Florida are making them unaffordable for many young families and those getting ready for retirement. Some are heading to fast-growing cities like Las Vegas or Seattle, where real estate isn't as expensive and there is a possibility of finding a good job. Some people, who don't necessarily need employment, are turning their attention to less-glamorous destinations, like small-town Missouri.

TYPICAL MISSOURI WEATHER—BRANSON

Temp. (F°)	Jan.	April	July	Oct.	Rain	Snow
Daily Highs	48	74	94	76	40"	7"
Daily Lows	27	49	71	49		

We recently interviewed a couple from the Los Angeles area who sold their home for $375,000 with a nice profit but couldn't find another home they liked for under $450,000. After looking around the country for another hometown, they discovered Branson, Missouri, a place with plenty of entertainment and recreation on an Ozark lake. They bought an even larger home—three bedrooms, three baths—for $99,000. Had they chosen some smaller and less well-known town, they could have duplicated their buy for $70,000.

Many of Missouri's small towns might be too "countrified" for your taste. Check around to see whether out-of-state people are relocating there also. Just because you can buy a nice home for under $60,000 doesn't make the location a wonderful place to retire.

Oklahoma

Some very pleasant and scenic retirement locations bring people from all over the country to enjoy economical retirement. However, Oklahoma also has some rather dreary-looking places. You'll do well to stick with the prettier places because that's where the out-of-state retirees congregate. Being the only "outsider" in a small town in Oklahoma could be a downer for those used to more sophisticated settings.

Grand Lake o' the Cherokees/Tenkiller Lake is part of a large network of lakes on the fringes of the Ozark Mountains. Some of the nation's best real estate values are found here, tucked away among picturesque forests, Ozark hills, and unsophisticated small towns. The Grand Lake is large enough for good-sized sailboats and permits private boat docks.

TYPICAL OKLAHOMA WEATHER—TULSA

Temp. (F°)	Jan.	April	July	Oct.	Rain	Snow
Daily Highs	46	72	94	75	39"	9"
Daily Lows	25	50	72	50		

Not far away is Bartlesville, a city that has preserved Oklahoma hospitality and affordable living, yet is relatively cosmopolitan. Its affluence is due to the Phillips Petroleum company headquarters here. Folks seem to come from all parts of the nation to work, and eventually retire, here.

Texas

Austin and San Antonio are two of our Texas favorite spots for big-city relocations—if you like big cities. Fortunately, there are numerous small towns within easy commuting distance from either city. For part-time work, your chances are probably as good here as anywhere. Austin is one of the country's high-tech centers, and there's a certain amount of modern industry in San Antonio.

Texas has a long coastline on the Gulf of Mexico, and two of the more popular towns there, Corpus Christi and Galveston, suffer from split personalities. On the one hand, there are lots of seasonal tourists. On the other hand, there are the cities' full-time residents. The trick to retiring on a budget in Corpus or Galveston is finding a home away from the tourist crush. The payoff is a mild climate with great gulf fishing and endless beaches. Padre Island has several small communities that attract retirees, especially the half-year types.

TYPICAL TEXAS WEATHER—AUSTIN						
Temp. (F°)	Jan.	April	July	Oct.	Rain	Snow
Daily Highs	59	79	95	81	32"	1"
Daily Lows	39	58	74	59		

For those who can create a pleasant retirement lifestyle without having to work, there are several towns in the Texas Hill Country, scattered between San Antonio and around Austin. Among our favorites are Kerrville, Wimberly, and Georgetown, and they really aren't all that far away from large city conveniences.

Border towns with easy access to Mexico for shopping and cheap pharmaceuticals, such as Brownsville and El Paso, rank very low in cost of living. Modern American conveniences and old Mexican charm blend to give these places a distinctive character.

Along the Rio Grande Valley, small cities such as Harlingen and McAllen are the choice of countless part-time retirees. However, more and more retirees are making this region their permanent home. Those who can stand summer heat will find rock-bottom housing prices here. In addition to the sweet aroma of citrus blossoms in December, residents enjoy a particularly colorful Christmas because of the abundance of poinsettias throughout the area. The Mexican city of Reynosa sits across the river from McAllen and is a popular shopping destination.

Western/Southwestern States

The Southwest has much less rainfall and humidity than the rest of the country. While some regions are very dry and hot, especially in the summer, the very low humidity makes the air feel comfortable. In Las Vegas a temperature of 95°F is downright comfortable, whereas 95°F in Florida would make you a prisoner in your air-conditioned home.

Winters in most southwestern locations are very mild, often with typical daytime high temperatures higher than 70°F. While it can get chilly in the evening, things warm quickly as soon as the sun comes out. Except in the mountains, you rarely see snow in most southwestern communities, and even in the high elevations the snowfall is sparse. In fact, precipitation of any kind is scanty, ranging from as little as 3 inches of rain yearly in Yuma to as much as 21 inches in Flagstaff. Compare this with 52 inches of rain annually in Gainesville, Florida.

The truly hot summers in many southwest locations aren't something you can conveniently ignore; you'll need some kind of air-conditioning. The good news is that inexpensive "swamp coolers" do wonders because of the low humidity. Trying to use these contraptions back East would indeed turn your living room into a swamp before long.

Arizona

Arizona is a state with varied climates and landscapes. It includes some of the most expensive places to live in the entire region, such as Scottsdale and Carefree, as well as some of the most inexpensive, places like Bullhead City and Payson. The low-desert locations are exceptionally hot in the summer, yet pleasant in the winter. The higher mountain towns see snow in the winter but have delightful summers. Just about anywhere you choose to retire in Arizona will place you with neighbors who've moved here after retirement.

TYPICAL ARIZONA WEATHER—TUCSON

Temp. (F°)	Jan.	April	July	Oct.	Rain	Snow
Daily Highs	64	80	99	84	11"	1"
Daily Lows	38	50	74	57		

Ajo and Bisbee are two mining towns that drew bargain-hunting retirees when large mining corporations suddenly closed down operations, sending the towns into economic tailspins. Property values dropped to almost giveaway prices. The real estate markets in both towns have recovered to some extent, but prices are still attractive. A large number of the residents today are retirees who hail from all parts of the country.

Lake Havasu City, Parker, and Bullhead City are three low-desert retirement towns on the banks of the Colorado River. They all offer great real estate bargains. Very hot in the summer but pleasantly warm and dry in the winter, the area loses population when the snowbirds fly away in late April. Bullhead City is just across the river from Laughlin, Nevada, one of the fastest-growing casino complexes in southern Nevada. The gambling palaces love to hire retired or semiretired employees for the casinos in a wide variety of jobs. According to the local chamber of commerce, about 80 percent of Bullhead City residents are retirees!

Yuma, near the Mexican border, is another low-cost retirement area, with subdivisions of inexpensive homes. Hot summers are the drawback, yet more and more people are staying year-round as time goes on. Thank goodness for air-conditioning. Senior-citizen services appear to be excellent.

Another of our discoveries is the town of Payson, about an hour north of Phoenix. Only an hour or so from Phoenix and the city's ovenlike summers, Payson is tucked away in the cool shade of enormous pine trees and snow in the winter. Payson is a great place for budget living. The community features mobile homes and inexpensive homes on forested lots. Because of its higher elevation and pleasant summers, Payson has traditionally been a weekend getaway from Phoenix.

Nevada

Nevada is an exciting state. Much of it is uninhabitable desert, yet new settlers are arriving daily. One of the fastest-growing states, its two major cities, Las Vegas and Reno, are booming. Nevada is a new frontier, a place of new beginnings with a go-for-broke attitude. It's a place where men and women can wear string ties, western jeans, and snakeskin boots and not look out of place. To me, Nevada represents the Old West.

More than half of the population resides in the vicinity of either Las Vegas or Reno. These are truly boomtowns, with construction and expansion continually under way. As new subdivisions spread out from the city centers, lower-cost housing becomes available, with affordable neighborhoods of older homes. Although the cost of living is not low, employment opportunities and gambling excitement make life here worthwhile for some. Competition between casinos forces them to offer tremendous values in restaurant food and entertainment, which makes going out easy on a shoestring budget. The good part about retirement for many is the opportunity for part-time work. Local casinos often make it a point to hire senior citizens as part-time workers. The bad part is that too many people have a weakness for gambling and high life. Those with weakness for craps tables and alcohol might consider smaller Nevada towns with fewer temptations.

TYPICAL NEVADA WEATHER—LAS VEGAS

Temp. (F°)	Jan.	April	July	Oct.	Rain	Snow
Daily Highs	56	77	104	82	4"	1"
Daily Lows	33	50	76	54		

Throughout the state there are smaller cities and towns that are being passed over by newcomers who insist on the excitement of Las Vegas and Reno lifestyles. Yet each has its own special Old West flavor, and because gambling is legal in Nevada, you'll find slot machines and blackjack just about anywhere. Towns we especially like are Virginia City, Pahrump, and Carson City. But there are dozens of possibilities.

New Mexico

New Mexico has traditionally been a popular place for retirement, with places like Santa Fe, Taos, and Albuquerque the favorites. Each of these places has its own personality, and they won't fit everyone's requirements. Santa Fe is rather expensive, and Taos can be provincial. We've found a few lesser-known and relatively inexpensive places to recommend.

TYPICAL NEW MEXICO WEATHER—ROSWELL

Temp. (F°)	Jan.	April	July	Oct.	Rain	Snow
Daily Highs	55	77	94	76	10"	12"
Daily Lows	27	47	69	48		

Roswell has been receiving many favorable reviews in magazines and books as a retirement destination. It's a nice-looking town, and local boosters are eager for newcomers to move in. Historic Silver City has a picturesque, turn-of-the-century downtown and some excellent housing opportunities. Its higher-altitude location moderates the summer climate. Another mountain location, Ruidoso, has an incredibly lovely ambience, with tall pines and a rushing river flowing through town. Carlsbad is a small city that actively encourages retirees to relocate. The local chamber of commerce is very helpful. Carlsbad's main drawback is its location so far from the closest metropolitan area, El Paso. An exceptionally economical if not scenic location, Truth or Consequences is in the desert not far from a large lake for water recreation. Housing is particularly inexpensive here, although much of the area is not exactly upscale. Our impression is that these places would be for full-time retirees, rather than those who expect to find employment.

Colorado

Most of Colorado is in a mountain setting—rugged peaks covered with ice and snow and mountain slopes covered with green forests that turn golden with fall aspens dominate Colorado's landscapes. Majestic mountains everywhere. Mountain passes above 10,000 feet are common, such high altitudes that some folks often have trouble breathing. When they do catch their breath, the mountain scenery immediately takes it away again.

TYPICAL COLORADO WEATHER—COLORADO SPRINGS

Temp. (F°)	Jan.	April	July	Oct.	Rain	Snow
Daily Highs	41	60	85	65	15"	43"
Daily Lows	16	33	57	37		

Denver is the largest city, a clean city with pleasant, tree-shaded residential areas, and an abundance of affordable, quality apartment buildings. The city of Denver has several top-quality and very livable neighborhoods but also several low-cost districts for those looking for economy over quality. Most older homes are built of brick—according to legend, because an early-day mayor owned a brick factory, so he ordered all homes to be constructed of brick. Maybe it's not true, but the brick construction does add a special touch to Denver's architectural flavor. The city is ringed by suburbs within easy commuting distance of the many high-tech industries located in the Denver complex. From there, it's an easy trip downtown for work, shopping, theater, or cultural events.

For skiing, several towns come to mind, with Steamboat Springs at the top of the list. Economical real estate can be found in most all of the smaller towns scattered throughout the state, all of them close to outdoor recreation. Grants Pass is one of the larger places with low-cost housing, but job prospects may not be all that great.

Pacific Coast States

Here you'll find the most varied climates in the country—perhaps on the entire continent. From desert terrain that makes the Sahara look like an oasis, to rain forest, to sunny beaches fringed by palm trees, to mountains with year-round snowpack, the Pacific Coast states have it all. In a matter of a few hours you can leave the mountain ski slopes and be swimming in the Pacific. You can live in a coastal town where temperatures seldom reach the mid-seventies, even in July and August, yet it never snows or freezes. Nearby places have hot summers and snow-free winters, yet they are forty-five minutes from snow country, where a 3-foot snowfall overnight is a common occurrence.

The Pacific Coast is also a study in economic and social contrasts. Here you'll find some of the most expensive real estate in the nation, yet not far away is housing that compares favorably with places in the Deep South. Some of the most densely packed metropolitan areas are just a few miles from small, rural towns that offer real country living. And, as in the

Southwest, much of the land in the Pacific Coast region is in the public domain. Virtually all of the national forests and state lands are open to the public. These open lands can be within an hour's drive of the center of enormous cities like Los Angeles and Seattle.

One other condition is very different from the rest of the country: Beaches are all public. By law, all beachfronts must be open to anyone who cares to go there. Public passage must be provided. This is in stark contrast with the Atlantic Coast and, to a great extent, the Gulf Coast. There, valuable waterfront properties include the beach, and trespassers are unwelcome. Even some rivers in the Pacific Coast region have guaranteed public access. That is, the first 10 feet of riverbank are available for recreational use. All of this public access to the shore and rivers means a great deal to anglers, beachcombers, and picnickers.

California

California has some of the most expensive places to live in the country, ranking just behind New York City. But you can find inexpensive areas where high prices haven't caught up. There are so many places to consider here that it's difficult even to make suggestions.

For year-round mild climate, the entire Pacific Coast is the place to go. Along the northern coast, air-conditioning is unknown, winter brings almost no snow, and some very inexpensive housing can be found there. Many small towns, such as Fort Bragg and Mendocino, dot the coastline south toward San Francisco. From Santa Barbara south, you'll have the admired Southern California climate: warm, sunny summers and cool but rarely cold winters. At the opposite extreme, desert living is inexpensive in towns like Indio, Desert Hot Springs, and Brawley. Expect hot weather here.

To the east, away from the Pacific Ocean and tucked away in California's northern mountains, are several little-known retirement gems. Outdoor recreation is available year-round, and property is inexpensive. Redding is a small city with a low cost of living. The highway east from Redding winds through several likely locations, with the town of Burney being a good candidate for retirement. The region is lush with evergreen forests and close to deep lakes and mountain streams for bass and trout.

TYPICAL CALIFORNIA WEATHER—SACRAMENTO						
Temp. (F°)	Jan.	April	July	Oct.	Rain	Snow
Daily Highs	53	71	93	78	17"	—
Daily Lows	38	45	58	50		

Some folks prefer the four-season climates of the Sacramento and San Joaquin Valleys, with mild winters but hot summers approximating those back East. Not all communities are affordable here, but you'll encounter a few localities with inexpensive homes. Clinging to the banks of the Sacramento and Feather Rivers as they wend their way toward San Francisco Bay are several towns worth investigating. Dunsmuir and Mount Shasta are at the upper reaches, and Paradise, Oroville, and Marysville are very popular for inexpensive retirement. These towns are near Gold Country and the foothills of the Sierra Nevada. Interesting retirement towns in the Gold Country include Tuolumne, Angels Camp, Fiddletown, and Calaveras.

Oregon

Oregon has always been popular with Californians looking for affordable retirement locations. It's become so popular that prices have risen to match demand. However, wages and prices are low compared with where retirees are coming from—high-priced California cities such as San Francisco and Los Angeles. Oregon has no sales tax but manages to make it up with high property taxes.

Inland Oregon valley cities, with quality living, access to outdoor sports, and low housing, are popular with California retirees. The winters are mild with very little snow, and the surroundings are green year-round. Despite Oregon's reputation for rain, this area receives about half the precipitation of most eastern and Midwestern cities but without the oppressive winter weather.

Especially inexpensive is a group of small communities scattered along the scenic highway that winds its way across the mountains toward the ocean at Crescent City. This area is known as the Illinois Valley, named after the Illinois River that runs through here. You'll find several "wide spot in the road" communities such as O'Brien, Kirby, and Selma. Cave Junction is one example of small-town living with rock-bottom real estate prices and pleasant surrounding countryside. Good fishing and hunting are bonuses.

TYPICAL OREGON WEATHER—EUGENE						
Temp. (F°)	Jan.	April	July	Oct.	Rain	Snow
Daily Highs	46	61	83	65	46"	6"
Daily Lows	34	39	51	42		

All along the Oregon coast, interspersed between beaches and cliffs, are places such as Brookings, Coos Bay, Florence, Gold Beach, and Port Orford. The weather here is some of the mildest in the nation, with almost no frost, and temperatures higher than 75°F rare. Residents refer to the area as Oregon's "banana belt." There's some justification: Flowers bloom all year locally, and about 90 percent of the country's Easter lilies are grown here. Retirees comprise an estimated 30 percent of the population. Along the Columbia River, you'll find some interesting retirement towns such as Hood River, The Dalles, and, farther upstream, Hermiston. Inland, in the high-desert country, Klamath Falls and Pendleton are also worth a look.

Washington

Although it's the most northernmost state on the West Coast, Washington's western region has mild winters, much of them almost snow- and ice-free, and cool summers. The coastal region is famous for rain, just as the central and eastern portions of the state are famous for being dry. About 25 percent less rain falls on Seattle than on most of Florida, but rain typically falls gently for hours at a time in Seattle, in contrast to Florida's typically brief but intense thunderstorms. It just *seems* like there's more rain. By way of contrast, much of western Washington is dry—if there were much less rainfall it would be desert.

TYPICAL WASHINGTON WEATHER—OLYMPIA

Temp. (F°)	Jan.	April	July	Oct.	Rain	Snow
Daily Highs	44	59	77	61 ·	51"	18"
Daily Lows	31	36	49	39		

Washington is replacing Oregon as the traditional place for Californians to retire. The state's electronics and aerospace industries are bringing skilled workers from all parts of the country to join the steady stream of Californians who have been leapfrogging over Oregon to land in Washington. Those with high-tech skills could find employment opportunities around the Seattle and Puget Sound areas.

A few of Washington's towns seem to be continually in economic doldrums, with real estate prices and rentals about the lowest we've seen anywhere. The U.S. Department of Housing and Urban Development has converted repossessions into subsidized housing. If you can qualify, you might find very inexpensive rents.

Vancouver, Washington, just across the Columbia River from Portland, offers reasonable housing costs and mild weather as well as an ideal tax situation. Why? The state of Washington does not collect state income taxes, yet it provides substantial property tax relief to low-income senior citizens. However, the state does have a sales tax. Vancouver residents handle this quite well; they simply cross the Columbia River into Oregon when making major purchases because Oregon has no sales tax! As for winter weather, you'll never need a snow shovel in Vancouver.

Index

About the Author

John Howells and his wife, Sherry, have spent many months traveling by automobile, motor home, and airplane gathering the information needed to produce this book. They've interviewed retirees all across the country, collecting experiences, advice, and valuable insights on how to maintain successful retirement lifestyles.

A founding member of the American Association of Retirement Communities and a former member of its board of directors, John has written extensively on the topic of retirement. He is the author and coauthor of several books in the Choose Retirement series of The Globe Pequot Press, as well as several other nonfiction books, and regularly writes feature articles for *Where to Retire* magazine and such other periodicals as *Consumer's Digest* and *International Living*.

John and Sherry call two places home: Monterey, California, and a small village off the Pacific coast of Costa Rica. When they aren't traveling for research or pleasure, their time is spent divided between the two locations.